# Starting an Etsy® Business

## FOR

# DUMMIES®

## by Allison Strine and Kate Shoup

**WILEY**

John Wiley & Sons, Inc.

**Starting an Etsy® Business For Dummies®**

Published by
**John Wiley & Sons, Inc.**
111 River St.
Hoboken, NJ 07030-5774

www.wiley.com

For general information on our other products and services, please contact our Customer Care Department within the U.S. at 877-762-2974, outside the U.S. at 317-572-3993, or fax 317-572-4002.

For technical support, please visit www.wiley.com/techsupport.

Wiley also publishes its books in a variety of electronic formats and by print-on-demand. Some content that appears in standard print versions of this book may not be available in other formats. For more information about Wiley products, visit us at www.wiley.com.

Library of Congress Control Number: 2011935395

ISBN 978-0-470-93067-0 (pbk); ISBN 978-1-118-08902-6 (ebk); ISBN 978-1-118-08904-0 (ebk); ISBN 978-1-118-08907-1 (ebk)

Manufactured in the United States of America

10  9  8  7  6  5  4  3  2  1

WILEY

# About the Authors

By day, **Allison Strine** is a happy artist who takes unreasonable joy in her Etsy shop feedback comments. She is also the author of *LadyBirdLand!* (published by StoryPeople Press), a colorful book that brings her irrepressible creations to vibrant reality. At night, Allison is a not-very-good cook; wife to a right-brained hunk (or is it the left? — the one that's all about math and not really about art); and tucker-inner of two perfectly behaved, well-groomed children. Allison writes in the third person and hawks her wares at www. allisonstrine.etsy.com.

During the course of her career, **Kate Shoup** has authored more than 20 books, including *Not Your Mama's Beading, Not Your Mama's Stitching,* and *Rubbish: Reuse Your Refuse* (all published by John Wiley & Sons, Inc.), and has edited scores more. Kate also co-wrote a feature-length screenplay (and starred in the ensuing film) and worked as the Sports Editor for *NUVO Newsweekly.* When not writing, Kate, an IndyCar fanatic, loves to ski (she was once nationally ranked), read, craft, and ride her motorcycle. She also plays a mean game of 9-ball. Kate lives in Indianapolis with her lovely boyfriend, her brilliant daughter, and their dog.

# Dedication

**Allison Strine:** This book is for you, Etsy seller. I'm proud of you for being brave enough to put your crafty creations online. Now go out there, make something cool, and sell it on Etsy! I can't wait to see what you come up with.

**Kate Shoup:** For Heidi, as always.

# Authors' Acknowledgments

**Allison Strine:** Thanks go to Kate Shoup for being such a blast to work with. You made it easy, girl! At John Wiley & Sons, Inc., senior project editor Georgette Beatty was invaluable in keeping the wheels of progress smoothly in motion. Thanks also to executive editor Lindsay Lefevere — we couldn't have done it without you!

Thank you, Lloyd, for doing all the math for me; thank you, Olivia, for making your own lunch when I needed to write; and thank you, Ethan, for sharing ideas for the title of this book. I love you all!

**Kate Shoup:** The publication of any book is an enormous undertaking, and this one was no exception! Thanks go first to my excellent co-author, who — figuratively, at least — pried more than one razor blade from my fingers. Thanks, too, to Lindsay Lefevere for giving us the opportunity to tackle this exciting project, and to Georgette Beatty for her dedication and patience in guiding this project from start to finish. Thanks to copy editor Krista Hansing, who ensured that all the *i*'s were dotted and *t*'s were crossed, and to technical editor Sherry Truitt, who skillfully checked each step and offered valuable input along the way. Thanks to the composition team at John Wiley & Sons, Inc., for their able efforts. Thanks to the Etsy sellers and talented photographers who graciously allowed us to feature their gorgeous photographs. Finally, thanks to Etsy itself for enabling craftspeople the world over to make a living by selling their work online.

On a personal note, many thanks and much love to my beautiful and brilliant daughter, Heidi Welsh; to my incredible parents, Barb and Steve Shoup; to my wonderful sister, Jenny Shoup; to my brother-in-law, Jim Plant; to my nephew, Jake Plant; and to *mon ti lapin,* Francois Dubois.

## Publisher's Acknowledgments

We're proud of this book; please send us your comments at http://dummies.custhelp.com. For other comments, please contact our Customer Care Department within the U.S. at 877-762-2974, outside the U.S. at 317-572-3993, or fax 317-572-4002.

Some of the people who helped bring this book to market include the following:

*Acquisitions, Editorial, and Vertical Websites*

**Senior Project Editor:** Georgette Beatty

**Executive Editor:** Lindsay Sandman Lefevere

**Copy Editor:** Krista Hansing

**Assistant Editor:** David Lutton

**Editorial Program Coordinator:** Joe Niesen

**Technical Editor:** Sherry Truitt

**Editorial Manager:** Michelle Hacker

**Editorial Assistants:** Rachelle S. Amick, Alexa Koschier

**Cover Photo:** ©iStockphoto.com/artvea

**Cartoons:** Rich Tennant (www.the5thwave.com)

*Composition Services*

**Project Coordinator:** Sheree Montgomery

**Layout and Graphics:** Samantha K. Cherolis, Lavonne Roberts

**Proofreader:** Toni Settle

**Indexer:** Sherry Massey

**Special Help:** Heike Baird

**Publishing and Editorial for Consumer Dummies**

    **Kathleen Nebenhaus,** Vice President and Executive Publisher

    **Kristin Ferguson-Wagstaffe,** Product Development Director

    **Ensley Eikenburg,** Associate Publisher, Travel

    **Kelly Regan,** Editorial Director, Travel

**Publishing for Technology Dummies**

    **Andy Cummings,** Vice President and Publisher

**Composition Services**

    **Debbie Stailey,** Director of Composition Services

# Contents at a Glance

# Table of Contents

# Introduction

· · · · · · · · · · · · · · · · · · · · · · · · · · · · · · · · · · · · · · · · · · · · · · · · · · · · · · · ·

**D**oes this sound like you? You hate your day job. You trained as a teacher, but what you really want to do all day is knit. Or maybe you're busy waiting tables, but you dream of starting your own jewelry-making business. Or maybe your background is in law, but what you *really* love is constructing handbags out of gum wrappers. The problem? You've got bills to pay. It's not like people can just ditch their jobs to hand-craft Juicy Fruit purses all day, right?

Wrong. Thanks to Etsy (www.etsy.com), plenty of people have done just that: ditched their day jobs to start their own craft business, or supplemented their existing incomes by selling their own crafts. And armed with the information in *Starting an Etsy Business For Dummies,* you can become one of them!

What's Etsy? Etsy was created in 2005 to help artists and craftspeople sell their handmade wares online. (Since then, Etsy has evolved to also allow the sale of vintage items and craft supplies.) Etsy's mission, in its own words, is "to enable people to make a living making things, and to reconnect makers with buyers." Put another way, Etsy allows creative types to channel their passion for their craft into their life's work. If your dream is to "make a living making things," then Etsy is for you!

## About This Book

Above all, *Starting an Etsy Business For Dummies* is a reference tool. You don't have to read it from beginning to end; instead, you can turn to any part of the book that gives you the information you need when you need it. And you can keep coming back to the book over and over. If you prefer to read things in order, you'll find that the information is presented in a natural, logical progression.

## Conventions Used in This Book

To help you navigate this book, we include the following conventions:

- ✔ **Boldface** highlights key words in bulleted lists and action steps that you need to follow in a specific order.
- ✔ New terms and words that we choose to emphasize are in *italics*.
- ✔ Web addresses appear in `monofont`.

When this book was printed, some of the Web addresses we mention may have broken across two lines of text. If that happened, rest assured that we didn't include any extra characters (such as hyphens) to indicate the break. If you want to visit a Web site whose Web address has been broken, just type exactly what you see in this book, as though the line break didn't exist.

# What You're Not to Read

Sometimes we have information that we want to share with you, but it relates only tangentially to the topic at hand. When that happens, we either mark that information with a Technical Stuff icon or place that information in a sidebar (a shaded gray box). Even though it may not be mission critical, we think you'll find it worth knowing.

# Foolish Assumptions

When writing this book, we assumed that you want to run your Etsy shop as a proper business. Sure, it's possible to build and manage an Etsy shop with minimal effort, but that will yield only minimal results. We assume here that you're serious about making your Etsy shop a success and that you're willing to invest the time and energy to make that happen.

We also generally assume that you reside in the United States. Although most of the information discussed applies regardless of your geographic location, certain tidbits — such as matters related to taxation — are specific to U.S. residents.

# How This Book Is Organized

*Starting an Etsy Business For Dummies* is organized into six parts, and the parts are divided into chapters. In the following sections, we give you a quick preview of what to expect from each part so that you can turn to the part that interests you most.

## Part I: Basic Instinct: Grasping Etsy Basics

On a site like Etsy, which is as active as an Icelandic volcano, it's easy to get overwhelmed. The mission of this part is to help you stave off any Etsy-related anxiety. In addition to discovering what all the Etsy fuss is about, you step through the process of signing up for an Etsy account. You also nose around the Etsy home page, discover how to keep track of your Etsy account, and check out what Etsy has for sale. Finally, this part gives you the lowdown on staying safe on Etsy.

## Part II: If You Build It, They Will Come: Setting Up Your Etsy Shop

Are you ready to launch your own Etsy shop? If so, this part is for you. In it, you discover what you can — and can't — sell on Etsy. (Handmade, vintage items, and supplies are a yes; Beagle puppies, among other things, are no-gos.) You also find out how to make your Etsy shop stand out in the crowd. After that, you explore the important subject of setting your shop policies, as well as discover a foolproof method for pricing your work.

## Part III: She Sells Seashells (and More): Understanding the Etsy Selling Process

Selling an item that you've made (or ferreted out at, say, a rummage sale) in your Etsy shop involves just a few steps. First, you photograph it. Then you compose a snappy title and description. After that, it's a simple matter of listing it, selling it, and shipping it. Not surprisingly, however, each of those steps represents its own special area of expertise. The objective of this part is to get you up to speed so that you can complete each step in the process like a pro.

## Part IV: All Up in Your Bidness: Handling Business Matters

You're not just opening an Etsy shop; you're launching your own small business. You need to take it seriously if you want it to succeed! Reading this part helps you evolve from an artisan to an entrepreneur. Coverage includes such topics as marketing and branding your Etsy shop, providing unrivaled customer service, and handling financial matters such as taxes. Armed with the information in this part, you'll be takin' care of business in a flash.

## Part V: Commune System: Exploring the Etsy Community

Yes, Etsy is the best place ever if you're looking to sell gorgeous handmade and vintage pieces or crafting supplies. But Etsy is more than just an amazing online marketplace; it's also a vast and diverse community of super-special people. This part is devoted to covering all the ways you can participate in this amazing Net-based neighborhood, from joining teams and engaging in forum discussions to adding other Etsy sellers to your own Etsy circle and beyond.

## Part VI: The Part of Tens

In this part, we share our opinions on a variety of topics, offering ten tips we think sellers must know, ten strategies for marketing your shop, and ten pointers on saving money and time.

# Icons Used in This Book

Icons are those little pictures you see in the margins throughout this book, and they're meant to draw your attention to key points that can help you along the way. Here's a list of the icons we use and what they signify.

Some information is so important that it needs to be set apart for emphasis. This icon — like a string tied around your finger — is a friendly reminder of info that you'll want to commit to memory and use over the long haul.

This icon highlights information that's interesting but not completely crucial to your life as an Etsy shop owner. If you're crunched for time, feel free to skip information with this icon.

When you see this icon in the margin, the paragraph next to it contains valuable information on making your life as an Etsy seller easier.

This icon highlights common mistakes Etsy sellers make and pitfalls to avoid. An important part of achieving success is simply eliminating the mistakes; the information marked by this icon helps you do just that.

# Where to Go from Here

Glance through the Table of Contents and find the part, chapter, or section that flips your switch. That's the best place to begin. If you're just trying to get a sense of what's available on Etsy, you'll want to turn straight to Chapter 5. If you're itching to launch your own Etsy shop, Chapter 8 can step you through the process of building it from scratch. If your shop is up and running but you're a little unsure of how to handle business matters — say, paying taxes or choosing the right structure for your business — then you'll want to flip right to Chapter 18.

When you're finished reading this book, you'll want to invest some time reading The Etsy Blog (www.etsy.com/storque) and interacting with the larger Etsy community (get started at www.etsy.com/community). As your business grows, you'll undoubtedly encounter issues that this book doesn't discuss; when that happens, you're sure to appreciate these incredible resources.

# Part I

# Basic Instinct: Grasping Etsy Basics

# In this part . . .

On a site as active as Etsy, it's easy to get over-whelmed. This part is devoted to helping you stave off any Etsy-related anxiety. In addition to discovering what all the Etsy excitement is about, you'll step through the process of signing up for an Etsy account. You'll also explore the Etsy home page, discover the tools available to you for keeping track of your Etsy account, and check out what Etsy has for sale. Finally, this part provides the 411 on staying safe on Etsy. With these Etsy basics under your belt, you'll be primed to use Etsy to its fullest potential!

# Chapter 1

# Handmade for Each Other: Falling in Love with Etsy

## In This Chapter

▶ Understanding Etsy's purpose and how Etsy makes money

▶ Signing up for (and making your way around) Etsy

▶ Setting up your Etsy shop

▶ Understanding the selling process on Etsy

▶ Running your Etsy business with ease

▶ Exploring the Etsy community

*I*f your goal is to "make a living making things," then Etsy (www.etsy.com) is for you. Etsy was created specifically to enable artists and craftspeople to sell their wares online — "to reconnect makers with buyers." In short, Etsy enables creative types to channel their passion for their craft into their life's work!

In this chapter, we give you a bird's-eye view of Etsy — its purpose and business model, how to sign up for and navigate around it, and all sorts of good stuff about opening and running your own shop.

## Handmade Crusade: Understanding Etsy's Purpose and Business Model

Many people think of Etsy as a sort of eBay for arts and crafts. And you can see why: People use both Etsy and eBay to buy stuff from other individuals. Also, both sites charge listing fees and make a small commission on every sale. Plus, members use feedback to rate their transactions.

But the sites have big differences, too:

- ✔ Although Etsy is growing — as of December 2010, the site boasted 7 million registered users spanning the globe and facilitated $400 million in transactions — it's still the proverbial mouse to eBay's proverbial elephant.

- ✔ Etsy, which launched in 2005, doesn't use an auction format.

- ✔ Perhaps the biggest difference is that whereas anything goes on eBay, Etsy was created specifically to enable artists and craftspeople to sell their handmade wares online. Etsy itself puts it this way: "Our mission is to enable people to make a living making things, and to reconnect makers with buyers. Our vision is to build a new economy and present a better choice: Buy, sell, and live handmade." (Over time, the site has evolved to also allow the sale of vintage items and craft supplies; find out more about what you can and can't sell on Etsy in Chapter 7.)

Etsy is part of a larger movement against the homogenous nature of mass-produced items. This movement is typified by an organization called The Handmade Consortium (of which Etsy is a member), which notes:

> The ascendancy of chain store culture and global manufacturing has left people all dressing, furnishing, and decorating alike. The connection between producer and consumer has been lost. Buying handmade helps them reconnect . . .. We want people, whenever possible, to support independent creators and shop outside the big boxes.

More than just ensuring that you and your frenemy don't wind up wearing the same dress to the Academy Awards, Etsy and The Handmade Consortium assert that buying handmade results in an economy that's more sustainable, more environmentally responsible, and more socially responsible. Simply put, the Consortium has said, "It's better for people." (Check out www.buy handmade.org for more information.)

Lofty philosophy aside, Etsy is a business — meaning it needs to make money. So how does Etsy's business model work? Etsy stays afloat by charging sellers a fee for each item listed on the site. At this time, the listing fee is 20¢ per item. In addition, Etsy collects a commission from the seller for each item sold — currently, 3.5 percent of the total price of the item, not counting shipping. These fees, which you can pay using a credit card that you put on file with Etsy or using your PayPal account, are assessed at the end of each month.

## Moniker mystery tour: Probing the secret behind Etsy's name

The origins of Etsy's name are as murky as a drifter's past, but theories abound.

✔ Some say that the name Etsy is a play on the Latin phrase *et si,* meaning "and if."

✔ Others suggest that the name comes from the Greek *etsi,* meaning "so," "thus," or "in this way."

✔ Still others posit that Etsy derives from the Unix director /etc, pronounced "et-C," or that it's meant to call to mind the word *itsy,* as in "itsy-bitsy," or "cute," which, of course, many items on Etsy are.

Any attempts for clarification by Etsy are met with playful — but misleading — answers by Etsy's staff, ranging from "Etsy is an acronym for Expanded Truncated Structural Y" to "It means 'horny person' in Japanese.'" And although Etsy founder Rob Kalin once insinuated that the answer to this riddle could be found in Fellini's film *8½,* no one has yet managed to solve it.

# World Up: Introducing the World of Etsy

Just what can you do on Etsy? And how do you use it? This section scratches the surface.

## Upper register: Registering with Etsy

You don't need to register with Etsy to scope out what goodies are for sale. But if you're in the market to buy any of said goodies — or to communicate with other Etsy members or participate in the site's community features, such as its forums, teams, Virtual Labs, and the like — you need to create an account with the site. Fortunately, creating an account is simple and free. All you need to do is enter your name and e-mail address, and choose a user name and password. You don't even need to supply a credit card number!

If you plan to use Etsy to sell your own handmade, vintage, or supply items (and we assume so, because you're reading this book!), you need to take one more step: upgrading to a seller account. That step requires a major credit card (think Visa, MasterCard, Discover, or American Express) and other vitals, such as your address.

For step-by-step coverage of completing the registration process and signing in to your Etsy account, turn to Chapter 2.

## Homeward bound: Navigating the Etsy home page

Whether you're buying or selling, exploring or researching, Etsy's home page is your home base. It's the page that appears when you type www.etsy.com into your Web browser. You can also access Etsy's home page from anywhere on the Etsy site by clicking the Etsy logo in the upper-left corner of each page.

The Etsy home page includes several important sections:

- ✔ A set of links and a header bar along the top, which you can click to access various Etsy features
- ✔ Categories, Handpicked Items, Recently Listed Items, and Ways to Shop, which make finding the perfect item a breeze
- ✔ The Featured Seller and Recent Blog Posts sections, which give access to information about exceptional Etsy sellers and other important topics, respectively

For more information about these and other home page features, check out Chapter 3.

## Let us account the ways: Understanding Your Account

On Etsy, managing your account is easy. Etsy has grouped all the key settings and info in one easy-to-reach place: Your Account. Your Account, which you access by clicking the Your Account link that appears along the top of every Etsy page when you're logged in to your Etsy account, acts like an instrument panel of sorts. It displays all kinds of account-related info — items you've bought, feedback you've received, your public profile, your billing and shipping info, your Etsy bill, any Etsy-related apps you use, and various shop-related settings.

For help with navigating Your Account, turn to Chapter 4.

## For sale by artist: Discovering what's for sale on Etsy

Etsy features unique, one-of-a-kind handmade and vintage items — goodies you simply can't find anywhere else — along with supplies for crafting your own pieces. In fact, Etsy offers an incredible breadth of items for sale, from accessories to ceramics, jewelry to quilts, and everything in between. And because there's no middleman — you buy directly from artists and crafts-people — prices on Etsy are generally very reasonable. At the same time, your purchase can enable these skilled artisans to earn a living wage. It's a total win-win!

To help you find a specific item, Etsy supports a robust Search tool. With it, you can search for handmade items, vintage items, and supplies. You can also use the Search tool to locate a particular seller or shop. If you're just browsing, you'll appreciate Etsy's many browsing-related features, including Categories, Handpicked Items, Recently Listed items, Colors, the Treasury, Pounce, Shop Local, Time Machine, and Gift Ideas. You access these tools from Etsy's home page or from the Shop on Etsy page, which you access by clicking the Buy link along the top of any Etsy page.

For additional help, turn to Chapter 5.

## Safety first: Ensuring your safety on Etsy

No doubt about it, one of the highlights of Etsy is its thriving community of interesting, arty folk. But you may still find an occasional bad apple on the site. Take a few key steps to ensure your safety:

✔ To make sure that no one accesses your account without your authori-zation, you must choose a strong password. Select one that meets all the following criteria:

- It's at least eight characters long.

- It doesn't contain your user name or your real name.

- It doesn't contain a complete word.

- It differs from passwords that you've used in the past.

- It contains a mixture of uppercase letters, lowercase letters, numbers, symbols, and spaces.

For an added layer of protection, change your password every so often — say, every 30 to 90 days.

✔ Be on the lookout for scams. These often involve the use of money orders or cashier's checks, along with an offer to pay significantly more than is necessary to expedite shipping or to cover some other weird request. If you do get taken on Etsy, contact your financial institution on the double. Then report the situation to Etsy. You may also opt to alert your local law enforcement.

✔ Before you jump into a forum or team discussion, monitor it for a while. See whether the Etsians engaged in the discussion are people you really want to interact with. If a discussion goes south, simply disengage. Life's stressful enough; why embroil yourself in a conflict on a site that's supposed to be fun? Oh, and don't share your digits or other personal deets, such as where you live or work, on Etsy's forums or other public spaces. And if you decide to meet up with someone you've met on Etsy in person, pick a neutral, public place; let a friend or family member know about your plans; and be sure to bring a cellphone with you in case you need to call for help.

Chapter 6 covers important safety issues in more detail.

# Storefront and Center: Setting Up Your Storefront

The simple act of signing up for a seller account results in the creation of your Etsy shop. That shop, however, may strike you as incredibly plain, because it consists of a white page with only two gray bars and a few links. Fortunately, you can personalize it in several ways (and doing so makes a huge difference!):

✔ Uploading a banner (a graphic that runs across the top of the page)

✔ Including a shop title and shop announcement to describe your shop

✔ Using sections to organize your goods

✔ Populating your Etsy profile and choosing an avatar

As you set up your storefront, keep in mind that a major reason people shop on Etsy is to feel connected to the artists who make what they buy. If you want people to buy from *you,* make sure your Etsy shop reflects your personality! Are you serious? Then your shop should be, too. Ditto if you're whimsical, modern, traditional, edgy, or frilly. Let your personality shine through in your choice of banner, avatar, and other visual elements, as well as in your bio and other text-based elements. Not only will this increase your sales, but it may just help you make some friends along the way. (For more on setting up your Etsy shop, check out Chapter 8.)

Oh, one more pointer: As you set up your Etsy shop, you'll want to clearly lay out your shop policies — how much you charge for shipping, whether you accept returns, and so on. We cover smart policies in Chapter 9.

# Sell's Angels: Surveying the Etsy Selling Process

Putting up an item for sale on Etsy is a simple process:

1. **Create the item you're selling and determine how much it costs (with the help of the pointers we provide in Chapter 10).**

2. **Photograph your piece.**

   You can include as many as five pictures of each piece in your Etsy shop. The photos you provide must convey the shape, size, color, and texture of your piece, and also be easy on the eye.

3. **Compose a snappy title and description for your item listing.**

4. **List your item on the site and wait for someone to snatch it up.**

5. **When the item sells, ship it to the buyer (after you receive your payment, of course)!**

Okay, that's a broad overview. Of course, the process has a little more to it, but trust us: It's nothing you can't handle. After you read Part III, you'll be up to speed.

# Takin' Care of Business: Handling Business Matters

For some sellers, running an Etsy shop is merely a hobby — a way to make a little extra money on the side. For others, it's their day job, or "what they do." Regardless of which camp you're in, you need to treat your Etsy shop as a proper small business — building a brand, marketing your shop, and providing excellent customer service.

If you're in the latter category — someone who seeks to earn a living by selling on Etsy — you may choose to do even more. For example, you may opt to incorporate your business, obtain a business checking account, streamline your supply chain, use special tools to analyze your business, and so on.

Part IV covers all these topics and more, including how to handle tax matters and pair up with a friend to run an Etsy shop.

# Community Collage: Engaging in the Etsy Community

Sure, Etsy is a great place to buy and sell handmade pieces, vintage items, and supplies. But it's more than that: It's a community of creative, crafty people that just begs for participation. Etsy offers several tools that help you jump right in, including these:

- ✔ Public message boards, called forums
- ✔ Teams, for connecting with likeminded Etsy members
- ✔ Chat rooms, for chatting with other Etsy members in real time
- ✔ Virtual Labs, which are special chat rooms where Etsy staffers and members can run seminars, workshops, shop critiques, and other educational gatherings

You can also gather your favorite shops and sellers into your own Etsy circle, to keep up with their goings-on and more. And you can show your love on the site by "hearting" your beloved items and shops — that is, adding them to your favorites.

Other great resources for the Etsy community include The Etsy Blog (also called The Storque; check out www.etsy.com/storque), which acts as a neighborhood newspaper of sorts. The Etsy Blog, which serves up fresh content daily, boasts material ranging from tips for improving your Etsy shop, to information to help you perfect various crafting techniques, to glimpses into the lives of other Etsy sellers.

Etsy's e-mail newsletters are another great source of information and inspiration. And if you're among the more than 500 million people who maintain a Facebook account, you can connect with Etsy there, as well as on Twitter, and YouTube.

Etsy is super easy to use, but you'll still need a little help sometimes. Fortunately, Etsy maintains copious resources to help members find answers to all their burning Etsy-related questions, from help files to an interactive Help forum. Go to www.etsy.com/help for the scoop.

Ready to dive in? Flip to Part IV for all the details on engaging in the Etsy community.

# Chapter 2

# Let's Get This Party Started: Signing Up

*F*ather of Taoism Lao Tzu once said, "A journey of a thousand miles begins with one step." (He also said, "Silence is a source of great strength" and "The sage does not hoard"; we're still working on digesting those.) On Etsy, that one first step is becoming a registered user by signing up with the site. After that, you're ready to embark on your own Etsy journey! This chapter gives you all the info you need to register with Etsy.

## Sign Me Up! Becoming a Registered User

Anyone can browse Etsy to see what goodies are for sale. But if you're in the market to buy, or if you eventually want to open your own shop, you need to create an account with the site by becoming a registered user. It's easy and free! Just follow the guidelines in the following sections.

In addition to being able to purchase items on the site, registered users can keep track of their best-loved items or shops by "hearting" them, communicate with other Etsy members, and participate in the site's community features, such as the forums and Virtual Labs. Flip to Part V for more information about all these options.

# All about you: Submitting necessary info and confirming your account

Assuming that you have a computer and an Internet connection, becoming a registered Etsy user is super easy. Here's what you do:

1. **In your Web browser's address bar, type www.etsy.com and press Enter or Return.**

   Etsy's main page appears (see Figure 2-1).

2. **Click the Register link in the header bar.**

   The Register page appears (see Figure 2-2).

3. **Type your first name in the First Name field and your last name in the Last Name field.**

4. **Click the Male, Female, or Rather Not Say option button to specify your gender (or not).**

5. **Type your e-mail address in the Your Email field.**

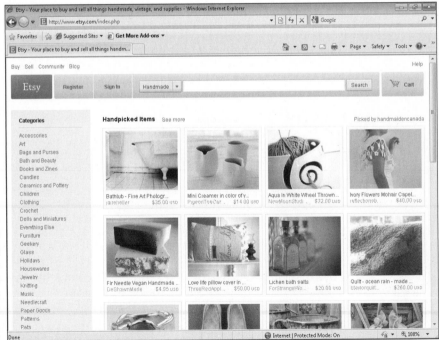

**Figure 2-1:** Click the Register link to start the registration process.

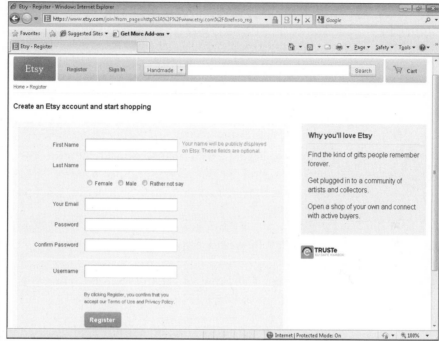

**Figure 2-2:**
Enter your
vitals to
create an
account.

**6. In the Password field, type the password you want to use to access your Etsy account.**

Create a password that's at least six characters — one that you can remember easily but that won't be too obvious to anyone else.

**7. Retype the password in the Confirm Password field.**

**8. In the User Name field, type the user name you want to use on Etsy.**

This name must contain between 4 and 20 letters or numbers (no spaces). Etsy notifies you if someone else has selected your user name; if so, try another one until you find one that's unique.

Take care in choosing your user name, because it's crazy important! If you decide to become an Etsy seller (and because you're reading this book, we figure that you're at least somewhat interested in doing so), your user name then becomes your shop name. What's more, you can't change your user name after you set it initially. For more information on selecting a user name, read the next section.

**9. To read the terms of use, click the Terms of Use link (find out more about the terms of use later in this chapter); you can also read Etsy's privacy policy by clicking on the Privacy Policy link (flip to Chapter 6 for more details).**

10. **Optionally, select the check box titled Sign Up for the Etsy Finds Newsletter.**

    If you do, Etsy will send you a daily Etsy Finds newsletter full of fantastic finds on the site. This newsletter is one of several Etsy newsletters available to you; you find out how to sign up for the rest in Chapter 20.

11. **Click the Register button.**

    Etsy creates your account and sends a confirmation e-mail to the e-mail address you supplied in Step 5.

    If you don't receive the confirmation e-mail right away, check your junk mail folder or your spam filter to make sure it wasn't intercepted.

12. **Open the e-mail from Etsy and click the link that it contains to confirm your account.**

    As shown in Figure 2-3, you're ready to go! Etsy sends you a second e-mail to officially welcome you to the site.

    If you can't click the link in your confirmation e-mail, you can copy it and paste it in your Web browser's address bar to confirm your account.

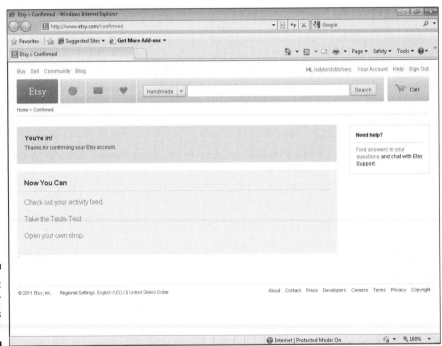

**Figure 2-3:**
Your account is created!

If you have trouble registering, contact Etsy's Support Team by e-mail at support@etsy.com.

## Yours for life: Choosing a solid user name

Friends and significant others may come and go. But you can count on one thing in this topsy-turvy world: the constancy of your Etsy user name. Yes, the user name you choose on Etsy is yours for life — not to mention the name with which your Etsy shop will be christened. Be sure to pick a good one!

Etsy generates two Web addresses for your shop, based on your user name. They look like this: http://username.etsy.com and http://www.etsy.com/shop/username.

When choosing your user name, keep these points in mind:

- ✔ Opt for a name that's easy to remember, that's easy to spell, and that contains no more than one or two words that flow well together.

- ✔ If you already have a following elsewhere — for example, at craft fairs, in art galleries, or somewhere else — consider using your own name as your user name. Using your own name may make it more difficult to maintain your privacy on the site, but it can help you capitalize on your real-world successes.

- ✔ Consider choosing a name that reflects what you sell. For example, if you specialize in selling refrigerator magnets, you may want to include the word *magnet* in your user name. Keep in mind, though, that this leaves little room for growth if you decide to expand your selection beyond the magnetic.

  Note that you can create multiple accounts to run more than one Etsy storefront — say, one for your thriving refrigerator magnet business and another for your hand-knit fingerless gloves enterprise. If you go this route, be aware that you must disclose all your user names in the user profile for each account. (Flip to Chapter 8 for more about filling out a profile.)

- ✔ Select a name that reflects your style — especially if you plan to open an Etsy shop. It won't do to select an elegant, refined name if you plan to sell wacky hand-knit balaclavas.

- ✔ For legal reasons, steer clear of trademarked words (including the word *Etsy*).

Etsy prohibits the use of words deemed racist or profane in user names.

# Signing away your firstborn: Reviewing the Terms of Use

Before registering with and using Etsy, take a moment to review the site's Terms of Use (Figure 2-4 shows them in part). To access the Terms of Use, click the Help link in the upper-right corner of any Etsy page; under Site Policy on the Help page, click Terms of Use.

If you're like a lot of people, you're probably wondering why you need to read Etsy's Terms of Use. Here's our answer: Violating any of the policies spelled out in the Terms of Use is grounds for expulsion from the site. The "But I didn't know it was a policy!" defense doesn't fly here!

In addition to its terms of use, Etsy maintains several other policy-related documents that you need to read, including the following:

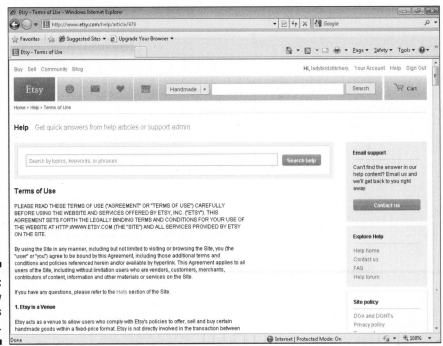

**Figure 2-4:**
Review
Etsy's terms
of use.

- ✔ **The DOs and DON'Ts of Etsy (www.etsy.com/policy/dosdonts):** This document outlines Etsy's expectations with respect to membership, conversations, transactions, feedback, shops and listings, flagging, and community.

- ✔ **Etsy Privacy Policy (www.etsy.com/policy/privacy):** This document clarifies how Etsy treats personal information that it collects and receives.

- ✔ **Etsy Copyright and Intellectual Property Policy (www.etsy.com/policy/ip):** This document spells out Etsy's policy with respect to copyright and intellectual property infringement.

- ✔ **Etsy's Trademark Guidelines (www.etsy.com/policy/etsymark):** This document states Etsy's guidelines for protecting its trademark.

# It's a Sign: Signing In

After you've created an account with Etsy, signing in is a snap. Simply direct your Web browser to Etsy and click the Sign In link in the header bar (you can see this link in Figure 2-1). Then, in the Sign In to Etsy screen, type your e-mail address or user name in the E-mail or User Name field, type your password in the Password field, and click the Sign In button (see Figure 2-5).

**Figure 2-5:** Use your user name or e-mail address and your password to sign in to your Etsy account.

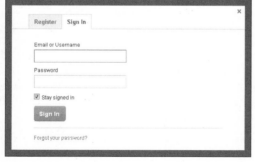

When you sign in to Etsy, you have the option of selecting the Stay Signed In check box. If you do, you can navigate away from the site and return again without having to sign in. Word of warning: Don't select this check box if you're on a public computer, such as one at a library or Internet cafe! Otherwise, after you leave the computer station, someone may access your Etsy account.

## I second the motion: Beware of opening a second account to change your user name

Actually, we lied earlier in this chapter. You can change your user name, but it involves opening a second account and then migrating to it. If all you do is buy stuff on Etsy, setting up a second account may not be a big deal. But if you've opened an Etsy shop and developed a following under your old user name, it can be a major ordeal. How?

✔ For one thing, there's no easy way to transfer items for sale from one shop to another; you have to do it by hand (and get hit with a second set of listing fees).

✔ Worse, your sales records, feedback, conversations, and other Etsy interactions don't transfer to your new shop.

The moral of the story: Think hard when you choose your initial user name and before you attempt to switch user names!

# Sellular Level: Registering for a Seller Account

If you want to join the ranks of people who earn — or supplement — their living on Etsy, you need to take one more step: Upgrade your Etsy account to seller status. To upgrade to a seller account, you must have a valid credit card on hand. Etsy accepts Visa, MasterCard, Discover, and American Express. Then follow these steps:

1. **Click Open Your Own Shop on the Confirm screen that you saw when you confirmed your account (refer to Figure 2-3); if that screen is no longer visible, sign in to your Etsy account and click the Sell link in the upper-left corner of the main page.**

   The Learn How to Sell on Etsy page appears. As shown in Figure 2-6, this page outlines what you can and can't sell on Etsy. (You discover more about this topic in Chapter 7.)

2. **Click the Sell on Etsy button in the upper-right corner of the page.**

3. **Enter your vitals in the Personal Info screen, shown in Figure 2-7; this information includes your full name, street, city, state, zip code, and country.**

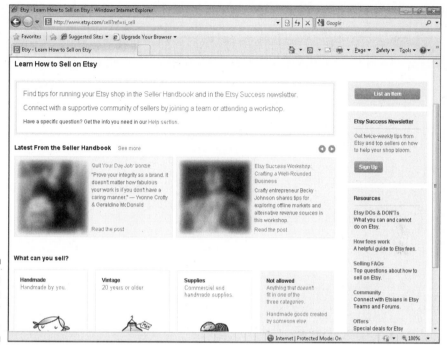

**Figure 2-6:**
Upgrade
to a seller
account.

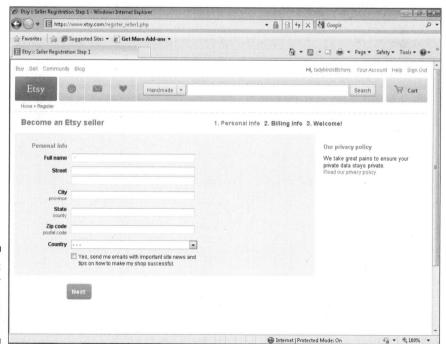

**Figure 2-7:**
Enter your
vitals on the
Personal
Info screen.

Since you're new to Etsy, why not select the check box at the bottom of the screen? That way, you'll receive e-mails containing site news and tips on how to make your shop successful.

4. **Click the Next button.**

5. **Etsy prompts you to enter your billing information, as shown in Figure 2-8; type the requested information (basically, information about your credit card, along with the billing address), select the I Agree with the Etsy's Terms of Use Agreement check box, and click the Validate Card button.**

   *Note:* When you click the Validate Card button, Etsy places a small charge on your card to validate it. Don't panic; it will be removed!

   Etsy then displays the Welcome screen shown in Figure 2-9, with info about listing items, fees, and more. (These topics are covered in more detail throughout the book.) Etsy also sends you an e-mail to confirm your upgrade to seller status.

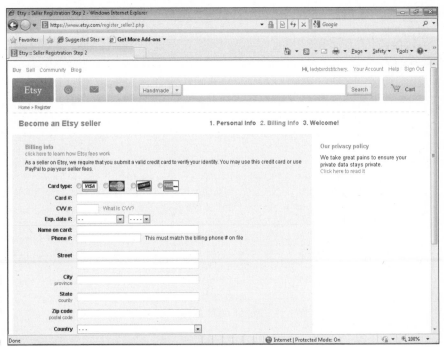

**Figure 2-8:**
Type your billing info.

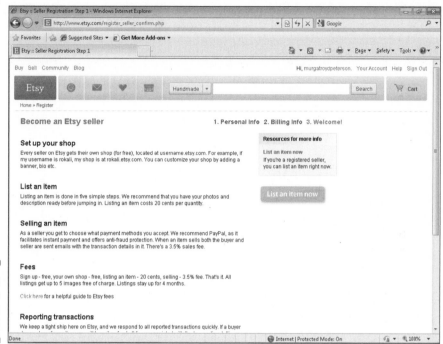

**Figure 2-9:**
Welcome
to being an
Etsy seller!

Absolutely nothing can stop you from opening an Etsy shop with, say, your grandma, your best friend, or the guy whose welding studio is across the hall from yours. (Etsy refers to shops run by or including goods crafted by more than one person as *collectives*.) But be aware that you can't attach multiple names to an Etsy account. That is, if you're the one who creates the account for the collective, your name — and your name only — is associated with that account (although you're required to add the name of everyone who participates in the collective to the shop's profile page). Etsy holds you responsible for all account-related activities. So even if you had nothing to do with the flame war that Grandma launched on the Etsy Ideas forum while using the collective's account, you're the one who'll be blamed for it. To find out more about running an Etsy collective, see Chapter 18.

# Chapter 3

# There's No Place Like Home: Discovering Etsy's Home Page

*H*ome. It's a word with many meanings. It's where you live. It's where your heart is. It's where you hang your hat. It's where the cows finally come. Simply put, it's a place to which one always longs to return.

Etsy's home page is no different. As you use the site, you'll find yourself always returning home — to the home page, that is. Whether you're buying or selling, exploring or researching, Etsy's home page is your home base. In this chapter, you explore the various features of the page and find out how to navigate from it. (*Note:* If your home page doesn't exactly match what we discuss here, don't freak out. Etsy regularly experiments with the layout of its home page.)

## Home Sweet Home: Viewing Etsy's Home Page

Etsy's home page is the page that appears when you type www.etsy.com into your Web browser. You can also access the home page from anywhere on the Etsy site by clicking the Etsy logo in the upper-left corner of each page.

As you can see in Figure 3-1, the Etsy home page includes several important sections

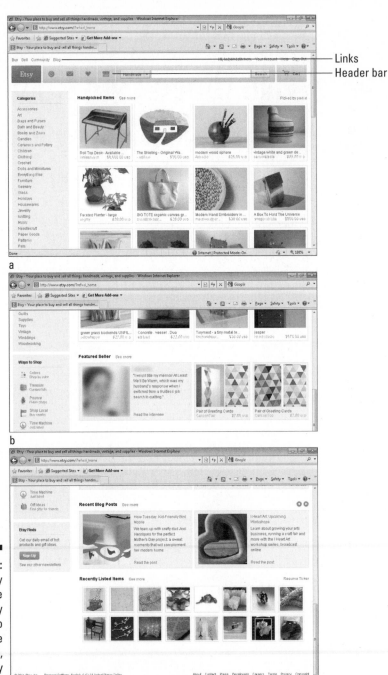

Links

Header bar

a

b

**Figure 3-1:**
The Etsy home page offers easy access to myriad site features, and it's easy on the eyes!

c

- ✔ Links (see Figure 3-1a)
- ✔ Header bar (see Figure 3-1a)
- ✔ Categories (see Figure 3-1a)
- ✔ Handpicked Items (see Figure 3-1a)
- ✔ Ways to Shop (see Figure 3-1b)
- ✔ Featured Seller (see Figure 3-1b)
- ✔ Etsy Finds (see Figure 3-1c)
- ✔ Recent Blog Posts (see Figure 3-1c)
- ✔ Recently Listed Items (see Figure 3-1c)

You delve into each of these sections in this chapter.

If you're signed in to Etsy, and you've made purchases on the site or flagged any shops or items as Favorites (known as *hearting* — see Chapter 21), you may also see a You Might Like section on your home page under Handpicked Items. This section features items similar to the ones you've bought or hearted.

# Hitting the Links: Exploring the Links at the Top of the Page

As with many Web sites, Etsy includes a series of links along the top of its home page to help you navigate the site. Clicking one of these links directs you to the link's associated page on the site.

These links don't appear just on the Etsy home page; they appear on every page on the site. This feature helps make Etsy extremely easy to navigate.

The links that appear vary depending on whether you're signed in to your account. If you're not signed in, you get the following links (see Figure 3-2):

- ✔ **Buy:** Click this link to access tools for buyers, such as Treasury, Pounce, Colors, and more. (As you find out later in this chapter, you can also access many of these tools directly from the home page, in the Ways to Shop area.) For more information about buying on Etsy, see Chapter 5.
- ✔ **Sell:** For quick access to tools and resources for sellers — including a helpful guide to how fees work and a link for listing items in your shop — click the Sell link. (Parts II through IV are devoted to selling on Etsy.)

✔ **Community:** For quick access to Etsy's community features — the teams and forums, as well as a list of upcoming events — click the Community link. Chapter 19 covers the Etsy community in more detail.

✔ **Blog:** The Etsy Blog, also called The Storque, is accessible from this link. This multifaceted blog plays host to any number of excellent posts relating to the handmade life, ranging from craft how-tos to tips for sellers and beyond.

✔ **Help:** For help with using the site, click the Help link. (You discover the details on getting help in Chapter 22.)

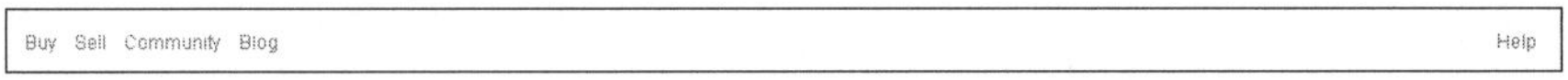

**Figure 3-2:**
If you aren't signed in to your Etsy account, just a few links are available.

Buy  Sell  Community  Blog                                                                                            Help

If you *are* signed in to your account, you'll see the aforementioned Buy, Sell, Community, Blog, and Help links. In addition, the following links appear (see Figure 3-3):

✔ **Hi, *user name* (where *user name* is your Etsy user name):** To view and edit your Etsy user profile, click this link. (For more on editing your user profile, see Chapter 8.)

✔ **Your Account:** Access the Your Account page by clicking this link. (You get the scoop on Your Account in Chapter 4.)

✔ **Sign Out:** To sign out of your account, click this link.

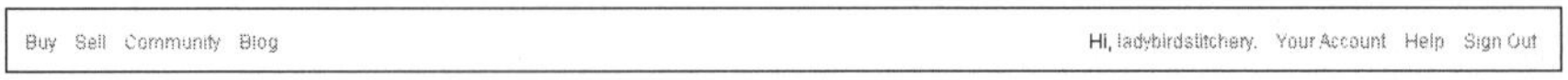

**Figure 3-3:**
Signing in to your Etsy account gives you access to additional links.

Buy  Sell  Community  Blog                                              Hi, ladybirdstitchery.  Your Account  Help  Sign Out

# Tonight's Headerliner: Exploring the Header Bar

To help you easily and quickly access the tools you need, every Etsy page, including its home page, contains a header bar with several links. As with the links along the top of the page, the appearance of the header bar differs depending on whether you're signed in to your Etsy account. If you're not signed in, the header bar contains the following links (see Figure 3-4):

✔ **Etsy:** No matter where you are on the Etsy site, you can return to the home page by clicking the Etsy logo in the header bar.

✔ **Register:** Click this link to register with the site, as you did in Chapter 2.

✔ **Sign In:** To sign in to your account, click this link (see Chapter 2 for more information).

✔ **Cart:** Click this link to view items in your shopping cart.

**Figure 3-4:**
Use the header bar to register or sign in to the site, as well as view items in your shopping cart.

When you sign in to the site, these links replace the Register and Sign In links (see Figure 3-5):

✔ **Activity:** If you opt to participate in the Etsy community — for example, by adding items or shops to your list of favorites, creating Treasury lists, or adding people to your Etsy circle — you'll see evidence of that activity in your Activity Feed, which you access by clicking this button. For more information, see Chapter 21.

✔ **Conversations:** A conversation — or convo, if you don't have time for all those extra syllables — is a communication with another member using Etsy's internal messaging system. To view any active convos, click this link. (You find out more about convos in Chapter 17.)

✔ **Favorites:** Etsy enables you to bookmark your favorite items as shops by adding them to your Favorites. In Etsy-ese, this is also called *hearting*. To view your Favorites, click this link. For more on hearting, see Chapter 21.

✔ **Shop:** This icon offers quick access to your Etsy shop.

**Figure 3-5:**
Use the header bar to access your activity feed, your convos, your favorites, and your Etsy shop.

Conversations    Favorites

Activity    Shop

Regardless of whether you're signed in to your Etsy account, the header bar also displays Etsy's Search tool, which you can use to locate the following:

✔ Handmade items

✔ Vintage items

✔ Supplies

✔ All items

✔ People and shops

If you're signed in, you can also use the search tool to search among your favorite items and your favorite shops.

Simply type a keyword in the Search field, click the down arrow to the left of the field and choose what you're searching for, and click the Search button. (Flip to Chapter 5 for more details on searching.)

# *Categorically Speaking: Viewing Categories*

In December 2010, Etsy sellers listed 1,518,859 items. Don't worry, though: These items are organized into categories — 31 categories, to be exact (see

Figure 3-6) — so you can easily find what you're looking for. Clicking a category (on the left side of the home page) reveals a list of items in that category, along with several clickable subcategories to help you narrow the field. Whether it's Geekery you seek or Crochet you covet, Etsy's categories can help you find the item that's just right.

**Categories**

Accessories
Art
Bags and Purses
Bath and Beauty
Books and Zines
Candles
Ceramics and Pottery
Children
Clothing
Crochet
Dolls and Miniatures
Everything Else
Furniture
Geekery
Glass
Holidays
Housewares
Jewelry
Knitting
Music
Needlecraft
Paper Goods
Patterns
Pets
Plants and Edibles
Quilts
Supplies
Toys
Vintage
Weddings
Woodworking

**Figure 3-6:**
From
Accessories
to Wood-
working
—and
everything
in between!

# Pick Me! Pick Me! Checking Out Handpicked Items

The Handpicked Items section of Etsy's home page, shown in Figure 3-7, features goodies assembled into a Treasury list by a fellow Etsy user. (You find out more about Treasury lists later in this chapter.) Etsy staffers then pluck this Treasury list from obscurity and plant it front and center on the site's home page. Often these items, which change several times a day, center on a particular color, style, holiday, or theme. If you're just browsing, the Handpicked Items section represents a great launching point.

**Figure 3-7:**
You'll find plenty to drool over in the Handpicked Items section of Etsy's home page.

# How Do I Love Thee? Let Me Count the Ways: Exploring Different Ways to Shop

Remember in *When Harry Met Sally* how Sally had her own unique way of ordering at a restaurant? "I just want it the way I want it," she explained. The same is true with shopping on Etsy. Not everyone wants to do it in the same way! Fortunately, Etsy offers several tools to enhance your shopping experience, located in the Ways to Shop area of the site's home page (see Figure 3-8).

**Figure 3-8:**
When it comes to ways to shop, Etsy offers tons of options.

## Colors

If you're looking to find the perfect bejeweled complement for your chartreuse-hued smoking jacket, check out Etsy's Color tool. With this tool, you simply click a color on the palette to view random items for sale in that color.

When you list an item in your Etsy shop, you can apply a "color" tag to it. That is, if the item is predominately puce, you can add a "puce" tag. You find out more about tagging the items you list in Chapter 13.

## Treasury

Etsy's vast community of members is a great resource for finding amazing items for sale on the site. To tap into this community, visit the Etsy Treasury. There you'll find what Etsy describes as an "ever-changing, member-curated shopping gallery" comprised of lists of items. These Treasury lists, which contain 16 items each, may focus on a particular color or theme — think pink! Or Africa! Or *Battlestar Galactica*! — or they may simply contain that member's favorite Etsy finds. The Treasury, which is searchable, isn't meant for self-promotion. Instead, its purpose, according to Etsy's help information, is to enable members to "acknowledge and share the many cool things for sale on Etsy." You discover how to create your own Treasury in Chapter 21.

## Pounce

Want to find the newest, freshest shops — so fresh, in fact, that they haven't yet enjoyed their first sale? Then Pounce is the tool for you. Using Pounce in Undiscovered mode, you can view random listings from undiscovered sellers. You can also use Pounce in Just Sold mode to view shops that just enjoyed a sale. Click the Pounce Again button to display additional items. It's fun!

## Shop Local

Everyone knows how important it is to shop local. For starters, it keeps money and jobs in your community. In addition, because the seller ships your item only across town instead of across the country, buying local blunts your impact on the planet.

It likely comes as no surprise that an organization like Etsy is hip to the whole "shop local" thing. Its Shop Local feature displays the most recently updated shops in your area. With Shop Local, you can find — and buy from — Etsy sellers right in your hometown. Just enter your town and state in the search field (if it's not pulled automatically from the info you supplied to Etsy when you signed up for an account). Easy!

To ensure that your shop appears in Shop Local, you must enter your hometown in your user profile. To find out how, turn to Chapter 8.

## Time Machine

You don't need a DeLorean to go back in time. You just need to visit Etsy's Time Machine page. There you can scroll through items using three viewing modes: Just Listed, Expiring Soon, and Just Sold. Click the Back in Time button to scroll backward through the displayed listings.

Technically, clicking the Time Machine link in the Ways to Shop box on Etsy's main page directs you to the Time Machine[2] page. This page represents an iteration from the original Time Machine page, which displayed listings in a sort of Hitchcock-y spiral format.

## Gift Ideas

Remember that old Reese's Peanut Butter Cups slogan, "Two great tastes that taste great together"? That's kind of what Gift Ideas for Facebook Friends is like: a perfect fusion of Etsy and Facebook. When you use this tool, Etsy trolls your Facebook friends' profiles and suggests gift ideas based on the information it finds.

To use the tool, follow these steps:

1. **Click the Gift Ideas link on the Etsy home page.**

2. **On the Gift Ideas page, click the Choose a Facebook Friend button.**

3. **If this is the first time you've used this tool, Etsy prompts you to allow access to your Facebook information; click Allow.**

4. **Select a friend from the list that appears and click Okay.**

   (Note that you can search for a friend by typing the first few letters of her name in the search box.) Etsy suggests items that your friend may like, based on the information on her Facebook profile.

If having your Etsy world collide with your Facebook universe skeezes you out, you can disconnect the two accounts. To do so, sign in to your Facebook account, open the Account menu in the top-right corner of the screen, choose Privacy Settings, click the Edit Your Settings link under Apps and Websites, click the Etsy link under Applications You Use, and click the X button to the right of the Etsy entry that appears.

# Baby, You're a Star: Meeting the Featured Seller

Every two days or so, Etsy staffers introduce a new Featured Seller — someone who displays ingenuity, sells well-made items, and populates each listing with interesting descriptions and top-notch photos. The Featured Seller appears on Etsy's home page (see Figure 3-9), with a link to an interview with that seller and to item listings in that seller's shop.

**Figure 3-9:**
See who's making noise on Etsy with the Featured Seller feature!

 If you're just starting out on Etsy, reading up on the Featured Seller is a great way to ferret out tips and tricks for becoming a successful seller — not to mention become totally inspired!

# Finders, Keepers: Signing Up for Etsy Finds

If you want to receive Etsy's daily e-mail that's chock full of goodies for sale on the site, click the Sign Up button under Etsy Finds (see Figure 3-10). Click the See Our Other Newsletters link to sign up for additional newsletters, such as Etsy Fashion, Etsy Weddings, Etsy Dudes — the list goes on. (Flip to Chapter 20 for full details on getting Etsy news.)

**Figure 3-10:**
Signing up for the Etsy Finds newsletter is a snap.

# The Velvet Blog: Reading Recent Blog Posts

To view new blog posts at a glance, scroll down to the Recent Blog Posts section of Etsy's home page (see Figure 3-11). There you'll find headlines from newly posted content on The Etsy Blog. If you see a headline that looks interesting, click it to read the post. To view additional headlines, click the arrow buttons. Click the See More link to land on the main page for The Etsy Blog (which we describe in more detail in Chapter 20).

**Figure 3-11:**
Keep up
with The
Etsy Blog at
a glance.

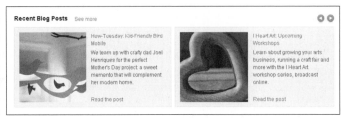

# Ooh, 1 Want That! And That! And That! Viewing Recently Listed Items

As sellers list new items, those items appear in the Recently Listed Items section of the Etsy home page (see Figure 3-12). If you're looking to land the very latest goodies, or if you just want to get a sense of how active the site is, park your eyeballs here for a few minutes and prepare to be amazed. To see more recently listed items, click the See More link. If the updates stall, click the Resume Ticker link.

**Figure 3-12:**
Don't be
surprised to
find yourself
mesmer-
ized by the
constantly
updated,
recently
listed items.

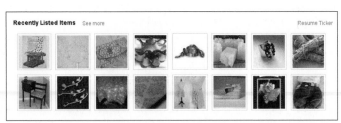

# Chapter 4

# Account Trackula: Navigating Your Account

**In This Chapter**

▶ Opening the Your Account page

▶ Tracking purchases, dealing with feedback, and tackling other account-related tasks

▶ Accessing shop settings

**M**anaging your Etsy account is super easy. Why? Because Etsy has gathered all the key settings and info in one easy-to-reach place: Your Account. Your Account acts like a dashboard of sorts, giving you access to all manner of account-related info — items you've bought, feedback you've received, your public profile, your billing and shipping info, your Etsy bill, any Etsy-related apps you use, and various shop-related settings. In this chapter, you find out about the ins and outs of Your Account.

## Total Access: Accessing Your Account

After you sign in (following the instructions in Chapter 2), you can access Your Account with one click of the mouse, on the Your Account link that appears on every Etsy page. When you click this link, you'll see a page like the one shown in Figure 4-1. (Actually, we fibbed a little. If you haven't yet posted an item for sale on Etsy, your page won't show item listings like this one does; it'll show a page that prompts you to list an item ASAP. We hope you'll forgive us!) As you can see, loads of links run along the left side of the page; read on to find out where they lead.

By default, Your Account displays items currently for sale on its main page. To change this display, click the Settings link, click the Preferences tab, open the Your Account Shortcut drop-down list, choose Orders (Sold) or Your Purchases, and click the Update Preferences button.

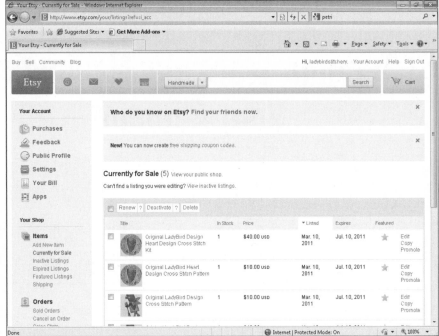

**Figure 4-1:**
You can access Your Account with one click of the mouse.

# Final Accountdown: Checking Out Options under Your Account

Etsy groups several account-related settings in one area in Your Account. These include options related to purchases, feedback, your Etsy profile, settings, your Etsy bill, and Etsy apps. For more info, read on.

## Buy crazy: Tracking your Etsy purchases

Anything that you buy on Etsy appears on the Purchases page, shown in Figure 4-2. To access this page, simply click the Purchases link on the left side of Your Account. You may view your purchased items to review an item's invoice (by clicking the Invoice link) or to reconnect with a seller (by clicking her user name and choosing Contact or Shop from the list of options that appears). (Check out Chapters 14 and 18 for info on invoices, and see Chapter 17 for details on communicating with other folks on Etsy.)

Notice that you can filter purchases by month and year, for easier viewing.

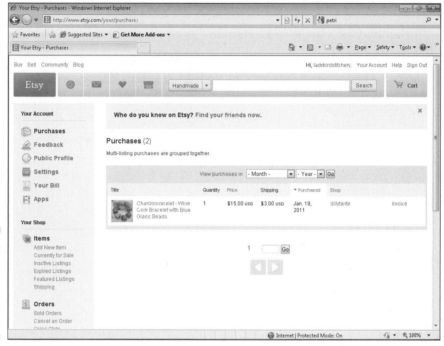

**Figure 4-2:**
Keep track
of your Etsy
purchases
on this
page.

## Baby got feedback: Checking your feedback

To get a sense of your rep on Etsy, check out your feedback in Your Account. Simply click the Feedback link along the left side of the Your Account page; then click the Completed Feedback tab to see the scuttlebutt (see Figure 4-3). You can also leave feedback for other members and view appreciation photos in this area of Your Account.

For more on leaving feedback, check out Chapters 5 and 17.

## Public eye: Viewing your public profile

Your Etsy public profile is just what it sounds like: a page where other Etsians can go to learn all about you and your Etsy shop. Populating your public profile is a big part of running a successful Etsy shop; after all, a big reason people shop on Etsy is to forge a personal connection with the people who make what they buy. You populate your public profile from, well, the Your Public Profile page; you find out all about populating your public profile in Chapter 8. To access this page, click the Public Profile link on the left side of the Your Account page.

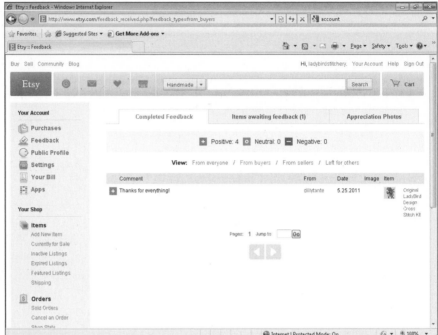

**Figure 4-3:**
View and leave feedback here.

# Revision quest: Revising your account settings

On Etsy, viewing and changing your account settings — such as your password; e-mail address; language, currency, and other preferences; privacy settings; shipping address; billing info; and e-mail notification settings — is a breeze. To access all these settings, click the Settings link on the left side of Your Account; then click the tab you need — Account (displayed by default, as shown in Figure 4-4), Preferences, Privacy, Shipping Addresses, Billing, or E-mails.

# I'm just a bill: Viewing your Etsy bill

Although it's true that the best things in life are free, it's also true that there's no such thing as a free lunch. If you opt to sell your handmade or vintage goodies on Etsy, you have to pony up each month. To see how much you owe, click the

Your Bill link in Your Etsy; you can pay your bill by clicking the Make a Payment Now button on the page that appears. For more on paying your Etsy bill, as well as on how much it costs to list an item on Etsy, flip forward to Chapter 18.

## Appy ending: Tracking your Etsy apps

As you discover in Chapter 18, loads of apps are available for Etsians to enjoy. (An *app* is just a piece of software designed to help you perform a specific task.) For example, you'll find apps to help you run your Etsy store, compile Etsy treasuries, and more. You can access apps connected to your Etsy account on the Apps page (see Figure 4-5), which you view by clicking the Apps link on the left side of Your Account. To see a list of available Etsy apps, click the App Gallery link on the Apps page.

Note that, for the most part, Etsy hasn't developed these apps; third-party vendors create them. If you have trouble with one, you need to contact the vendor, not Etsy.

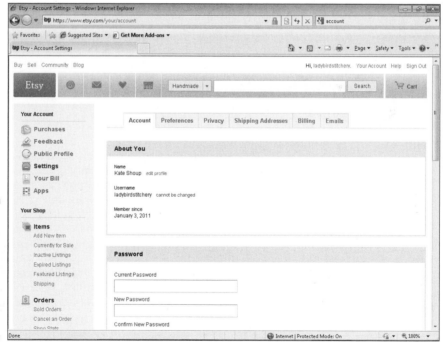

**Figure 4-4:**
Use this page to view and change your Etsy account settings.

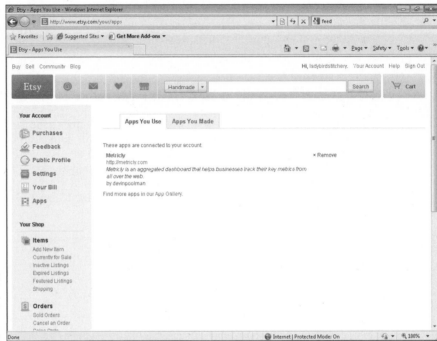

**Figure 4-5:**
Access your
Etsy apps.

# Shop Girl: Familiarizing Yourself with Your Etsy Shop Settings

Your Account does more than enable you to keep track of purchases, monitor your feedback, change your public profile, adjust your account settings, view and pay your Etsy bill, and keep track of Etsy apps (as we note earlier in this chapter). You can also use Your Account to administer your Etsy shop. Specifically, links in the Your Shop section on the left side of Your Account allow you to manage item listings, handle orders you've received, change your shop settings, and promote your shop (see Figure 4-6).

This area also includes links to seller resources, such as Etsy's super-handy Seller Handbook, which is a crazy-thorough compendium of articles about selling on Etsy, and the site's App Gallery (see the preceding section).

## Listful thinking: Managing item listings

The Items links in the Your Shop area give you easy access to tools that enable you to do the following:

- ✔ Add new item listings
- ✔ View, edit, renew, deactivate, and delete items currently for sale
- ✔ Manage draft listings
- ✔ View, edit, activate, and delete inactive item listings
- ✔ View, edit, renew, and delete expired listings
- ✔ View, edit, and rearrange featured listings
- ✔ Apply shipping profiles to multiple listings (you learn about shipping profiles in Chapter 9)

You find out how to do all these tasks (except for applying shipping profiles to multiple listings) in Chapter 13.

**Figure 4-6:**
Use these links to manage your Etsy shop.

# *Order up: Handling sold items*

With the Orders links in the Your Shop area, you can do the following:

- ✔ View and track sold items (see Chapters 14 and 15 for more details)
- ✔ Find out how to cancel an order (covered in Chapter 17)

✔ View daily and monthly sales stats (discussed further in Chapter 18)

✔ View reported cases — that is, nondelivery cases reported by buyers

If a buyer doesn't receive your item, she can report the problem to Etsy. Any nondelivery reports appear on the Reported Cases page, which you access by clicking the Reported Cases link. For more information about handling reports, see Chapter 17.

## Bump, setting, spike: Changing shop settings

The Shop Settings links give you access to tools that enable you to do the following:

✔ Establish the look of your shop and broadcast information about your shop and policies (covered in Chapters 8 and 9)

✔ Establish shipping profiles and accepted payment methods, accept sales tax, and set your preferred currency (discussed in Chapter 9)

✔ Access shop options, vacation mode settings, and Web analytics, and download shop data to a spreadsheet application (see Chapter 18 for additional details)

## Go through the promotions: Promoting your shop

With literally millions of Etsy shops for buyers to choose from, making yours stand out is imperative. Your Account provides easy access to several tools to help you achieve just that. For example, you can use these tools to do the following:

✔ Generate coupons

✔ Reserve a spot on the Etsy Showcase, to boost sales

✔ Build your own Etsy Mini, for showing off your Etsy inventory on your own personal Web site

✔ Add an Etsy tab to your Facebook page

These tools are major topics of conversation in Chapter 16.

# Chapter 5

# Buy and Buy: Finding and Purchasing Items on Etsy

## In This Chapter

▶ Discovering Etsy's allure for buyers

▶ Searching for items on Etsy

▶ Understanding how transactions work

▶ Leaving feedback after a purchase

*Y*ou've set up your Etsy account. You've gotten your bearings on the Etsy home page. You've explored the ins and outs of using Your Account. After all that work, you deserve a break!

You know as well as we do that there's no better way to recharge than to engage in a little retail therapy. And there's no better way to engage in a little retail therapy than to shop — you guessed it — on Etsy. In this chapter, you discover how, and why, to buy on Etsy.

## Gimme One Reason: Understanding Why You Should Buy on Etsy

Why buy from Etsy? Simple: Where else are you going to find a handmade bracelet featuring images of *The Golden Girls* cast in resin?

Of course, even if you don't maintain a shrine for Rue McClanahan in your foyer, you can find plenty of compelling reasons to buy on Etsy. Consider just a few:

✔ Etsy features unique, one-of-a-kind handmade and vintage items — goodies you simply can't find anywhere else.

✔ Etsy offers an incredible breadth of items for sale, from accessories to ceramics, from jewelry to quilts, and everything in between.

✔ If you're in the market for craft supplies, Etsy is for you. At last count, Etsy's Supplies category listed nearly a million items, including beads, buttons, fabric, yarn, paper, stamps, and more.

✔ Because there's no middleman — you buy directly from artists and craftspeople — prices on Etsy are generally very reasonable. At the same time, your purchase can help these skilled artisans earn a living wage.

✔ Buying on Etsy can make you a savvier seller. As a customer, you'll develop an eye for which selling practices work and which don't.

# Go Fish: Using Etsy's Search Tool

If you've landed on Etsy with the idea of finding a specific item or certain items that relate to a particular theme — say, aardvarks or jai alai — you'll be grateful for the site's robust Search tool. With the Search tool, you can search for handmade items, vintage items, and supplies. You can also use it to locate a particular seller or shop, and to search among items and shops you've hearted.

To use the Search tool, follow these steps:

1. **While on Etsy's home page, type a keyword or phrase in the Search field, located on the right side of the header bar.**

   As you type your keyword or phrase, Etsy displays Search Suggestions — that is, links for items that may constitute a good match. Etsy culls these suggestions from recent searches performed by other folks on the site. If one of these Search Suggestions matches what you're looking for, simply click it to view a list of relevant items.

2. **Click the down arrow to the left of the Search field and choose one of the following from the list that appears (see Figure 5-1):**

   • Handmade

   • Vintage

   • Supplies

   • All Items

   • People

   • Shops

**Figure 5-1:**
Specify the type of item you want to find, or indicate that you want to locate a particular Etsy shop.

If you're logged in to your Etsy account, you'll see two other options: Your Favorites and Your Favorite Shops. Choose these to search for items or shops you've hearted, respectively. (Don't know what hearting is? Flip to Chapter 21 for details.)

**3. Click the Search button.**

Etsy returns a list of items that match your criteria (see Figure 5-2). If you searched for a specific person on Etsy, the list contains people whose user names start with the keywords you typed.

**Figure 5-2:**
Etsy displays your search results.

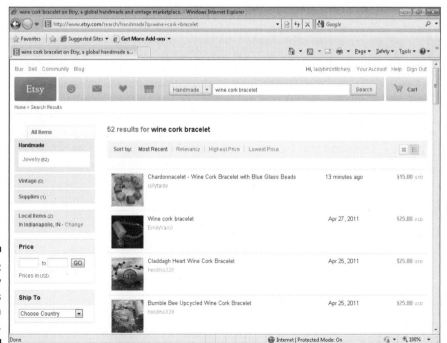

4. **Optionally, sort the search results by clicking the Most Recent, Relevancy, Highest Price, or Lowest Price link (as shown in Figure 5-2).**

   To narrow your search results to items in a particular category (say, Jewelry), click the category link on the left side of the screen, as shown in Figure 5-2.

5. **Click an item in the list to view its item listing.**

   If you searched for a person, click her user name to visit her profile page.

*Note:* When you launch a search from a page other than the Etsy home page, you may notice that the options in the list shown in Figure 5-1 change. For example, when you start your search from the Treasury, you see a Treasury option in the list. By selecting this option, you can limit your search to the Treasury. Likewise, when you start your search from a category page, such as the Geekery page, you see a Geekery option in the list, enabling you to limit your search to items in that category. And when you launch your search on an Etsy shop page, you can limit your search to items in that shop. (Check out Chapter 3 for an introduction to Etsy's Treasury feature, categories, and more.)

If your search efforts fail to yield useful results — for example, Etsy returns too many matches — try these techniques:

✔ To search for a specific phrase, surround it with quotation marks. For example, suppose that you want to find items related to the movie *Roman Holiday.* Of course, searching for the phrase *Roman Holiday,* without quotation marks, returns pages that contain the phrase *Roman Holiday.* However, it also returns pages that simply contain the individual words *Roman* and *Holiday,* which likely have nothing whatsoever to do with Audrey Hepburn's romp across Roma. Enclosing the phrase in quotation marks limits the results to pages that contain the phrase only.

✔ To exclude pages with a certain word from your results, precede the word you want to exclude with a minus sign. For example, suppose that you want to find listings that pertain to mustangs (as in, the horses). To omit listings that relate to the Ford Mustang automobile, you could add *-Ford* to the search string. (Note that there's no space between the minus sign and the word.)

Searching is great when you have some idea of what you're looking for. But what if you just want to poke around the site? In that case, you'll enjoy Etsy's many browsing-related features. These include Categories, Handpicked Items, Recently Listed items, Colors, the Treasury, Pounce, Shop Local, Time Machine[2], and the Facebook Friends tool. You can access these tools from Etsy's home page or from the Shop on Etsy page, which you access by clicking the Buy link in the header bar. For help in using these tools, refer to Chapter 3.

# Transactions Speak Louder Than Words: Delving into Transaction Details

As you browse or search the gajillionty-leven items available for sale on Etsy, you're bound to find a thing or two (or five) that you simply cannot live without. Fortunately, Etsy makes buying a breeze. As you find out in the following sections, all you do is add the item to your cart, check out, arrange for payment, and submit your order.

Before you buy, take a moment to view the seller's feedback score. To do so, click the Feedback link in her shop's home page or her public profile. If the seller boasts positive feedback, you can feel confident buying from her. If not, you may want to reconsider your purchase. (You find out more about feedback later in this chapter.) You also want to check the store's policies by clicking the View Shop Policies link that appears in the item listing.

## Affairs of the cart: Adding an item to your cart and checking out

To add an item to your cart and check out, follow these steps:

1. **Click the Add to Cart button found on the listing page for the item you want to buy (see Figure 5-3).**

2. **Etsy displays your shopping cart (see Figure 5-4).**

   If you want to continue shopping, click the Keep Shopping button. (If you click Keep Shopping, you can return to your cart at any time by clicking the Cart link along the top of every Etsy page.) Otherwise, click the Ship To down arrow and choose the country where you want the item shipped. Etsy updates your Shipping and Order Total information.

   Got cold feet? No worries. You can remove the item from your cart by clicking the Remove link. You can also click the Contact Shop link to launch a convo with the shop owner. This option is helpful if you have questions about the item. (Flip to Chapter 17 for the scoop on convos.)

3. **Under How You'll Pay, indicate how you want to pay for the item.**

   Note that the options available here may differ by shop. Typical options include PayPal or credit card, money order, and check.

**Figure 5-3:**
Click the
Add to Cart
button to
add an item
to your Etsy
shopping
cart.

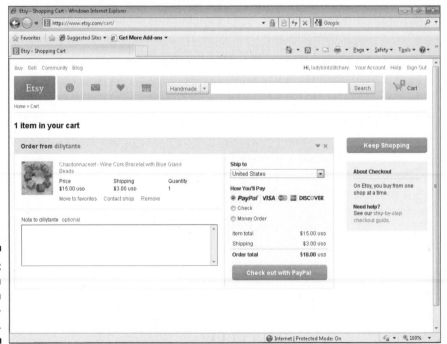

**Figure 5-4:**
The item
appears in
your shop-
ping cart.

Some Etsy sellers issue coupon codes for their shops. When a seller issues a coupon code, a special Shop Coupon Code field appears on the page shown in Figure 5-4. If you have a coupon code for the shop you're buying from (maybe you grabbed a coupon code from a blog, or the seller posted it in her Etsy shop), you enter it in the Shop Coupon Code field and click the Apply button. Etsy updates your Order Total information.

4. **Optionally, type a note to the seller in the Notes section.**

    Adding a note is especially important if the item you bought offers different options, like color or size.

5. **Click the Check Out button.**

    Note that the exact verbiage on this button differs depending on which payment method you choose in Step 3.

## Pays of our lives: Paying for your item

What happens after you add an item to your card and check out depends on which payment option you choose — PayPal or credit card, money order, check, or "other." The following sections describe these options in more detail.

If your shopping cart contains items from multiple shops, you must pay each seller individually. You have to complete the checkout process for each shop separately.

### Paying with PayPal or credit card

If you chose to pay via PayPal, a PayPal window opens, where you can log in to your PayPal account. After you do, a Review Your Information page opens (see Figure 5-5). Follow these steps:

1. **Verify your shipping address.**

    To change the address, click the Change link and choose from the list of alternate addresses that appears. To add a new address, click the Add a New Address link and follow the onscreen instructions.

2. **Choose your method of funding.**

3. **Review your information and click Continue.**

    PayPal returns you to the Etsy site. To find out how to submit your order, read on.

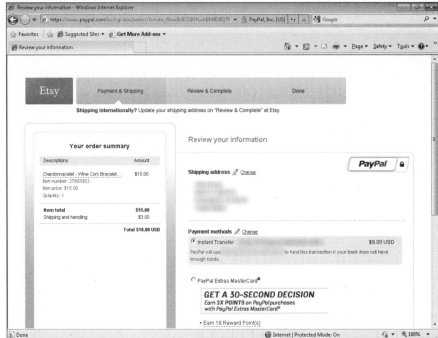

**Figure 5-5:**
Pay via
PayPal.

Don't have a PayPal account? Don't worry. Setting one up is as easy as pie. You can even do it from Etsy during the checkout process. Simply choose PayPal as your payment method and click the Check Out with PayPal button. Then when you're prompted to pay, follow the onscreen instructions to register for a PayPal account.

Note that, in some cases, you may also be able to use PayPal to pay for your purchase with a credit card, even if you don't have a PayPal account. To do so, again choose PayPal as your payment method and click the Check Out with PayPal button. Then when you're prompted to pay, click the Continue Checkout link on the left side of the page. Enter your contact and credit card info; decline when asked whether you want to create a PayPal account.

### Paying via other means

If you opted to pay via check, money order, or "other" (say, magic beans), you'll want to convo the seller to make the appropriate arrangements. (See Chapter 17 for the full scoop on convos.)

# *Submissionary position: Submitting your order*

Before you submit your order, take a moment to review the order summary.

✔ If the shipping address shown isn't correct, click the Change Shipping Address link, click your preferred address in the list that appears, and click Continue. If the address you want doesn't appear in the list, click the Ship to a New Address option button and enter the address in the fields that appear.

✔ If something related to your payment details is out of order, simply click the Back button on your browser to return to the Shopping Cart page and choose the desired payment option.

If all the order details are error free, click the Submit Order button to submit your order (see Figure 5-6). In addition to displaying a special confirmation screen, Etsy e-mails you to confirm your order. All you have left to do is install yourself in the proximity of your mailbox until your item arrives.

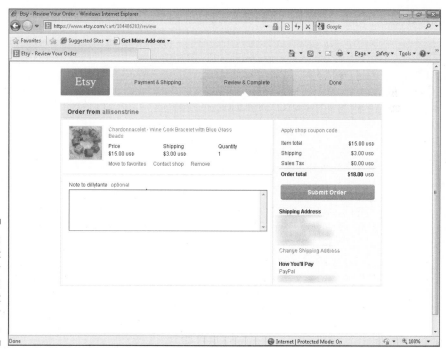

**Figure 5-6:** Submit your order by clicking the Submit Order button.

As you wait for your purchase to arrive, if you need to review your order information, simply sign in to your Etsy account, click the Your Account link along the top of any Etsy page, click Purchases, and click the item's invoice to view it. Note that the invoice includes the seller's e-mail address, in case you need to contact her. You can also contact the seller by clicking the Contact link in the invoice.

# Feedback Is Forever: Leaving Feedback After You Buy

After you receive your item, take a moment to leave feedback about the transaction. When you leave feedback about a sale, you indicate whether the experience was positive, negative, or neutral. You also have the opportunity to share your comments about the transaction. Other Etsy users can then view this feedback to determine whether a particular seller is reliable.

Your feedback affects your seller's feedback score — and, by extension, her reputation on the site. It's super important that you issue feedback consistently, fairly, and honestly.

Although leaving feedback is purely optional, doing so is a good idea; it helps ensure that everyone feels safe shopping on Etsy. Note that you have 120 days to leave feedback after the conclusion of a sale.

To leave feedback, follow these steps:

1. **While signed in to your Etsy account, click the Your Account link along the top of any Etsy page.**

2. **Click the Feedback link on the left side of the screen.**

   The Feedback page opens, with the Items Awaiting Feedback tab displayed (see Figure 5-7).

3. **Click the Positive, Neutral, or Negative option button under the transaction you want to rate.**

   If you've had a negative experience with a seller, first see if you can hammer out whatever issue is bothering you via e-mail or a convo. Often conflicts on Etsy are simply the result of a misunderstanding.

4. **Optionally, type a comment about the transaction or the seller.**

   If the transaction was super great, why not make the seller's day by saying something super nice in the comment field?

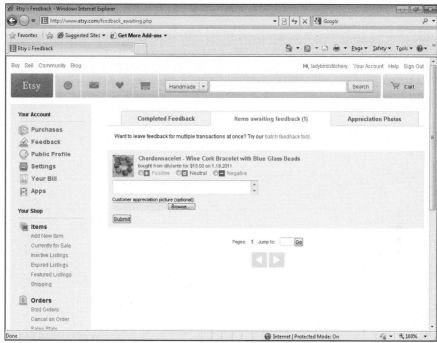

5. **If you want, upload an appreciation photo for the seller.**

   This photo may be an image of you wearing the item you bought, a photo
   of the item in its new home on your bookshelf, or simply something silly
   to make your seller smile. Appreciation photos are a great way to share a
   little love on Etsy! To upload an appreciation photo, just click the Browse
   button; then locate and select the photo on your computer.

6. **Click Submit.**

   Etsy posts your feedback on the site.

# Chapter 6

# Safe Word: Maintaining Privacy and Safety on Etsy

Aₛ the saying goes, it's all fun and games until somebody gets hurt. On Etsy, as in life, safety is paramount. Just as you wear a seatbelt when you drive, you wear a helmet on your bike, and you wear knee pads during roller derby, you must take the appropriate steps to remain safe on Etsy. In this chapter, you discover the precautions you must take to ensure your security and maintain your privacy on Etsy.

## Oh, Behave! Adhering to Etsy's Do's and Don'ts

Every Etsy member must make it a point to peruse the site's do's and don'ts (see Figure 6-1). This page spells out everything you need to do to avoid committing a potentially embarrassing gaffe on the site. (To view this page, click the Help link that appears along in the upper-right corner of every Etsy page; under Site Policy on the Help page, click the DOs and DON'Ts link.) In brief, it covers the following:

✔ **Membership:** This section of Etsy's Do's and Don'ts outlines how members must behave on the site, specifies whether members can transfer ownership of an Etsy account to another party, clarifies the ins and outs of maintaining multiple accounts, specifies the scenarios under which collectives may be formed (see Chapter 18 for the scoop), and more.

✔ **Conversations:** These do's and don'ts pertain to the use of conversations, or convos (which we discuss more in Chapter 17). Although members may use convos to build friendly relationships with each other, they're intended primarily for communicating about transactions. Under no circumstances should you use convos to send spam, to harass another member, or to interfere with a transaction.

✔ **Transactions:** Here Etsy defines what a transaction is, clarifies its role in any transaction, and spells out policies relating to transactions both for buyers and for sellers. This section also indicates what to do when the buyer doesn't pay up, what happens when a seller doesn't deliver, what recourse a buyer has when an item isn't up to snuff, and more. (Brush up on the basics of transactions in Chapter 5.)

✔ **Feedback:** As you find out in Chapter 5, Etsy members rely on feedback to gauge a buyer or seller's reputation. This section of Etsy's Do's and Don'ts indicates the rules regarding leaving feedback and cites situations in which feedback may be removed or altered.

✔ **Shops and Listings:** See this section of Etsy's Do's and Don'ts for guidance on handling issues relating to your Etsy shop and any listings you post there. This section includes details on what you can and can't sell on Etsy, how you need to tag the items you list, and more. (Parts II and III explain the basics of opening and running an Etsy shop.)

✔ **Flagging:** Members can use Etsy's flagging features to alert the site to potential problems. This section of Etsy's Do's and Don'ts spells out when flagging is appropriate and what happens when someone or something is flagged. You find out more about flagging later in this chapter.

✔ **Community:** In this section of Etsy's Do's and Don'ts, members discover what Etsy deems appropriate behavior on the site's various community features, including its forums, chat rooms, Virtual Labs, and teams (see Chapter 19 for more about these features). This section takes special care to remind members that these areas are public, meaning that people need to use common sense when sharing personal information on them. It also emphasizes the importance of treating everyone on the site with respect and kindness.

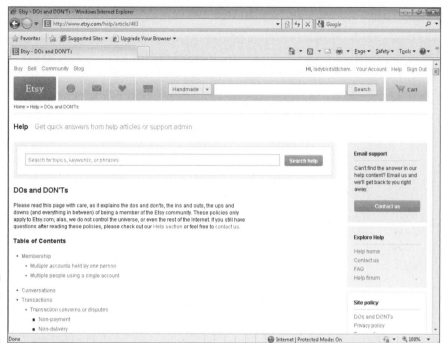

**Figure 6-1:**
Etsy's do's
and don'ts.

# Private Party: Guarding Your Privacy on Etsy

Just because you're on Etsy doesn't mean you want everyone there all up in your business. Fortunately, Etsy takes your privacy seriously; you can take several steps to guard your privacy on Etsy.

If you're particularly concerned about maintaining your privacy, consider using a P.O. box as your address when conducting business on Etsy. That way, even if you buy or sell an item on the site, your home or work address remains unrevealed.

## Privacy, please: Understanding Etsy's privacy policy

Like all reputable Web sites, Etsy maintains rigorous standards with respect to privacy. These standards relate to the following:

✔ How Etsy collects and treats personal information

✔ How Etsy handles service-related announcements and administrative messages

✔ What types of tracking technology Etsy uses

✔ How Etsy uses *cookies* — that is, small bits of data from the site that are stored on your computer's hard drive

✔ Measures Etsy takes to ensure that transactions on the site are secure

To view this privacy policy, shown in Figure 6-2, click the Help link that appears in the upper-right corner of every Etsy page; under Site Policy on the Help page, click the Privacy Policy link.

As you read Etsy's privacy policy, you may notice the TRUSTe seal prominently displayed at the top. TRUSTe is an independent, nonprofit organization whose mission is to promote the use of fair information practices. This seal indicates that Etsy complies with TRUSTe's privacy standards, meaning that you can click with confidence. Oh, and for those of you over the pond, Etsy also complies with the E.U. Safe Harbor framework. Set forth by the Department of Commerce, this framework outlines standards for collecting, using, and retaining data from the European Union.

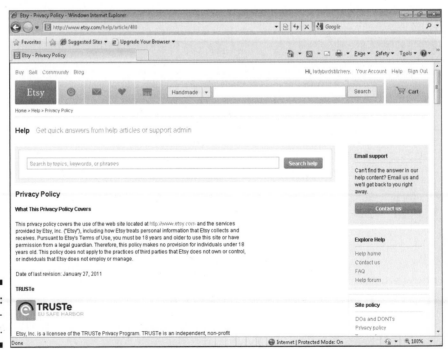

**Figure 6-2:**
Etsy's privacy policy.

## Leave me alone! Changing your privacy settings

By default, anyone who visits your Etsy page can view your favorites. However, you may prefer to keep this information private. Maybe you use Etsy to buy gifts for others, and you don't want them to be tipped off to gift ideas that you've hearted if they visit your page. Or maybe you don't want to alert your atheist boyfriend to your secret guilty pleasure: *Touched By an Angel*–themed soaps. Whatever your reason, you can easily change your privacy settings to keep your favorites on the down low. You can also limit your "findability" by hiding your info from other Etsy members who use Etsy's Find Your Friends feature to find real-world friends on the site. (Chapter 21 has more on finding friends on Etsy by importing your contacts into the site.) Here's how to do so after you log in to your Etsy account:

1. **Click the Your Account link along the top of any Etsy page.**

2. **Click the Settings link on the left side of the Your Account page.**

3. **Click the Privacy tab at the top of the page.**

4. **In the Favorites section of the Privacy tab, shown in Figure 6-3, click the Only You (Private) option button to select it.**

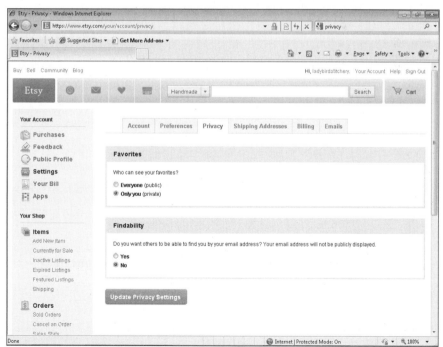

**Figure 6-3:**
Change your privacy settings.

5. **In the Findability section, click the No option button to prevent other Etsy members from finding you when they use Etsy's Find Your Friends feature.**

6. **Click the Update Privacy Settings button.**

## Close sesame: Choosing a strong password

When you set up your Etsy account, you're prompted to select a password to prevent others from accessing your Etsy account (see Chapter 2 for details). Unfortunately, many people opt for decidedly lame passwords — their birthdays, their kid's name, the word *password,* or something equally easy to guess.

To ensure that no one accesses your account without your authorization, you need to set a strong password. A strong password has the following characteristics:

✔ It's at least eight characters long.

✔ It doesn't contain your user name or your real name.

✔ It doesn't contain a complete word.

✔ It differs from passwords you've used in the past.

✔ It contains a mixture of uppercase letters, lowercase letters, numbers, symbols, and spaces.

Don't use the same password on multiple sites. Otherwise, if someone figures out your password for one site, that person will have access to all your online accounts.

For an added layer of protection, you need to periodically change your password — ideally, every 30 to 90 days. To change your password, log in to your Etsy account and follow these steps:

1. **Click the Your Account link along the top of any Etsy page.**

2. **Click the Settings link on the left side of the Your Account page.**

   You should land automatically on the Account tab, but if you don't, click the Account tab at the top of the page.

3. **In the Password section of the Account tab, shown in Figure 6-4, type your current password in the Current Password field.**

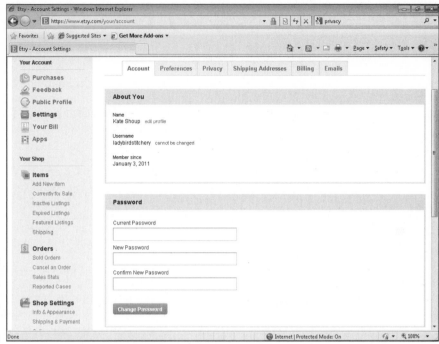

**Figure 6-4:**
Change
your Etsy
password.

4. **In the New Password field, type your new password.**

5. **Retype your new password in the Confirm New Password field.**

6. **Click the Change Password button.**

If you're worried about forgetting your password, you can write it down — but make sure you store it somewhere safe and private. If you forget your password *and* where you wrote it down, you have to contact Etsy at support@ etsy.com to ask for help (after upping your daily dose of gingko biloba, of course). Ditto if you forget your user name.

If you've signed on to your Etsy account using a public computer — for example, one at your local library or in an Internet cafe — be sure you log off when you're finished. Otherwise, the next person who uses it will be privy to your account information.

# Safe Passage: Keeping Yourself Safe on Etsy

The good news is, since its inception in 2005, the Etsy community has grown like Shaquille O'Neal in the ninth grade — a lot. Unfortunately, that growth has made the site all the more attractive to scammers and other flim-flammers, not to mention just plain jerks. In this section, you find out how to keep yourself safe on the site.

## Scam I am: Avoiding scams on Etsy

Etsy's not just home to artists and crafters; it's also a congregation of con artists and shafters. As you use Etsy, be on the lookout for scams.

On Etsy, most fraudulent activities involve the use of money orders or cashier's checks. For example, if someone contacts you with a vague offer to buy something in your Etsy shop via money order or cashier's check, but offers to pay more than is necessary to expedite the item or includes some other weird request or instructions, beware. This interaction is typically an attempt to relieve you of your merchandise.

Some of these scammers operate by purchasing an item — usually something expensive — and indicating that they'll pay by money order or cashier's check, but they tack on a substantial amount along with a request to, say, buy them a new notebook computer and ship it to them along with your valuable piece. The catch? The money order or cashier's check is really a forgery. The end result: Not only does the scammer effectively steal your item, but you reward her by buying her a computer!

If anyone asks you to front her some cash or some other expensive item, pronto, your answer should be a polite but firm "N to the O, no."

Sometimes people do have gift emergencies. They need one of your kitten-soft hand-knit scarves, like, yesterday. But sometimes people will foster a sense of urgency in an attempt to prey on your kindly nature — for example, begging you to ship an item right away, even though their cashier's check or money order hasn't cleared. Don't be reeled in by this tactic!

Given how many scams involve the use of cashier's checks and money orders, you may reasonably choose not to accept those forms of payment for items in your Etsy shop. (We discuss forms of payment in Chapter 9.)

Beyond these very obvious examples, how do you determine whether the person you're dealing with on Etsy is on the up-and-up? If she has engaged in countless transactions and received reviews as glowing as Kate Winslet's skin, then you can probably proceed without fear. (For help with checking a seller's reviews — or, in Etsy parlance, her feedback — refer to Chapter 5.) But trust your instincts. Assuming that you're not Billy Idol, those hairs on your neck are standing on end for a reason. Pay attention to them.

So what do you do if you get taken on Etsy? First, contact your financial institution, on the double. Second, report the situation to Etsy. (See the next section for details.) You may also opt to alert your local law enforcement.

## Safety dance: Staying safe in Etsy's public places

As any regular Etsy user will tell you, one of the great things about using the site is its robust community of interesting, arty folk. But as with any community — especially online — not everyone on Etsy is on the up-and-up. For this reason, it's critical to take steps to keep yourself safe on Etsy's public places, such as its forums and teams (which we describe in detail in Chapter 19). Keep a few points in mind:

- ✔ **Lurk before you leap.** Before jumping into a forum or team discussion, monitor it for a while. See whether the Etsians engaged in the discussion are people you want to interact with.

- ✔ **Don't hesitate to exit left.** If a discussion goes south, simply disengage. Life's stressful enough; why embroil yourself in a conflict on a site that's supposed to be fun?

- ✔ **Limit personal information.** Don't share your digits or other personal details, such as where you live or work, on Etsy's forums, teams, or other public spaces.

- ✔ **Avoid oversharing.** Although participating in the Etsy community can foster a sense of closeness among members, avoid the temptation to over-share. If you wouldn't be comfortable sharing something with, say, your boyfriend's grandmother, then it probably doesn't belong on Etsy, either.

- ✔ **Think before you connect in real life.** Although using Etsy is certainly a great way to pick up a new BFF and even fall in love (for proof, search for the Etsy Love Stories series on The Etsy Blog at www.etsy.com/ storque), take care before you agree to connect with other Etsy users in real life. If you do decide to meet in person, pick a neutral public place — somewhere you'll feel comfortable. Hip a friend or family member to your plans, and be sure to bring a cellphone.

✔ **Be nice.** If you're kind to others online, chances are, others will be kind back. Not only is it bad karma to knowingly insult or harass another Etsy member, but it's against the site's rules. Abusive behavior can get you kicked off the site for good.

# Brooklyn, We Have a Problem: Reporting Issues to Etsy

Suppose you run across a problem while using Etsy. For example, maybe you find yourself engaged in a dispute with another Etsy member. Or perhaps you've stumbled across an item that shouldn't be sold on the site (in other words, it isn't handmade, vintage, or a craft supply). Or perchance some dastardly character has swindled you out of an item in your Etsy shop. If so, you can report it. Here's how:

1. **While logged in to your Etsy account, click the Help link that appears along the top of any Etsy page.**

   The Help page opens.

2. **Click the Contact Us button under E-mail Support.**

   The E-mail Etsy Support page opens (see Figure 6-5).

3. **Click the Select a Topic down arrow.**

   The Select a Topic drop-down list opens.

4. **To "flag" a shop or item that you think is in violation of Etsy's rules, choose Report Something You Saw in a Shop or Listing. To report another type of problem, such as harassment, choose Help with Disputes, Harassment, or a Suspicious Convo.**

5. **Type a subject for your message.**

6. **Type your message.**

7. **Optionally, you can click the Choose a File button to attach a file.**

   For example, if you've uncovered an item that shouldn't be sold on Etsy, you can capture a screen shot of the item's listing page and attach the image file to your message.

8. **Click Submit.**

   Etsy notifies you that your report has been submitted; it also sends you a confirmation e-mail.

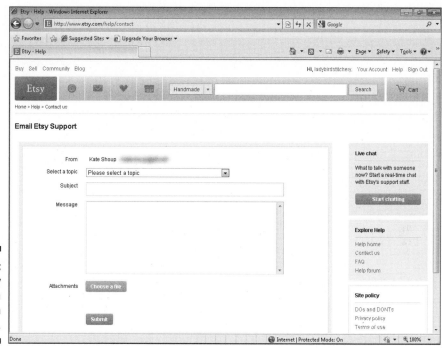

**Figure 6-5:**
It's easy
to report a
problem on
Etsy.

# Part II

# If You Build It, They Will Come: Setting Up Your Etsy Shop

The 5th Wave                    By Rich Tennant

"Oh, we're doing just great. Philip and I are selling jelly jar candles on Etsy. I make the candles and manage the listings, and Philip sort of handles the supplies."

# In this part . . .

If your goal is to launch your own Etsy shop, this part is the one for you. Here you'll discover what you can — and can't — sell on Etsy. (In case you're wondering, drugs, live animals, and firearms, among other things, aren't allowed.) You'll also find out what steps you can take to make your Etsy shop stand out in the crowd. After that, you'll explore the important, yet oft-overlooked, subject of shop policies, as well as discover a foolproof method for pricing your work.

# Chapter 7

# Sell Coverage: Understanding What You Can and Can't Sell on Etsy

## In This Chapter

▶ Figuring out what you can sell on Etsy

▶ Determining what items Etsy doesn't allow

▶ Understanding the consequences of selling prohibited items

$M$any people think of Etsy as a sort of eBay for arts and crafts. Indeed, Etsy and eBay *are* similar — people use both sites to buy stuff from other individuals; the sites' business models, which involve charging listing fees and taking a small commission on every sale, are clearly related; and members use feedback to rate sellers.

But the differences are hard to ignore. For starters, unlike eBay, Etsy doesn't use an auction format. Furthermore, although Etsy is certainly growing, it's significantly smaller than eBehemoth. But the biggest and most obvious difference is that, unlike eBay, where sellers can list pretty much anything (anyone need a ghost in a jar?), sellers on Etsy are limited to selling items that meet Etsy's strict criteria. In this chapter, you discover what you can — and can't — sell on Etsy.

For more information about what you can and can't sell on Etsy, see the site's "Do's and Don'ts" page (www.etsy.com/policy/dosdonts). Specifics appear in the "Shops and Listings" section of this page. If you don't find your answer there, check Etsy's Site Help forum. (You find out more about forums in Chapter 19.)

# Yes, We Can! Figuring Out What You Can Sell on Etsy

In a nutshell, you can sell three types of items on Etsy (see Figure 7-1, which you can find by clicking the Sell link at the top of any Etsy page):

- ✔ Handmade items
- ✔ Vintage goods (20 years or older)
- ✔ Supplies for crafting

In the following sections, we describe these three categories in detail and address questions you may have about them.

Some items transcend these categories. For example, you may have vintage or handmade items that also qualify as supplies. If your inventory includes items like these, you need to decide which category applies best.

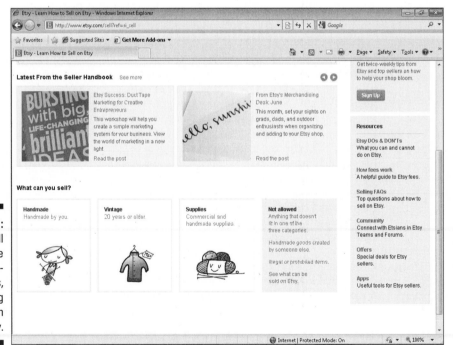

**Figure 7-1:**
You can sell handmade items, vintage goods, and crafting supplies on Etsy.

## *The Handmaid's Tale: Selling handmade items*

Etsy's primary *raison d'être* is to serve as a marketplace for handmade goods, with no mass-produced items allowed. But the site isn't for selling just *any* handmade goods. Etsy sellers must offer handmade goods *made by them* (or by members of their Etsy collective — flip to Chapter 18 for more about collectives). Selling an item that someone else made, even if it was painstakingly crafted by hand, isn't permitted.

Naturally, this requirement raises a few key questions:

✔ **What if you upcycle or otherwise alter an existing item?** Up-whatting? *Upcycling* is the process of fashioning new, higher-quality items out of useless materials or products that you would otherwise throw away. So maybe you specialize in making purses out of old license plates. Or perhaps you screen-print your own designs onto mass-produced T-shirts. In both cases, you're covered. In Etsy's view, items that are altered by hand in this manner can still be considered "handmade." Note, however, that Etsy doesn't feel that way about items that you've simply tailored, restored, or repaired.

✔ **What if you craft an item yourself from a kit?** Etsy doesn't view items that you've created using a "ready to assemble" kit as being handmade, unless you substantially alter the design as you work. So if you were planning to profit from your passion for paint-by-number, you may need to rethink your position.

✔ **What if someone helps you make your item?** For example, maybe you have an assistant who, under your supervision, assists with a portion of the creative process. Or perhaps you've enlisted a third-party vendor to handle some aspects of your workflow, such as printing your artwork onto greeting cards. Either way, you're golden. Etsy understands that more than one pair of hands may need to touch your item. It's also okay by Etsy if you have an assistant help you with such shop-related tasks as listing items in your Etsy shop, shipping items, communicating with buyers, keeping records, and so on. But you cross a line if that assistant or vendor handles most of the work involved in the item's creation.

✔ **What if you creatively repackage a commercial item?** Nope. No matter how great the finished product is, you can't list a gift basket stuffed with nonhandmade items and try to pass off the package as a handmade good.

The whole point of Etsy is to enable artisans and craftspeople to connect with buyers. Etsy is more than an online craft fair; it's an attempt to build an alternative, artisanal economy of sorts — one that eschews mass production. If your inventory isn't in line with this philosophy, Etsy may not be the marketplace for you.

## *Oldies but goodies: Offering vintage items*

Although Etsy was originally conceived as a marketplace for handmade goods, it also serves as an excellent venue for vintage goods and collectibles. Items can range from bags to books, clothing, electronics, furniture, jewelry, toys, and beyond.

So how old does something have to be in order to be considered vintage? It depends on who you ask. But if you ask Etsy, the answer is 20 years old. Unless your item was manufactured during Kurt Cobain's lifetime (or before), you need to find another venue for it.

## *Supplies and demand: Selling supplies*

In an effort to support its crafty community, Etsy allows the sale of commercial crafting supplies on the site: beads, buttons, fabric, findings, paper, patterns, tools, trim, wire, wool, and what-not. Shipping and packaging supplies are also acceptable.

What's not allowed: items that, although perhaps considered commercial crafting supplies, are ready for use as is — think mass-produced dollhouse furniture and the like. Ditto for mass-produced goods that may be used in conjunction with handmade items but aren't crafting supplies themselves. In other words, although your handmade lip gloss is a totally legitimate item on Etsy, selling the mass-produced brush you use to apply it as a separate item isn't kosher.

Do you have a closet full of crafting supplies? If so, consider culling your collection and listing your leftovers on Etsy. Not only will you pull in a little extra cash, but you'll give those goodies a new lease on life.

# *Just Say No! Understanding What's Not Allowed on Etsy*

You know what you can sell (thanks to the previous section): handmade items (when you've made them), vintage goods, and supplies. You may assume, then, that as long as your item fits into one of those categories, it's acceptable for sale on Etsy. But you know what happens when you assume! In the following sections, we describe the items and services that Etsy doesn't allow.

## *Achtung, baby: Knowing what items are prohibited*

Any number of items may meet the aforementioned criteria but aren't permitted on Etsy. One obvious example is items that are illegal; every Etsy seller is responsible for following all local laws. Other prohibited items include the following:

- Alcohol
- Drugs, druglike substances, and drug paraphernalia
- Firearms and weapons
- Live animals and illegal animal products
- Motor vehicles (automobiles, motorcycles, boats, and so on)
- Pornography
- Real estate
- Recalled items
- Tobacco

In addition, Etsy prohibits the sale of items that

- Promote hatred toward people or demean them based on race or ethnicity, gender or gender identity, disability, or sexual orientation
- Promote or glorify illegal activity
- Promote or glorify harmful acts

---

### Risqué business: Selling mature items on Etsy

Although Etsy prohibits the sale of pornography, it permits the sale of NC-17 items — think goods that involve a depiction of male or female genitalia or sexual activity, a depiction of graphic violence, or profane language. However, sellers who list such items must comply with certain policies to ensure that Etsy remains appropriate for a G-rated audience. Specifically, items of this sort must be tagged with the word *mature* and must contain the word *mature* in their titles. That way, users can restrict searches to omit these listings by including the exclusionary term "NOT mature" in their searches. Furthermore, the first thumbnail image of the item must be appropriate for general audiences, although additional images may show the item in all its mature splendor.

Also, although you can sell items that contain mature content or profane language, you may not use this type of content or language in your user name, profile, item titles, item tags, avatar, banner, shop announcement, or shop section titles.

## Service says: Selling only certain services

In general, you can't sell your services on Etsy. The site is designed as a marketplace for goods. So even if you're the best dog-walking, house-sitting masseuse this side of the Mississippi, you can't list your services on Etsy. You're not even allowed to avail yourself to members seeking your skills in the realm of tailoring, restoring antiques, retouching old photos, and the like.

If, however, your service results in a new, tangible item, you may offer it for sale on the site. For example, you may sell your services as a graphic designer, offering custom logos for clients, delivered via a digital file. Or maybe you give workshops; in that case, as long as participants leave your class with an actual physical object — an instructional booklet, a finished project, or what have you — it counts.

# Off with Her Head! Knowing What Happens If You Break a Rule

If you list a prohibited item or service on Etsy, vigilant staffers or other site members may flag it for Etsy's review. (Note that you're not privy to information about who flagged your item.)

In extreme cases, Etsy may delist your item immediately. More typically, however, Etsy will contact you to attempt to remedy the problem. Generally, you'll simply be asked to remove the prohibited item from your shop. If you fail to do so, Etsy will remove it for you. In egregious cases, Etsy may also opt to suspend or even terminate your selling privileges. Note that, as a seller, you will still be responsible for any outstanding fees if Etsy removes an item or suspends or terminates your account.

# Chapter 8

# Come on In! Creating an Eye-Catching Storefront

*W*hen you first create your Etsy shop, you'll no doubt be struck by one thing: its incredible plainness. In fact, when you visit your shop page (which you can easily do by clicking the Shop icon in the header bar that appears on every Etsy page after you sign in), all you'll see is a plain white page with two gray bars and a few links. Although minimalists among you may cheer this aesthetic, the rest of you will likely be itching to make some changes.

Fortunately, you can personalize your Etsy shop in any number of ways: by adding a banner, including a shop title and a shop announcement to describe your shop, and using sections to organize your goods. You can also personalize your shop by populating your Etsy profile; certain items that you add, such as your profile picture, or avatar, will appear on your shop page, too. This chapter shows you how.

We've said it before and we'll say it again: A major reason people shop on Etsy is to feel connected to the artists who make what they buy. To make sure people buy from *you,* you want your Etsy shop — and the items you list there — to reflect your personality. Whether you're serious or whimsical, modern or traditional, edgy or frilly, let your individuality shine through in your choice of banner, colors, and fonts, as well as your avatar and other visual elements. Your choice of words in your bio and other text-based elements also needs to reflect your personality. By revealing your true self in your Etsy shop, not only are you likely to increase your sales, but you may just make some friends along the way!

Don't forget to proofread all the text in your Etsy shop — your shop title, shop announcement, section titles, bio, and so on. Running a shop that's riddled with spelling and grammatical errors sends shoppers the wrong message — namely, that you're sloppy, lazy, and/or incompetent. That image isn't likely to win you any buyers!

# Mind Your Banners: Adding a Banner to Your Shop Page

To personalize your Etsy shop, you can add a banner — a graphic that runs across the top of the page. You can make this banner from scratch using any number of graphics programs.

Don't just create a banner willy-nilly. The banner you create needs to give viewers some idea of what they'll find in your shop and has to reflect the aesthetic of the items you make in some way. It also must tie in with your overall branding. (You find out more about branding in Chapter 16.)

If you have commitment issues, fear not. You can change your banner anytime you want. For example, you can change your banner to reflect promotions that you're running or update it seasonally to keep your shop looking fresh.

If you've developed a strong brand identity for your shop, you want your banner to incorporate your shop name, photos of your work, or even your shop slogan (assuming that you have one), all using the color palette you've selected for your brand. In the following sections, we note popular programs that you can use to design a banner and then provide basic steps on the designing process.

## Get with the program! Checking out programs for creating banners

You can create your own banner using just about any image-editing software you like — even free stuff online. Here are just a few image-editing tools to choose from:

- **Photoshop (www.photoshop.com):** Like Tylenol and Kleenex, Photoshop is so ubiquitous, it has crossed over into the general vernacular. It's by far the most respected and full-featured image-editing program available today. It's also among the most expensive and complicated to use (although Adobe, the maker of Photoshop, does offer a cheaper, scaled-down version called Photoshop Elements, which has more than enough bells and whistles to do the job).

- **GIMP (www.gimp.org):** This free, downloadable image-editing tool is nearly as powerful as its costly counterpart, Photoshop — albeit somewhat clumsier in design. It's great for performing essential image-editing tasks like resizing, editing, and cropping. You can even use it for more advanced purposes, such as adjusting levels and the like.

- **Picasa (www.picasa.com):** Offered free from Google and available for download for both Mac and Windows, Picasa supports basic photo-editing functionality, including color enhancement and cropping.

  The only downside? You can't create new images within Picasa; you can only edit existing ones. If you use Picasa, you have to use some other image-editing program to create a basic version of your banner, and then import that version into Picasa for enhancement purposes.

- **Picnik (www.picnik.com):** Picnik, also owned by Google, enables you to edit images free, directly from the Web site. It also offers lots of artsy and fun fonts and filters.

  As with Picasa, you can't use Picnik to create new image files; you have to import an existing file into the site before you can prettify it.

If you use a Windows PC, you can also use the Paint program, which was included free with your computer. Yet another option is to use the software that came with your digital camera.

## Signage says: Walking through the basic steps

Unfortunately, we can't cover the ins and outs of creating a banner using all the different programs in the preceding section. But to give you a basic idea of how it's done, we step you through the process using GIMP (which, again, you can download for free) to create a simple banner:

1. **Open GIMP.**
2. **Click File and choose New.**

   The Create a New Image dialog box opens (see Figure 8-1).

3. **Type 760 in the Width field.**
4. **Type 100 in the Height field.**
5. **Make sure Pixels is selected in the drop-down list.**

   Whatever program you use, the key to creating a banner is ensuring that it's cropped correctly to fit properly on your Etsy shop page. All banners must be 760 pixels wide and 100 pixels high.

**Figure 8-1:**
Create a
new file for
your banner
in GIMP.

6. **Click OK.**

GIMP creates a new image in the dimensions you specified (see
Figure 8-2).

7. **Using the program's various tools, create your banner (see Figure 8-3).**

For guidance using GIMP's various features, see the program's help
information; just click Help at the top of the screen.

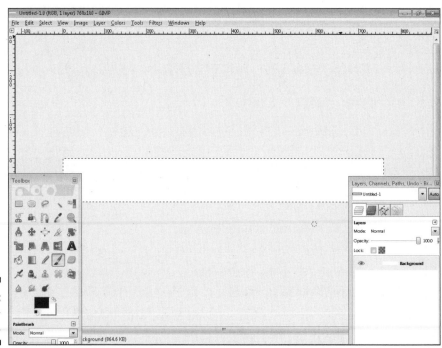

**Figure 8-2:**
A blank ban-
ner appears.

**Figure 8-3:**
Design your
banner in
GIMP.

8. **To save your banner, click File and choose Save As.**

   The Save Image dialog box opens (see Figure 8-4).

**Figure 8-4:**
Save your
banner in
GIMP.

9. **In the Name field, type a descriptive name for your banner file.**

10. **If you want to save your banner file somewhere other than the folder shown, click the plus sign next to the Browse for Other Folders entry, and then locate and select the folder where you want to save the file.**

11. **Click the plus sign next to the Select File Type (By Extension) entry, and then locate and select the JPEG Image option.**

12. **Click the Save button.**

    GIMP prompts you to export your file.

13. **Click the Export button.**

    GIMP prompts you to select a compression setting.

14. **Drag the Quality slider all the way to the right, for maximum image quality; then click the Save button.**

    GIMP saves your banner file in the folder you chose.

If you're no Rembrandt, why not let the pros take over and invest in a professionally designed custom banner? Many talented designers offer this service from their own Etsy shops. Try searching Etsy for "Etsy shop banner" and see what comes up.

## Load 'em up: Uploading your banner

After you've created your banner, it's time to upload it to your Etsy shop. Here's how:

1. **While logged in to your Etsy account, click the Your Account link along the top of any Etsy page.**

   The Your Account page opens.

2. **Click the Info & Appearance link, under Shop Settings, on the left side of the page.**

   The Info & Appearance page opens, with the Info & Appearance tab displayed.

3. **Scroll down to the Shop Banner Image section and click the Browse button (see Figure 8-5).**

4. **Locate and select your banner file; then click the Open button.**

5. **Click the Save button.**

   Etsy uploads your banner to your shop.

6. **To view your banner, click the Shop icon that appears in the header bar (see Figure 8-6).**

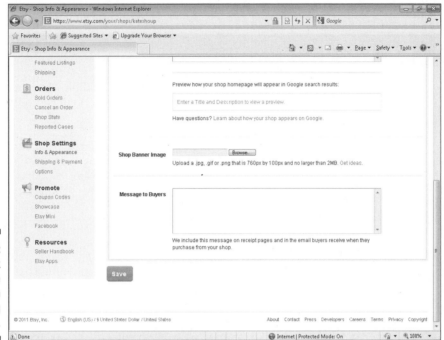

**Figure 8-5:**
Click
Browse
to begin
uploading
your banner.

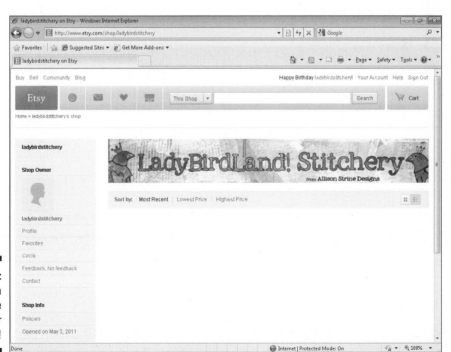

**Figure 8-6:**
What a
difference
a banner
makes!

# Title Wave: Adding a Shop Title and Announcement

Looking for a way to tell visitors what your shop's about? Look no more. Etsy enables you to include a shop title and shop announcement on your shop's main page:

- ✔ Think of your shop title as a tagline of sorts. It needs to briefly sum up what your shop is about. For example, if you sell, say, belt buckles, your shop title — which appears just below your user name on your Etsy shop page — may be "Keep Your Pants On . . . With Becky's Belt Buckles."

- ✔ The shop announcement, which appears just below your banner, is a great way to, well, announce things about your shop. For example, you may use it to trumpet the types of items you sell, the variety of materials or ingredients you use, or your artistic philosophy. Alternatively, your shop announcement may broadcast when your next sale will be or share your shop policies.

If your shop focuses on high-end, pricier items, you can use your shop announcement to indicate why. Maybe you use only the finest materials, or perhaps you employ a particularly difficult technique to craft your pieces. Either way, you can share this information with prospective buyers in your shop announcement.

To add a shop title and announcement to your shop, log in to your Etsy account and follow these steps:

1. **Click the Your Account link along the top of any Etsy page.**

   The Your Account page opens.

2. **Click the Info & Appearance link, under Shop Settings, on the left side of the page.**

   The Info & Appearance page opens, with the Info & Appearance tab displayed.

3. **Type your shop title in the Shop Title field, under Info & Appearance.**

4. **Type your shop announcement in the Shop Announcement text box, under the Shop Title field (see Figure 8-7).**

5. **Click the Save button.**

   Etsy adds your shop title and shop announcement to your shop.

6. **To view your shop title and shop announcement, click the Shop icon that appears in the header bar (see Figure 8-8).**

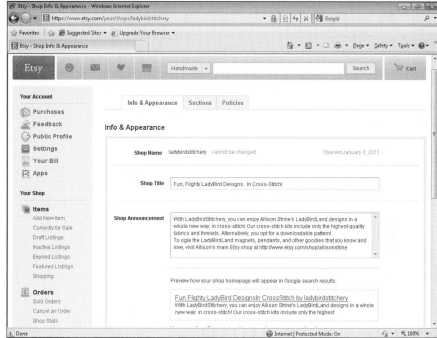

**Figure 8-7:**
Type the
text for your
shop title
and shop
announce-
ment.

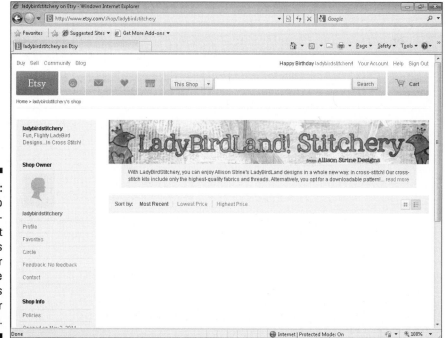

**Figure 8-8:**
Your shop
announce-
ment
appears
under your
banner; the
shop title is
under your
user name.

*Note:* Your shop announcement can be as short or as long as you want. Just be aware that if it's more *Anna Karenina* than haiku, not all of it will be visible by default. To read it in its entirety, click the Read More link that appears after the first few lines (see Figure 8-9).

**Figure 8-9:**
View the shop announcement in its entirety.

**ladybirdstitchery's Shop Announcement**

With LadyBirdStitchery, you can enjoy Allison Strine's LadyBirdLand designs in a whole new way: in cross stitch! Our cross-stitch kits include only the highest-quality fabrics and threads. Alternatively, you opt for a downloadable pattern!
To ogle the LadyBirdLand magnets, pendants, and other goodies that you know and love, visit Allison's main Etsy shop at http://www.etsy.com/shop/allisonstrine.

Close

TIP

The first 160 characters of your shop announcement, along with your shop title, are used as the meta description for your shop. In English, that means if someone uses a search engine to search for keywords that appear in your shop title or announcement (as well as section names and your bio, discussed in a moment), your Etsy shop will appear in their search results. So you want to make sure that you include the really important stuff — what you sell, what it's made of, and so on — right up front. You find out more about using search engine optimization (SEO) to boost traffic to your Etsy shop in Chapters 12 and 16.

# Section Leader: Setting Up Sections

What if, when you went to your grocery store, everything was set out haphazardly — with the milk alongside the charcoal briquettes, the kitty litter next to the radishes, the cheese by the sardines? You'd never be able to find everything you needed to buy! That's why grocery stores are organized into sections and aisles: so you can find what you're looking for.

Why should your Etsy shop be any different? Fortunately, Etsy enables you to organize your items by section. For example, if you sell different types of items — say, magnets, notebooks, and picture frames — you can use sections to organize your shop by item. Even if you don't sell different types of items — maybe you're all about knit caps — you can use sections to organize your goods by, say, yarn type, size, or price. You're allowed ten sections in all, as well as the default All Items section that's available in every shop.

To create a section, log in to your Etsy account and follow these steps:

1. **Click the Your Account link along the top of any Etsy page.**

   The Your Account page opens.

2. **Click the Info & Appearance link, under Shop Settings, on the left side of the page.**

   The Info & Appearance page opens, with the Info & Appearance tab displayed.

3. **Click the Sections tab.**

   The Shop Sections page opens (see Figure 8-10).

4. **Click the Create New Section link.**

5. **Type a name for the new section in the field that appears.**

   The name can contain as many as 24 characters.

In addition to using your shop title and shop announcement, Google uses your section titles as keywords for search. Opt for section titles that double as likely keywords. (Check out Chapters 12 and 16 for more about search engine optimization.)

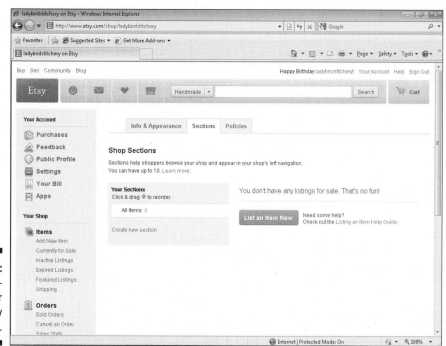

**Figure 8-10:**
Create sections for your Etsy shop.

6. **Click the Save button.**

   Etsy creates a section, using the name you typed.

7. **Repeat Steps 4–6 to add more sections.**

8. **To change the order in which sections appear, click the icon to the left of the section and drag it to the desired spot in the order.**

To change a section's name, click its Edit link, type a new name for the section, and click the Save button. To delete a section, click the trash can icon next to it. Etsy prompts you to confirm the deletion; click OK. (Note that deleting a section doesn't delete the listings in that section.)

If you haven't created any shop listings yet, you can't view sections on your shop's main page. After you create a listing, however — and assign it to a section — that section gets listed along the left side of your Etsy shop page. You find out how to create a shop listing and assign that listing to a section in Chapter 13.

# All about Me: Populating Your Profile

Yes, we know. It's much more fun to talk about other people than it is to talk — let alone write — about yourself. But part of the reason people shop on Etsy is that they want to feel a personal connection with the living, breathing artists and craftspeople who make what they buy. And the only way they can feel a personal connection with you is to read a little bit about you. That's where your Etsy profile comes in.

An Etsy profile can include the following tidbits:

- Your profile picture (also known as your avatar)
- Your name
- Your gender
- Your city
- Your birthday
- The date you joined Etsy
- Your bio
- A list of your favorite materials

We explain how to add this information to your profile in the following sections.

# *Just the facts, ma'am: Adding basic details*

To add basic details to your Etsy profile, you must access it from the Your Account page. Log in to your Etsy account and follow these steps:

1. **Click the Your Account link along the top of any Etsy page.**

   The Your Account page opens.

2. **Click the Public Profile link on the left side of the screen.**

   An editable version of your profile page appears (see Figure 8-11).

3. **To add a profile picture, also known as an avatar, to your profile, click the Browse button (see Figure 8-11a); in the dialog box that opens, locate and select the image you want to use.**

   Alternatively, to repurpose your Facebook profile picture for use on Etsy, click the Use Your Facebook Profile Picture link. (For help with choosing an avatar, see the next section.)

4. **If you want, indicate your gender.**

   If you prefer to keep that information private, select the Rather Not Say option button.

5. **Type your city in the City field.**

   As you type, Etsy displays a list of matching locales; click your town in the list to select it.

   By entering your location, you enable Etsy buyers to find your shop using the Shop Local tool. Chapter 3 has more information about this feature.

6. **Use the Month and Day drop-down lists to enter your birthday.**

7. **Type your bio in the About box.**

   You find out what constitutes a good bio later in this chapter.

8. **In the Favorite Materials box (see Figure 8-11b), indicate which materials you like to use, separating each entry with a comma and a space.**

   You can add as many as 13.

9. **If you want your profile to include your shop, any favorite items or shops, any Treasury lists you've compiled, and any teams you've joined, leave the check boxes at the bottom of the screen checked.**

10. **Click the Save Changes button.**

    Etsy saves the changes you made to your profile.

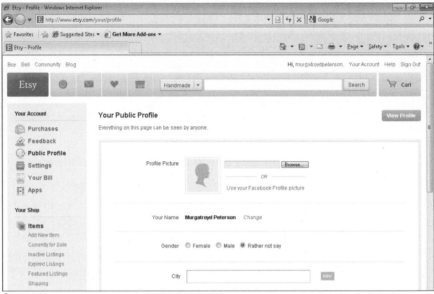

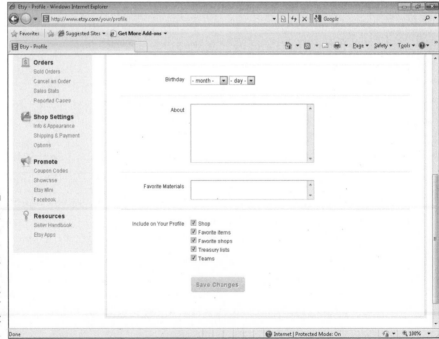

**Figure 8-11:** To populate your profile, click the Public Profile link on the Your Account page.

11. **To preview your profile, click the View Profile button.**

Etsy shows you how your profile will appear to others (see Figure 8-12).

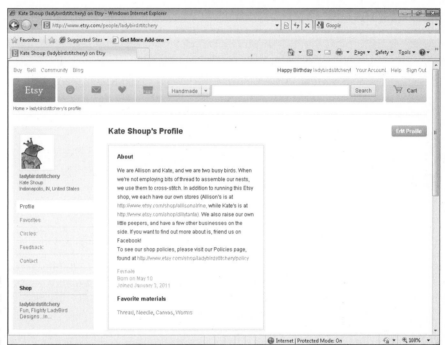

**Figure 8-12:**
Preview
your profile.

# *Avatar Hero: Choosing an avatar*

Your profile picture, or *avatar,* isn't just something people see when they peruse your profile page or visit your shop. It's the image that represents both you and your store across the site. When you post on a forum, your avatar appears next to it. Ditto when you comment on The Etsy Blog or participate in teams or online workshops. You want to select an avatar that reflects well on you and your shop.

So what type of image do you want to choose? Consider a few ideas:

✔ **Your store logo:** If you've developed a logo for your Etsy store, consider using it as your avatar. It's a great way to reinforce your brand on the site. (Flip to Chapter 16 for details on developing a logo.)

✔ **A product shot:** Using a product shot as your avatar is an excellent way to convey what you sell in your store. It's like having a little window right into your shop. (Chapter 11 has the scoop on taking great product shots.)

✔ **An emblematic image:** Suppose that you make lavender sachets. In that case, an image of, say, a field of lavender may serve as your avatar. It's not exactly a product shot (that is, you're not selling the field), but it's emblematic of your product.

✔ **A picture of you:** Although some Etsy peeps view this practice as a tad narcissistic, you may consider using a photo of yourself for your avatar — particularly if it reflects the overall aesthetic of your shop or if you're wearing or holding an item you sell.

Be aware that avatar images are quite small — 75 by 75 pixels, to be exact. You can't use that panoramic shot you took of the Sistine Chapel ceiling (or, at the very least, you'll need to crop it).

## Biohazard: Writing a winning bio

For many crafty types, the idea of writing anything — let alone a piece about themselves — is about as enticing as spelunking in Yucca Mountain. But a succinct, clever, well-written profile is essential to the success of your Etsy shop. Why? Lots of reasons. For example:

✔ Your bio enables buyers to see who they're buying from. Through your bio, you become a bona fide human being in your buyer's eyes.

✔ Your bio lets you toot your own horn a bit. Maybe your work has been recognized in some way. Or maybe you studied your craft at the most prestigious school around. If so, you want to make sure that everyone who visits your shop knows about it!

In the following sections, we explain how to write a first draft of your bio, edit it effectively, and polish it with a few extra details.

### Quiz show: Starting with a few essential questions

If writing your bio seems a bit daunting, don't freak out. Writing your bio is a process, just like anything else. It starts with writing down answers to a few key questions:

✔ Who are you?

✔ What's your educational and/or artistic background?

✔ What do you make? Do you have a signature product? If so, what's the story behind that product?

✔ What do you enjoy most about making the things you sell?

✔ What are your hobbies?

✔ What are you passionate about?

✔ Who or what inspires you?

Armed with your answers, you're ready to write the first draft of your bio. Notice that we said "first draft." That's code for "Don't try to be perfect right out of the gate." For now, just put your pen to the paper (or your fingers to the keyboard) and see what comes out. The idea is to tell buyers a little bit about yourself, your business, and the products you sell.

Some people write their bios in first person, while others opt for third person. Our view? Unless you're the queen or you play in the NBA, stick with first person.

### The tweak shall inherit the earth: Tweaking your first draft

With your first draft complete, it's time to tinker and tweak. As you do, try incorporating some or all of these tips:

✔ **Say hello.** If you were the proprietor of a real-world boutique, you'd certainly greet customers as they entered your store. Do the same for folks visiting your Etsy shop. While you're at it, thank them for stopping by. It's just good manners.

✔ **Start strong.** The first few pages of a novel need to grab readers by the throat and shake them until their lunch money falls out of their pockets (figuratively speaking). Likewise, the first paragraph of your Etsy bio needs to seize buyers by the eyeballs to convince them to read on. (Again, we're talking figuratively; *actually* seizing someone by the eyeballs would probably subject you to litigation.)

✔ **Be friendly and approachable.** This strategy will yield substantially better results than taking the opposite tack — being rude and inaccessible. Also, a little bit of humor can go a long way.

✔ **Tell a story.** An anecdote about how your business started or a story about the spark behind your store name may be just the thing to pull a buyer in.

✔ **Go the fictional route.** If it's true that all fiction is autobiographical, why not opt for a clever fictional "bio"?

✔ **Keep it short.** It's your Etsy bio, not *War and Peace*. A few short paragraphs will do.

- ✔ **Break your information into sections.** For most people, reading large blocks of text is about as appealing as chewing gum pried off the floor of a subway car. People perusing your profile will appreciate your use of sections, with titles, to break up your information.

- ✔ **Proofread.** Before you post your bio, triple-check it to make sure that it doesn't contain any spelling or grammatical errors. Better yet, ask your English-major friend to check it for you.

- ✔ **Be professional . . . sort of.** No, you don't have to wear pin-striped suits and practical pumps and drive a no-nonsense four-door sedan. But you do need to project an air of competence — even if your shop is all about fun. You want to be taken seriously as a seller, right?

The tone of your bio needs to match the tone of your shop and products. If your business is about whimsy, a stuffy bio just won't do!

### Extra! Extra! Adding a few extras

In addition to sharing your story with readers, you can use your bio to include the following information:

- ✔ **Press clippings:** If you or your business has garnered a nod in the media, don't hesitate to provide a link to the story in your bio. Just don't go too crazy with the clippings. Having links to more than a few may make your shop seem more corporate than co-op.

- ✔ **Shop policies:** Yes, your shop policies really belong on your Shop Policies page. But nothing's stopping you from including a brief list of policies in your bio as well. For example, you can include your accepted forms of payment, shipping terms, return details, and so on. You can then link the buyer to your policy page for more information. (Flip to Chapter 9 for information on setting shop policies.)

- ✔ **Product info:** If you find yourself answering the same question about one of your products over and over again ("Yes, the sweaters are knit from hair shed by my hamster"), consider spelling out the information in your bio.

- ✔ **Disclaimer:** If your product merits a disclaimer, you can include it in your bio. For example, if you sell vintage items, you may want to include a disclaimer indicating that your goodies are old and used. If you sell, say, copper jewelry, you can mention in your disclaimer that your pieces may turn people's skin green. Or if you craft toys but they aren't meant for babies, you can include a disclaimer to that effect.

- ✔ **Contact info:** Do you maintain a Facebook page or Web site for your business? What about a Twitter feed? If so, include a link to it in your bio.

- ✔ **Charitable giving:** Many Etsy sellers donate a portion of their take to charity. If you're one such seller, you can indicate that in your bio.

# Chapter 9

# Policy Academy: Establishing Your Shop's Policies

***

*In This Chapter*

▶ Understanding policy basics

▶ Choosing policies for payment

▶ Setting shipping policies

▶ Establishing your policy for returns and exchanges

▶ Setting up your Shop Policies page

***

*R*ules. Who needs 'em? In a word, you. Or, to be more precise, your Etsy shop. As you set up your Etsy shop, it's critical that you lay some ground rules for buyers. You want to establish clear store policies, especially with respect to payment, shipping, and returns and exchanges. That way, your customers know what to expect if they buy from you and will feel more confident and at ease. Setting clear policies also enables you to head off problems down the road.

Although developing your shop policies will likely be an ongoing process — and one that will probably result in a set of policies that's as unique as the items you sell — this chapter can help you get started.

Keep in mind that although you can avert a lot of crises by establishing clear store policies, you'll still face the occasional conflict with customers. When that happens, you need to take three actions: Communicate, communicate, and communicate. Oh, and one more thing: Communicate. For more on dealing with disagreements and other customer service issues, see Chapter 17.

## *Fair and Square: General Policy Tips*

Before we get into policy specifics in the rest of this chapter, we want to talk in general terms about what, apart from honesty, constitutes a good policy. A good policy has two key characteristics:

✔ **It's fair.** Yes, you put policies in place to protect your business. But a good policy also protects your customers. Your shop policy needs to be one for which you would be grateful if, through some amazing breach in the time–space continuum, *you* were your customer.

✔ **It's simple.** Although it's important to use your words, you don't want to use too many of them when crafting your shop policies. Keep your policies simple, clear, and concise.

One more thing: When it comes to setting your shop's policies, you have a lot of leeway. As we mention earlier in this chapter, shop policies are often as unique as the items they sell. That being said, you do need to adhere to Etsy's terms of use (www.etsy.com/policy/terms) and respect the site's Do's and Don'ts (www.etsy.com/policy/dosdonts). And of course, you must comply with all local and federal laws.

# Financial Matters: Establishing Payment-Related Policies

Perhaps the most important policies you need to consider relate to payment. After all, you started your Etsy shop in the hopes of pulling in a few Benjamins, right? As you craft your payment-related shop policies, you want to cover these points (for more on these, read on):

✔ **Payment methods:** What forms of payment will you accept? PayPal? Personal checks? Money orders? Shiny beads?

✔ **Sales tax:** Are you obligated to collect sales tax? If so, you'll appreciate Etsy's tax calculator, which automatically assesses a sales tax for buyers in the specified area. (Not sure whether you need to collect sales tax? See Chapter 18 for more info.)

✔ **Preferred currency:** On Etsy, the default currency is U.S. dollars. However, you can price your items using any of 20 other currencies.

*Note:* You also need to decide how much time you'll allow buyers when it comes to paying for items in your shop. Will you require immediate payment, or will you give buyers a little more leeway — say, 24 hours, three days, or some other period? After you decide, you need to post this info and all other payment-related policies on your shop's Shop Policies page, as we explain later in this chapter. (If buyers go the PayPal route, they'll automatically have to pay right away.)

# You're so money: Setting your payment methods

When you set up your Etsy shop, you need to decide what forms of payment you'll accept and then take the necessary steps to configure your shop accordingly. You find out how in the following sections.

### Exam cram: Examining your options

You can set up your Etsy shop to accept the following forms of payment:

- ✔ **PayPal:** As the most popular payment method used on Etsy, PayPal offers several advantages:

  - It's fast; electronic payments are instantly deposited into your PayPal account.

  - Transferring money from your PayPal account to a bank account is a breeze — and free.

  - PayPal offers protection from fraud for buyers and sellers alike, along with tools to expedite shipping.

  Although not everyone loves PayPal — some fear it's vulnerable to fraud; others have a beef with its customer service — it's the clear leader in terms of payment methods on Etsy.

  Don't have a PayPal account? No worries. Opening one is as easy as pie. Simply type www.paypal.com in your Web browser's address bar, click the Sign Up link at the top of the page, and follow the onscreen prompts. As a seller, consider opting for either a Premier or a Business account; that way, buyers will be able to use PayPal to buy your goodies with a credit card.

- ✔ **Money order:** Some people are simply old school. They prefer the time-honored system of paying by money order over using newfangled digital solutions like PayPal. Fortunately, Etsy allows you to accommodate these buyers. The downside? Unlike with PayPal, payment isn't rendered immediately. You must wait for the buyer to snail-mail you the money order (or send it via some other type of delivery service).

- ✔ **Personal check:** Allowing payment by personal check offers the same basic advantages and disadvantages as permitting payment via money order: You indulge the Luddites, but you have to wait for delivery of payment.

- ✔ **Other:** If you want, you can accept additional payment methods — say, cashier's checks, Beanie Babies, or Beagle puppies. If you opt to accept other forms of payment, be sure to indicate on your Shop Policies page what types you accept. (You find out how later in this chapter.)

If you choose to accept personal checks, money orders, or cashier's checks as payment, do so with care. These forms offer less protection from fraud. Never, never, ever, never ship an item to a buyer until her personal check, money order, or cashier's check clears, no matter how nicely she asks!

### *Preferential treatment: Specifying your preferences*

When you've decided what forms of payment to accept, you need to indicate your preferences on Etsy. Here's how:

1. **While logged in to your Etsy account, click the Your Account link along the top of any Etsy page.**

    The Your Account page opens.

2. **Click the Shipping & Payment link, under Shop Settings, on the left side of the page.**

    The Shipping & Payment page opens.

3. **Click the Payment Methods tab.**

    The Payment Methods page opens (see Figure 9-1).

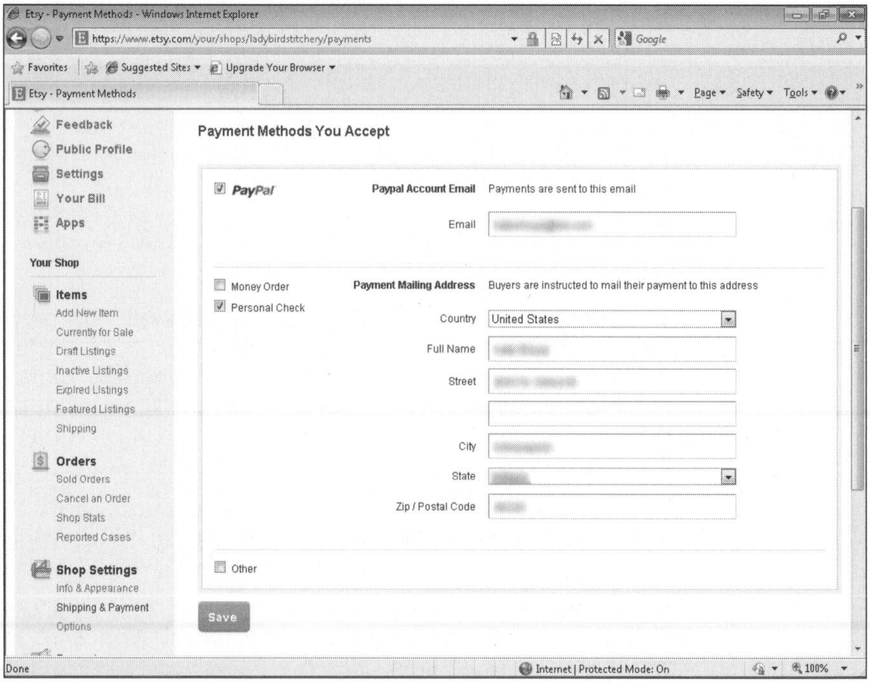

**Figure 9-1:**
Indicate
what
payment
methods
you accept.

4. **Select the PayPal, Money Order, Personal Check, and/or Other check boxes.**

5. **If you selected the PayPal check box, type the e-mail account you use to access your PayPal account under PayPal Account E-mail.**

6. **If you'll accept personal checks, money orders, cashier's checks, or other forms of payment that must be mailed to you, enter your mailing address under Payment Mailing Address.**

7. **Click the Save button.**

    Etsy saves your settings.

Note that this is a global shop setting. Any items that you list in your shop will offer these payment options.

# Death and taxes (well, taxes anyway): Collecting sales tax

If, after checking the local laws in your area and consulting a smarty-pants accountant, you've determined that you must collect sales tax, you can easily do so. In fact, with Etsy's tax calculator, you can collect sales tax during the checkout process. When you do, Etsy automatically assesses a sales tax for buyers in the region that you specify.

To set up Etsy's tax calculator, log in to your Etsy account and follow these steps:

1. **Click the Your Account link along the top of any Etsy page.**

    The Your Account page opens.

2. **Click the Shipping & Payment link, under Shop Settings, on the left side of the page.**

    The Shipping & Payment page opens.

3. **Click the Sales Tax tab.**

    The Sales Tax Settings page opens (see Figure 9-2).

4. **If you live in the United States, click the State drop-down list and choose your state.**

    If you live in Canada, choose your province from the Canada drop-down list; if you live elsewhere, choose your country from the Other Countries drop-down list. Then skip to Step 6.

5. **Click the Add Tax Rate button.**

    The United States (or Canada or Other Countries) box expands to include additional settings, as shown in Figure 9-3.

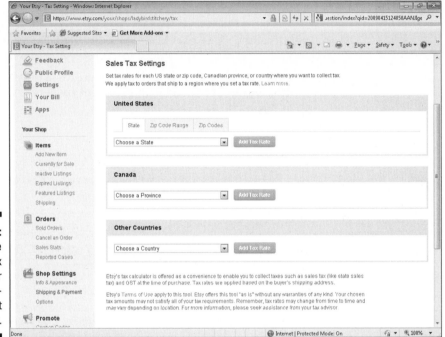

**Figure 9-2:**
Set up the
Etsy tax
calculator
to automati-
cally collect
taxes.

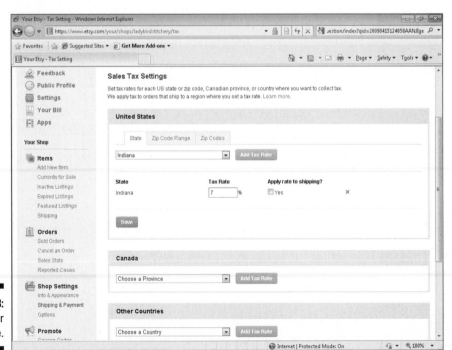

**Figure 9-3:**
Enter your
tax rate.

6. **Enter your state's tax rate in the Tax Rate box.**

7. **If the laws in your area require you to charge sales tax on shipping fees, select the Apply Rate to Shipping check box.**

8. **If local laws require you to assess a sales tax on buyers from specific zip codes, click the Zip Code Range or Zip Codes tab, enter the applicable zip code range or zip code, and repeat Steps 5 and 6.**

9. **Click the Save button.**

    Etsy saves your settings.

You find out more about collecting sales tax in Chapter 18.

## Currency events: Setting your preferred currency

Most Etsy sellers hail from the ol' U. S. of A., which is one reason the site's default currency is the U.S. dollar. Of course, plenty of Etsy sellers call other countries home. If you're in that latter group, or if you find that your buyers tend to be clustered in a particular region abroad, you'll be pleased to know that you can list items and receive payments in a different currency (assuming that it's one of the other 20-plus currencies supported, including Australian, Canadian, Hong Kong, New Zealand, and Singapore dollars; British pounds; E.U. euros; Japanese yen; Israeli shekels; Mexican pesos; Thai baht; and more).

Here's how you set your preferred currency:

1. **While logged in to your Etsy account, click the Your Account link along the top of any Etsy page.**

    The Your Account page opens.

2. **Click the Shipping & Payment link, under Shop Settings, on the left side of the page.**

    The Shipping & Payment page opens.

3. **Click the Currency tab.**

    The Shop Currency page opens (see Figure 9-4).

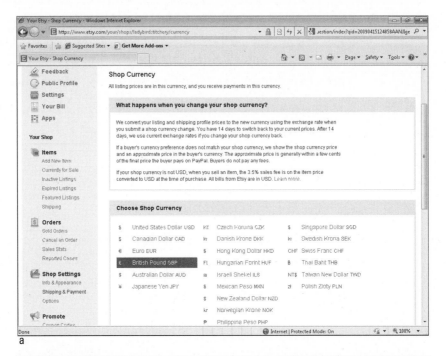

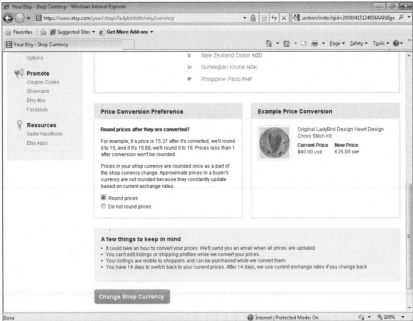

**Figure 9-4:**
Set your
preferred
currency.

4. **Click the currency you want to use (refer to Figure 9-4a).**

5. **If you want prices to round up after they're converted, click the Round Prices option button under Price Conversion Preference. Otherwise, click the Do Not Round Prices option button.**

   A preview of the converted price appears in the Example Price Conversion area (see Figure 9-4b).

6. **Click the Change Shop Currency button.**

   Etsy saves your settings.

# Ship Shape: Establishing Your Shipping Policies

Unless you enjoy keeping customers in the dark about how and when they can expect to receive their items, you'll want to outline a clear policy with respect to shipping.

## Special delivery: Picking basic shipping policies

As you develop your shipping policy, consider these areas:

- ✓ **What shipping carrier you'll use:** Do you plan to ship via USPS? FedEx? UPS? DHL? Pony Express? Delivery owl? (For help in choosing a shipping provider and making other shipping-related decisions, see Chapter 15.)

- ✓ **Which delivery option you'll select from your shipping carrier:** Say that you've opted to ship via USPS. Will you choose first class? Priority Mail? Media Mail?

- ✓ **Whether you'll include delivery confirmation or insurance:** Smart money has you providing both — especially for higher-priced items. That way, if a package gets lost en route, you're covered.

- ✓ **Whether you're willing to ship internationally:** If you are, decide whether you or the buyer will be responsible for any Customs fees incurred.

- ✓ **How you'll handle combined shipping:** Many sellers discount shipping when buyers purchase multiple items from their Etsy shop at once. Although you're certainly not obligated to do so, adopting this practice can be a good way to increase sales.

✔ **How quickly you'll ship the item:** Some sellers promise to ship items within 48 hours of receiving payment. Other sellers plan weekly trips to the post office, mailing all the items they've sold in the past seven days in one fell swoop.

If you make custom items, you want to account for the time it takes to make the item when estimating how quickly you'll ship it.

✔ **Your willingness to upgrade:** Sometimes buyers need their items quickly. To accommodate those buyers, consider offering expedited shipping — for example, overnighting the item.

✔ **How you'll package items you ship:** Will you send your piece in a padded envelope or a box? Do you recycle packaging materials? Is gift wrapping available?

After you decide on your basic policies, you can add them to your shop's Shop Policies page, as we describe later in this chapter.

## Ship happens: Creating a shipping profile

Suppose that you plan to stock your shop with items of a similar size — say, jewelry, magnets, greeting cards, or stuffed patchwork wiener dogs. In that case, it may behoove you to create a shipping profile. A *shipping profile* is simply a collection of shipping-related settings that you can apply to an item listing in one fell swoop instead of entering them one by one.

Before you create a shipping profile, you want to sort out how much it costs to ship your item based on its size, weight, and shipping method. If you plan to ship internationally, you need to get a handle on how much that method will cost as well. For help, contact your shipping provider. (You find out about choosing a shipping provider in Chapter 15.) Note that you want to factor in any costs associated with packaging your item when calculating your shipping charges.

To create a shipping profile, log in to your Etsy account and follow these steps:

1. **Click the Your Account link along the top of any Etsy page.**

   The Your Account page opens.

2. **Click the Shipping & Payment link, under Shop Settings, on the left side of the page.**

   The Shipping & Payment page opens, with the Shipping Profiles tab displayed (see Figure 9-5).

3. **Click the Create a New Profile link.**

   The Create a New Shipping Profile page opens (see Figure 9-6).

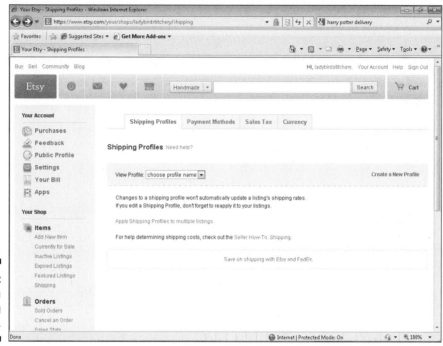

**Figure 9-5:**
Create a
shipping
profile here.

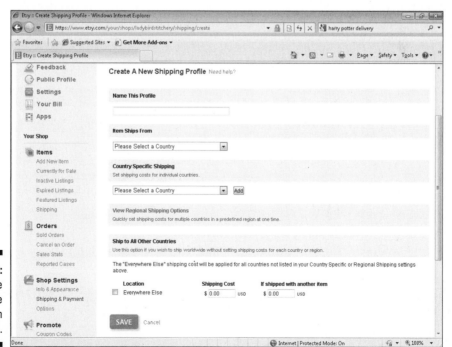

**Figure 9-6:**
Enter the
profile
details on
this page.

4. **In the Name This Profile field, type a descriptive name for your profile.**

   For example, if the profile is for items in your jewelry line, type Jewelry.

5. **Click the Items Ship From drop-down list and choose your country of residence.**

6. **If you want to set shipping rates on a country-by-country basis, click the Country Specific Shipping drop-down list and choose a country; then click the Add button.**

   The Country Specific Shipping area expands to include a Shipping Cost field and an If Shipped with Another Item field.

7. **Enter the shipping cost for buyers in the selected country in the Shipping Cost field, and then type the cost for shipping for purchases sent with another item in the If Shipped with Another Item field.**

8. **Repeat Steps 7 and 8 to add more countries to your shipping profile.**

   Don't forget to add your country of residence in the Country Specific Shipping area!

9. **To quickly set options for an entire region, such as the European Union, click the View Regional Shipping Options link.**

   The View Regional Shipping Options area expands to include a drop-down list.

10. **Click the Regional Shipping drop-down list and choose the region for which you want to set shipping options; then click the Add button.**

    The Regional Shipping area expands further to include a Shipping Cost field and an If Shipped with Another Item field.

11. **Enter the shipping cost for buyers in the selected region in the Shipping Cost field, and then type the cost for shipping for purchases sent with another item in the If Shipped with Another Item field.**

12. **If you're willing to ship anywhere in the world, click the Everywhere Else check box to select it.**

13. **Enter the shipping cost for buyers in all other countries in the Shipping Cost field, and then type the cost for shipping for purchases sent with another item in the If Shipped with Another Item field.**

14. **Click the Save button.**

    Etsy saves your shipping profile.

If you need to, you can edit your shipping profile. To do so, follow Steps 1–3 to access the Shipping Profiles tab, click the View Profile drop-down list and choose the desired profile, adjust your settings as needed, and click the Save button.

# Return to Sender: Handling Returns and Exchanges

Obviously, you want all your customers to love your items. But — no disrespect — sometimes they won't. (What? We said "no disrespect"!) When that happens, you need to refer buyers to your policy on returns and exchanges.

Your policy for returns and exchanges needs to cover the following:

- ✔ **Whether you accept returns or exchanges:** Some sellers do, some sellers don't. Be sure to spell out your policy on both regularly listed items and custom pieces.

  Some items aren't conducive to being returned — think panties, swimsuits, bath and beauty products, and the like.

- ✔ **Under what circumstances returns or exchanges are permitted:** Some sellers accept returns or exchanges for any reason, the theory being that they want their customers to be happy, no matter what. Other sellers allow returns or exchanges only in certain circumstances — for example, if the item doesn't fit correctly or if it was damaged en route.

- ✔ **How long customers have to return or exchange an item:** If you do allow returns and exchanges, you want to lay down the law on how long customers have to contact you with their concerns and send their item back to you — for example, one week, two weeks, or 30 days.

- ✔ **Who pays to ship the item back to you:** Do you cover shipping costs, or does the buyer?

After you select your return and exchange policies, it's time to add them to your shop's Shop Policies page, as we describe in the next section.

# Policy Wonk: Setting Up Your Policies Page

With your policies established, all that's left is to share them with your buyers. Fortunately, your Etsy shop includes a special Shop Policies page, where you can do just that. In the following sections, we list the page's sections and explain how to populate the page with your shop's specific information.

## Introductory offer: Introducing the sections

The Etsy Shop Policies page includes the following sections (Figure 9-7a shows the top of the page, and Figure 9-7b shows the bottom).

Your Shop Policies page doesn't have to be all business. Although it includes information of a serious nature, there's nothing to stop you from letting your quirky personality creep in.

It's a good idea to read other shops' policies. You're almost certain to run across great policies that you never thought of implementing. To view a shop's Shop Policies page, display the shop's main page and then click the Policies link on the left side of the screen, under Shop Info.

### Welcome

The Welcome area is a great place to, well, welcome customers to your shop. You can also talk a bit about your shop, the pieces you sell, and your overarching philosophy as an artist or craftsperson. Here's an example of a solid Welcome statement:

> Welcome to LadyBird Stitchery! Thank you so much for visiting. Our cross-stitch kits include only the highest-quality fabrics and threads. Alternatively, you can opt for a downloadable pattern! We hope you find something here to love. Please check back often, as we regularly add new kits and patterns!

### Payment

This area is where you spell out any policies that relate to payment: forms of payment you accept, whether (and for whom) you charge sales tax, your preferred currency (assuming that it's not the default, U.S. dollars), how long buyers using methods of payment other than PayPal have to pay for their goodies, and so on. Check out this example of a strong Payment statement:

> LadyBird Stitchery accepts payment via PayPal and personal check, although Beagle puppies are also an acceptable form of compensation. If you opt to pay by personal check, please send your payment within 48 hours of placing an order; otherwise, we'll have to cancel your order and relist your item. (If you need a little more time, just let us know. We're nice people! Really!) Indiana buyers are subject to a 7% sales tax. (Sorry, neighbor!)

a

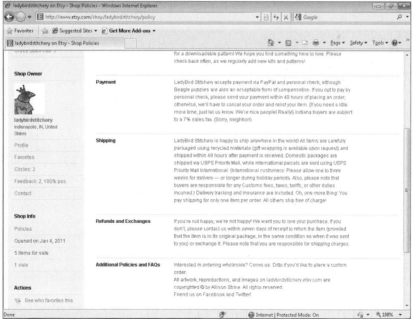

**Figure 9-7:**
An Etsy
shop's Shop
Policies
page.

b

## Shipping

Indicate your shipping policies here — how you ship items (and how quickly), whether you ship internationally, whether buyers can upgrade shipping to expedite delivery, how items are packaged, and so on. Here's an example of a thorough Shipping statement:

> LadyBird Stitchery is happy to ship anywhere in the world! All items are carefully packaged using recycled materials (gift wrapping is available upon request) and shipped within 48 hours after payment is received. Domestic packages are shipped via USPS Priority Mail, while international parcels are sent using USPS Priority Mail International. (International customers: Please allow one to three weeks for delivery — or longer during holiday periods. Also, please note that buyers are responsible for any Customs fees, taxes, tariffs, or other duties incurred.) Delivery tracking and insurance are included. Oh, one more thing: You pay shipping for only one item per order. All others ship free of charge!

## Refunds and exchanges

Here's where you say whether you accept returns or exchanges, and under what circumstances. You can also indicate how long customers have to contact you about an item they want to return or exchange, and who pays to ship the item back to you. Here's an example of a good Refunds and Exchanges statement:

> If you're not happy, we're not happy! We want you to love your purchase. If you don't, please contact us within seven days of receipt to return the item (provided that the item is in its original package, in the same condition as when it was sent to you) or exchange it. Please note that you are responsible for shipping charges.

## Additional info

You guessed it: This area is where you include any additional information that you want to share about you or your shop. For example, you can use this space to indicate that you welcome wholesale inquiries or accept custom orders. You can also include a copyright statement to scare off design poachers, as well as provide your contact information. Here's an example:

> Interested in ordering wholesale? Convo us. Ditto if you'd like to place a custom order.

> All artwork, reproductions, and images on ladybirdstitchery.etsy.com are copyrighted © by Allison Strine. All rights reserved.

> Friend us on Facebook and Twitter!

## *Population control: Populating the page*

To populate your Etsy Shop Policies page, log in to your Etsy account and follow these steps:

1. **Click the Your Account link along the top of any Etsy page.**

   The Your Account page opens.

2. **Click the Info & Appearance link, under Shop Settings, on the left side of the page.**

   The Info & Appearance page opens.

3. **Click the Policies tab.**

   The Shop Policies page opens (see Figure 9-8).

4. **In the Welcome text box (refer to Figure 9-8a), type a welcome message for your customers, share your philosophy, and enter any other bits you want to share.**

5. **In the Payment text box, indicate which payment methods you accept, along with your payment terms, deadline requirements, tax policy, cancellation policy, and the like.**

6. **In the Shipping text box, enter what shipping method you use, whether you're willing to upgrade shipping, whether you ship internationally, and so on.**

7. **In the Refunds and Exchanges text box (refer to Figure 9-8b), indicate whether you issue refunds and under what circumstances.**

8. **In the Additional Info text box, add any other policies you've established.**

9. **Click the Save button.**

   Etsy saves the changes you made to your Shop Policies page.

Be sure to proofread your policies before you post them in your Etsy shop. You don't want any grammatical errors or misspellings making you look like an idiot!

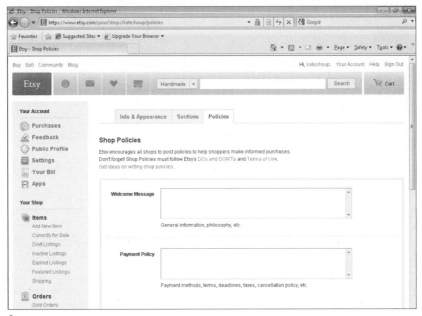

a

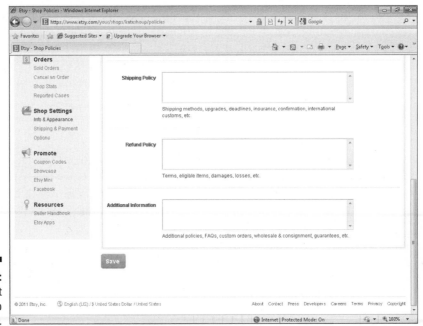

**Figure 9-8:**
Spell out
your shop
policies.

b

# Chapter 10

# Come on Down, the Price Is Right! Pricing Your Work

● ● ● ● ● ● ● ● ● ● ● ● ● ● ● ● ● ● ● ● ● ● ● ● ● ● ● ● ● ● ● ● ● ● ● ● ● ● ● ● ● ● ● ● ● ● ● ●

● ● ● ● ● ● ● ● ● ● ● ● ● ● ● ● ● ● ● ● ● ● ● ● ● ● ● ● ● ● ● ● ● ● ● ● ● ● ● ● ● ● ● ● ● ● ● ●

*Y*ears ago, a close friend developed a keen business idea: the million-dollar hot dog. The million-dollar hot dog would be just like any other hot dog, except that it would cost a million dollars. Yes, demand for the million-dollar hot dog may be low. But as our friend rightly points out, "You really only ever need to sell *one!*"

Ironically, as tempted as they may be to employ the million-dollar-hot-dog pricing model, most Etsy sellers err on the other end of the spectrum, under-pricing the pieces they sell. Often they're so thrilled that someone wants to buy something they made, it doesn't occur to them that they could've sold it for more. But just as overpricing your pieces has its problems (you never sell anything), so does underpricing your wares. Specifically, underpricing results in lost profits and, worse, the perception that your pieces are "cheap" — that is, products of low quality. Particularly with one-of-a-kind items like yours, customers use the piece's price to assess its value.

The trick, then, is to strike a balance with your pricing. You want to price your pieces high enough to cover your costs and turn a healthy profit. (After all, you're running a business.) But you need to price your items low enough that you can sell a reasonable volume of goods. Finding that sweet spot is the focus of this chapter.

As you become more adept and efficient at crafting your pieces and running your business, your profit margin will naturally improve.

# Formulaic Plot: Breaking Down Your Pricing Formulas

Hands down, one of our favorite *Saturday Night Live* sketches was the one with Chevy Chase as President Gerald R. Ford, taking part in a presidential debate. After being asked an extremely complicated question involving numerous dollar figures and percentages, Chase, sweating profusely, stammered, "It was my understanding that there would be no math during the debates. . . ."

No doubt, many Etsy sellers feel exactly the same way. After all, don't most of us become artists or crafters specifically to avoid ever having to do arithmetic? Unfortunately, if you hope to run a profitable Etsy shop, you need to get comfortable with doing a little math, especially when it comes to pricing your pieces. But don't freak out! We're not talking calculus here, or even trigonometry. All you have to learn are two very simple formulas:

> (Materials + Labor + Overhead) × 2 = Wholesale price
>
> Wholesale price × 2 = Retail price

In the following sections, we break down each item in the preceding formulas and show you how to put the formulas to work.

Offering products at different price points (using the preceding formulas) is a great way to increase your customer base. For example, say that you specialize in ceramics. In that case, you may make ceramic mugs to sell at a lower price point; simple, medium-size bowls to sell at a slightly higher price point; and ornate platters to sell at a premium price point. This structure enables you to reach a larger range of potential buyers, which may help you increase your overall sales.

## Material girl: Calculating the cost of materials

When calculating your cost for materials, include the price of every little component in your piece. For example, suppose that you sell handmade puppy plush toys for babies. Your material cost for each pup may include the following:

- ✔ Fabric
- ✔ Label
- ✔ Rickrack
- ✔ Stuffing
- ✔ Thread

When you calculate the costs of your materials, you need to consider only the price of what you used to produce one piece. For example, if you bought 3 yards of fabric when purchasing your supplies, for a total of $12, but you used only a third of that fabric to produce a single pup, you want to divide what you paid for the fabric by 3, to calculate your material cost for the fabric — here, $4.

## Labor pains: Figuring labor costs

While perusing the want ads in your local newspaper, suppose that you happened upon this listing:

> **Wanted:** A skilled professional to expertly fabricate our product by hand. Must also run every aspect of our business, including sourcing supplies, maintaining and marketing our shop, interacting with customers, and ensuring that items sold are artfully packaged and shipped to buyers. Pay: Nil.

Odds are, that's a job you'd pass up. Why, then, do so many Etsy sellers seem to pay themselves *nada* to run their shops? Don't fall into this trap! Your time is valuable. Like every working person, you deserve to be compensated for it. Your pricing formula needs to include the cost of your labor.

Calculating your labor costs requires you to first set an hourly rate for your time. Be sure to pay yourself a fair wage — one that accounts for the skill required to craft your piece. Also, think about how much you want or need to make for your time. (This consideration is especially important if you're looking to quit your day job.) Many professional crafters go with a rate in the neighborhood of $12 to $20 per hour.

If you're just starting out, you may opt for a lower hourly rate. You can give yourself periodic raises as your skills improve.

Another approach to figuring your hourly rate is to work backward. That is, figure out how much you need to be able to "bill" for each day and divide that by the number of hours you intend to work. For example, if you need to earn $80 a day to survive, and you plan to work four hours per day crafting the items you plan to sell, then you can simply divide $80 by 4, for an hourly rate of $20.

Armed with your hourly rate, you're ready to work out your labor costs. These costs must take into account the time it takes to do the following:

- ✔ Design a piece
- ✔ Shop for supplies for the piece
- ✔ Construct the piece
- ✔ Photograph the piece (see Chapter 11)
- ✔ Create the item listing for the piece, including composing the item title and description (see Chapters 12 and 13)
- ✔ Package and ship the item (see Chapter 15)

As with materials costs (described in the previous section), you can amortize some of the labor costs — that is, you can spread them out. For example, if it took you four hours to develop the design for a piece, but you plan to make 50 of them, you have to amortize those four hours over the 50 finished pieces. Similarly, you likely shop for supplies for several pieces at once, meaning that you can spread the time that you spend shopping across all the projects that you plan to craft using those supplies.

Let's use our plush toy pups as an example. Suppose that you spend four hours designing your toy, and another hour shopping for enough supplies to construct 50 units. Your labor cost — assuming that your hourly rate is $20 — is $100, or, spread out over 50 toys, $2 per toy. Suppose further that each toy takes 30 minutes to make, photograph, and package ($10 in labor). Your labor cost per toy is then $12.

If you clear more than $400 per year with your Etsy shop, you need to pay taxes on it — probably at a rate of about 30 percent. Especially if you plan to quit your day job and devote yourself exclusively to running your Etsy shop, you want to inflate your hourly wage to account for that. For more information about taxes, see Chapter 18.

## *Heads up: Adding up overhead*

In addition to calculating your costs for materials and labor (as we describe earlier in this chapter), you want to account for your overhead. Your overhead may encompass the following:

- ✔ Tools and equipment used in the manufacture of your products
- ✔ Office supplies
- ✔ Packaging supplies

> ✔ Utilities (for example, your Internet connection, electricity used to power your sewing machine, and so on)
>
> ✔ Etsy fees
>
> ✔ PayPal fees

*Note:* These costs don't include shipping. Be sure to calculate those costs separately and pass them along to the buyer. Chapter 15 has more details on calculating shipping costs.

As with your labor costs, you need to amortize your overhead costs. That is, you total your overhead and then spread out that cost over all the items you make. As a simple example, if you calculate your monthly overhead at $100, and you produce 100 pieces a month, your overhead is $1 per piece. Of course, this calculation gets tricky when your overhead involves purchases of such things as tools and equipment used in the manufacture of your products. In those cases, you want to amortize the items over their life span. For example, suppose that you buy a $250 sewing machine that you plan to use for five years. In that time, you anticipate that you'll sew 500 pieces. Your overhead for the machine is then 50¢ per piece.

If you simply can't face calculating all these overhead costs, try adding together your materials cost and your labor cost for each piece you make; then multiply the sum by 10 or 15 percent and call that your overhead. It won't exactly reflect your actual overhead, but it'll probably be in the ballpark.

## *Two-timer: Understanding the "times two"*

In the formula we provide earlier in this chapter, you may have noticed that, after adding together your costs for materials, labor, and overhead, you multiply the sum by 2. What's up with that? Simple. That "times two" is your profit. It's what you invest back in your business. If your sewing machine breaks, the "times two" is what you use to buy a new one. If you decide to expand your product line, that "times two" is where you find the capital you need to grow. Or you may just use your "times two" revenue to build a nice nest egg for your business or a fund to fall back on if times get tough.

Although some sellers may feel uncomfortable with all this two-timing, thinking that their labor costs are their "profit," don't make the mistake of omitting this part of the formula. Yes, you may be paying yourself to make your products, but if your business grows, that may not always be the case. Multiplying your costs by two enables you to ensure that your business is profitable, regardless of how it's structured.

## *Double or nothing: Pricing for wholesale and retail*

As the proprietor of your own small manufacturing business, you need to establish two prices for your goods: the wholesale price and the retail price. The wholesale price is for customers who buy large quantities of your item to resell it. That customer then sells your piece to someone else at the retail price, which is usually double the wholesale price.

We opt to multiply the wholesale price by 2 to determine the retail price. But some sellers may choose a higher number, multiplying the wholesale price by 2.5 or even 3 to determine the retail price, assuming that the market will bear that. Basically, the multiplier you choose is really up to you.

Another approach is to work backward, setting your retail price based on what you think people will pay for your item and then dividing that figure by 2 to establish your wholesale price.

Wait, don't say it. We know what you're thinking: "I'm going to sell my stuff only through my Etsy store, so I'll just charge everyone my wholesale price." Wrong! Even if you plan to sell your items exclusively through your Etsy shop, you need to establish both a wholesale price and a retail price, and you need to sell your pieces on Etsy at the retail rate. Why?

✔ First, even if you have no plans to expand beyond your Etsy shop, you don't want to cheat yourself of the opportunity to offer wholesale prices to bulk buyers, if the opportunity arises.

✔ Second, you'll almost certainly want to run the occasional sale in your Etsy shop; by pricing your goods for retail, you'll have some leeway to discount them as needed and still turn a profit.

If you do develop a wholesale business, it's especially important that you sell the pieces in your Etsy shop at the retail price. Otherwise, you're undercutting your wholesale customers! Unless it's your stated goal to alienate these customers, avoid this practice.

## *Some assembly required: Putting it all together*

To help you get comfortable with pricing your pieces, we run through a couple examples here. Let's start with the puppy plush toys that we introduce in the earlier section "Material girl: Calculating the cost of materials." Suppose the following:

✔ The cost of materials for each plush is $2.50.

✔ Your hourly rate is $20. Your amortized labor costs for designing the toy and shopping for supplies is $2 per toy. It takes you 30 minutes to create, photograph, and package each toy, or $10 per toy. So your total labor rate is $12 per toy.

✔ Your overhead for each piece is $1.10.

Your pricing equation then looks something like this:

($2.50 [Materials] + $12 [Labor] + $1.10 [Overhead]) × 2 = $31.20 (Wholesale price)

$31.20 (Wholesale price) × 2 = $62.40 (Retail price)

Consider another example. Suppose that you've designed a new bracelet for your jewelry line, and you need to determine how much to charge for it. The beads, findings, and thread you used to construct the bracelet put you back $12. Your labor rate is $14 per hour, and it takes you 45 minutes to make each bracelet (including amortized values for time spent on other business-related activities), which means that your labor cost is $14 × 0.75 = $10.50. Finally, suppose that your overhead for each bracelet is $1.75. Here's what your pricing equation looks like:

($12 [Materials] + $10.50 [Labor] + $1.75 [Overhead]) × 2 = $48.50 (Wholesale price)

$48.50 (Wholesale price) × 2 = $97 (Retail price)

# Eyes on the Price: Evaluating Your Prices

You've done it: You've used the pricing formulas in the preceding section to determine your wholesale and retail prices. You're finished, right? Wrong. These formulas simply deliver the price you need to charge for your piece to turn a healthy profit. To ensure that the price you've hit on is, in the immortal words of Goldilocks, "just right," you need to do a little research, as we explain in the following sections.

## Know thy enemy: Assessing your competition's pricing

Your first order of business is to scope out your competition, both on and off Etsy. What are they charging? If their prices are roughly in line with yours, you're probably in good shape. But what if they're significantly higher or, more likely, lower? In that case, put yourself in your prospective buyer's shoes and ask yourself the following questions:

✔ Would I buy my product or a competitor's product? Why?

✔ Is my product made of better materials than my competitors' products?

✔ Did crafting my product or my competitors' products require more skill?

✔ Is my product different or special in any way?

✔ What do I think my product is worth?

Your answers to these questions help you determine whether you need to adjust your price upward or downward. For example, if your product is better made than your competitor's, you may be able to adjust your price upward. Ditto if it required more skill to build. Of course, if the opposite is true, you may need to lower your price.

Your competition doesn't consist just of people who make an item similar to yours; it's anyone who's targeting the same market you are. Using the puppy plush toy example that we introduce earlier in this chapter, your competition wouldn't be only other shops that sell puppy plush toys; it would be any shop that makes toys or gifts for babies.

## Here's looking at you, kid: Studying your target market

In gauging your price, you need to consider your target market. Who, in your estimation, will buy your piece? How much disposable income does that person have? If your target market is 20-something hipsters, chances are, they're not quite as flush as, say, your 40-something set, so you may need to keep your prices lower. On the flip side, if that 40-something set is the market you're after, you may be able to command a higher price.

Has this ever happened to you? You're shopping for a gift — say, earrings for your sister — but the pair you've found is priced far below what you want to spend, so you don't buy the set, even though the earrings are gorgeous and you know she'd love them. People often shop for gifts with a certain price point in mind — say, $25 for a friend, or $50 for a family member. If your product is aimed at this market, ask yourself, who's the ultimate recipient for this gift? A best friend? An acquaintance? Someone's nephew? Then think about what most people would spend on a gift for that person, and price your piece accordingly.

## Floor it: Figuring out how to lower your prices

If your research has revealed that your prices will likely give your market sticker shock, you may need to lower them.

One approach may be to sell your pieces at your wholesale price. For the reasons cited in the earlier section "Double or nothing: Pricing for wholesale and retail," however, we don't recommend this strategy — you want a wholesale price in place to accommodate bulk orders, and you want some leeway in your pricing to run sales.

A better approach is to attempt to lower your own costs. Can you purchase your materials more cheaply from a different supplier? Can you spend less time making each piece? Or can you redesign your product to require less in the way of supplies or labor time — for example, omitting the decorative rick-rack piping on your plush pup? After you've managed to lower your costs, apply the formulas we talked about earlier in the chapter to determine the new price.

Don't lower your prices to compete with machine-made or imported items. Handmade items have more value and need to be priced accordingly.

## Up the ante: Knowing when to raise your prices

True, you need to lower your price in some circumstances, but other times you can charge — wait for it — *more*. See, people perceive some products to be more valuable than others. For example, consider the fact that some painters can command stratospherically high prices for their paintings. It's not because their raw materials were substantially more expensive — paint and canvas costs pretty much the same amount for everybody. And it's not that their paintings took longer to create. No, these paintings are insanely expensive because the public perceives their paintings to be valuable.

When pricing your items, see if you can take advantage of this "perceived value" and position your pieces as "premium" products. Maybe you use exceptional materials in crafting your piece. Or maybe you've developed a unique technique that makes your piece especially beautiful or durable. Note that buyers will also perceive your work as more valuable if you've developed a reputation as an artist — perhaps by showing your pieces at galleries or gaining publicity in some other way.

---

## Bundle up: Bundling your items

You may be able to increase sales by *bundling* your items — that is, selling multiple items together, as a package deal. For example, suppose that you specialize in making jewelry. Instead of selling a $20 pair of earrings and a $30 necklace separately, you may bundle them into a single listing for, say, $45. Offering value bundles — say, buy two, get one free — is another tactic. Yes, you'll make less than you would if you sold them separately, but you'll move more merchandise, you'll save on shipping, and your customer will feel like she's gotten a super deal.

---

Be sure to talk up your work in your shop announcement and item descriptions. Share why your pieces are valuable. For example, if you not only craft necklaces, but also make your own beads, be sure to say so. If you use only the best organic cotton to sew your baby clothes, include words to that effect. If you use a particularly difficult technique that only a few other people have mastered, spell that out, too. (Flip to Chapter 8 for details on creating a shop announcement, and see Chapter 12 for details on writing item descriptions.)

Sometimes the very act of tagging your piece with a higher price can make buyers perceive it as more valuable. Of course, that doesn't mean you should offer some useless doodad or otherwise unremarkable item at an outrageous price. (Remember the million-dollar hot dog we mention earlier in this chapter?) People will see right through that ploy. But if you offer an item that's beautifully crafted and truly unique, you may be able to capitalize on this phenomenon.

If demand for an item that you sell is so high that you simply can't keep up, it may be an indication that you've priced it too low. On the flip side, when items don't sell, many shop owners assume that it's because they're priced too high. However, your price may be too *low*. Before you start slashing prices in your store, try raising them. You may be pleasantly surprised by the result!

Many artists and craftspeople underestimate their worth. They lack confidence in their work and their vision. As a result, they inevitably underprice their pieces. Underestimating the value of your work doesn't just hurt you; it hurts everyone who's trying to earn a living by selling their handmade goods. Deflated prices are bad all the way around! If you suffer from this malaise, channel your inner Stuart Smalley: You're good enough, you're smart enough, and, gosh darn it, people like you!

# Something Old: Special Considerations for Pricing Your Vintage Items

If your Etsy shop specializes in the sale of vintage goodies rather than hand-made items, you can forget about everything that we discuss earlier in this chapter. No "formula" exists for pricing these types of items. Instead, you have to rely on your knowledge of the piece. Specifically, you want to be armed with the following information:

- **What is the piece?** Obviously, you want to know what, exactly, you have for sale.

- **How old is the piece?** Older pieces tend to be more valuable than newer ones.

- **What company manufactured the piece?** Certain manufacturers are held in higher esteem than others. That's why a Tiffany lamp is a lot more valuable than one made by another company and can command a much higher price.

- **What condition is the piece in?** Obviously, an item in good condition can command a higher price than one that appears to have passed through a farm thresher.

- **How desirable is the piece?** Items that are rare or highly collectible generate much more interest than your run-of-the-mill pieces.

When pricing a vintage item, you must also consider how much time you've invested in the piece, in both researching it and finding it in the first place. Finally, assuming that you bought the item (rather than, say, unearthing it in your Aunt Mildred's attic), you must take into account how much you paid for it, as well as any costs you incurred to clean it up, fix any broken bits, and so on.

Still not sure where to start? Try scoping out the competition. Search Etsy or, dare we say it, eBay to see if any other sellers have listed something similar. If so, how much are they charging? Assuming that your piece is in the same condition as theirs, it can give you a good starting point.

# How Low Can You Go? Having a Sale

Many businesses use any excuse to run a sale. ("It's Arbor Day! Take 20 Percent Off!") The idea is, they'll draw in loads of customers and move more merchandise. Although this may be an effective strategy for large, mass-market stores, it's not the best model for your Etsy shop. Running frequent sales not only devalues your work, but it trains your customers to buy from you only when you're running some type of promotion.

That's not to say, however, that you should never run a sale. For example, you may run a once-a-year sale to celebrate your store's anniversary. Or you may run a twice-a-year sale to let go of seasonal inventory.

When you do run a sale, you want to ensure that you still turn a profit on your items — or at least break even. Fortunately, you can easily do so if you use the formula outlined earlier in this chapter to price your goods and you list them at the retail price. You can then discount them by as much as 50 percent and still make money. (Of course, how much you actually discount your items depends on how desperate you are to get rid of them.)

If you do decide to run a sale, make sure you spread the word. Consider a few tips:

- ✔ Talk up your sale in the Etsy community. (For more on the Etsy community, see Chapter 19.)

- ✔ Tell all your Facebook friends and Twitter followers.

- ✔ Share the news on any blogs you maintain.

- ✔ Upload a special "sale" graphic for your shop banner and/or your avatar (see Figure 10-1). Check out Chapter 8 for details on creating shop banners and avatars.

- ✔ Post a notice about your sale in your shop announcement (see Chapter 8 for information on how to create a shop announcement).

- ✔ Include the word "SALE!" in your item title and description, and add a SALE tag. (You find out about item titles and descriptions, as well as tags, in Chapter 12.)

**Figure 10-1:**
Adding
a sale
banner to
your shop
draws
attention
to your
promotion.

# Part III

# She Sells Seashells (and More): Understanding the Etsy Selling Process

The 5th Wave          By Rich Tennant

"Try putting a person in the photo with the product you're trying to sell. We generated a lot of interest in our Etsy shop once Leo started modeling my hats and scarves."

## In this part . . .

*I*f you think about it, selling an item that you've made (or nosed out at, say, a rummage sale) in your Etsy shop involves just a few steps: photographing it, writing an engaging title and description, listing it, selling it, and shipping it. But each of those steps represents its own special area of expertise. This part is devoted to getting you up to speed so that you can complete each step in the process like a pro.

# Chapter 11

# Say Cheese! Photographing Your Wares

*E*ver heard the saying, "It's a vision thing"? Nowhere is this more true than on Etsy. Because shoppers on Etsy can't touch, smell, lick, or otherwise handle the goodies in your Etsy shop, they must evaluate each item based on sight. If you plan to sell on Etsy, it's up to you to supply potential buyers with excellent images of your products — beautiful photos that not only convey the shape, size, color, and texture of your pieces, but also reflect you and your broader brand identity.

At the risk of sounding like Barbara Cartland, your photos must elicit in potential buyers a deep, abiding thirst for your items that they can only satisfy with their purchase. Unfortunately, we can't teach you everything you need to know about photography to make that happen; after all, you can find entire libraries of books on the topic of becoming an expert photographer (like the latest edition of *Digital Photography For Dummies,* by Julie Adair King, published by John Wiley & Sons, Inc.). But this chapter *does* at least enable you to get your feet wet!

You can find lots of photography resources on Etsy. A good place to start is here: www.etsy.com/storque/seller-handbook/etsys-guide-to-photography-10979.

# I'll Take That-a-One! Choosing a Camera with the Right Features

Although you *can* use a film camera to take photos of your pieces and then use a scanner to digitize those images, we don't recommend it. All that film is expensive, and scanning your photos takes time. Truth be told, if you plan to use Etsy to sell your handmade pieces, you need a digital camera — and, no, the one on your phone doesn't count. It simply cannot deliver the level of quality you need to pique buyers' interest.

In the following sections, we describe some essential features that your digital camera needs to have, as well as a few extras that you may find helpful.

Read your camera's manual! Yes, we know, it's boring. But if you want to get the most out of your camera, you need to know what it can and can't do. If you've lost your manual, don't fret; chances are, you can download a digital version of the manual from your camera manufacturer's Web site.

If you're in the market for a new camera, get the best model you can afford. And don't be turned off by gently used models; these can be just the ticket for an Etsy seller, at a much lower price!

## Key club: Identifying key camera features

You don't need some fancy camera that can do everything for you *and* draw you a bubble bath afterward. A trusty digital point-and-shoot in the 4-megapixel range will serve you well, especially if it offers a few key features:

- ✔ **A macro setting:** This setting, typically represented by a flower icon, enables you to shoot extreme close-ups — critical when photographing smaller pieces, such as jewelry, or when you want to reveal the texture of an item.

- ✔ **Autofocus:** These days, pretty much all cameras offer autofocus. In most cases, you use it by pointing your camera at your subject and pressing the camera's shutter button halfway down; the camera automatically focuses on the subject. To capture the image, simply press the shutter button the rest of the way.

If you want the area of focus to be off center, just move your camera to the left or right while keeping the shutter button pressed halfway down; then, when you've achieved the desired composition, press the shutter button the rest of the way. (We talk about focusing your photos later in this chapter.)

✔ **A white balance setting:** With this setting, usually represented with a light bulb icon, you can help your camera identify pure white. The idea here is that if the camera can capture pure white correctly, it can correctly capture (and render) all other colors as well. Setting your camera's white balance before you shoot can save you a bushel of time later trying to correct the color in image-editing programs. (You find out more about image-editing programs later in this chapter.)

## Feature story: Considering extra features

A few other camera features may serve you well (see the nearby sidebar "Say what? Defining a few camera terms" if you need to brush up on technical camera talk):

✔ **An aperture-priority mode:** Although this feature is less "must have" and more "nice to have," aperture-priority mode helps you achieve the photography equivalent of a mullet: an image that's sharp in the front, blurry in the back. Simply engage aperture-priority mode, set your camera's f-stop as low as it goes, press the shutter button halfway down to autofocus on your item, and then snap your photo. (You can read more about the benefits of blurry backgrounds later in this chapter, in the section "Focus, People! Focusing Your Image.")

✔ **A manual mode:** Although you can certainly use the automatic settings on your digital camera, switching to manual mode gives you scads more control over your image's exposure. With manual mode, you can set the camera's aperture size, shutter speed, and ISO. In this way, you prevent the image from being underexposed (too dark) or overexposed (like Justin Bieber).

If your camera doesn't offer a manual mode, see if it supports a feature called exposure compensation. This feature enables you to instruct the camera to expose more or less than it normally would, given the lighting conditions.

# In Style: Styling Your Photos

Photographers who specialize in product shoots are no strangers to stylists — that is, people who work closely with the photographer and other professionals to ensure that the shot contains all the necessary elements. Indeed, high-profile shoots — for example, shoots for magazine advertisements, brochures, and the like — may well have multiple stylists on set, including prop stylists, food stylists, and wardrobe stylists, not to mention full-blown set designers.

## Say what? Defining a few camera terms

We throw a few new terms at you in the previous section — most notably, *exposure, aperture, shutter speed,* and *ISO.*

✓ *Exposure* refers to the amount of light that strikes a digital camera's sensor (which replaced the film in old-school cameras). Achieving proper exposure involves selecting the appropriate aperture size, shutter speed, and ISO.

✓ *Aperture* is the hole through which light passes en route from your camera's lens to the sensor. The size of the aperture affects the image's *depth of field,* which you read about in the later section "Focus, People! Focusing Your Image." You change the size of the aperture by changing the camera's f-stop setting. (Somewhat counterintuitively, a smaller f-stop value indicates a larger aperture.)

✓ *Shutter speed* refers to the amount of time the aperture is open, allowing light to pass through.

✓ *ISO* measures the sensor's sensitivity to light.

Note that changing one of the last three settings — the aperture size, the shutter speed, or the ISO — requires adjustments to the other two settings. For example, if you make the aperture larger, you need to increase the shutter speed and/or choose a less sensitive ISO to ensure that the resulting image isn't overexposed. The key is to strike a balance. (If all this information is freaking you out, simmer down. Just use your camera's automatic setting.)

Chances are, the shoots you conduct for your Etsy shop won't look anything like these affairs. But you can still adopt some of the style pros' practices when you're setting up your shoot. These extras include backgrounds, props, and live models to both complement and emphasize the pieces you photograph.

## *Background check: Using backgrounds*

Although white is the background color of choice for many Etsy sellers — it's crisp, simple, and neutral — it's not your only option. When choosing a background for your photo shoot, keep these points in mind:

✓ **Scout your environment for "everyday" backgrounds.** Do you have a garden? If so, consider using a plant or flower as your background (see Figure 11-1 for an example). Or maybe your living-room wall is exposed brick, another excellent background. Really, just about anything works — wooden tables, tile floors, stone walkways, wicker baskets, wooden crates, whitewashed fences . . . the list goes on. These natural backgrounds can serve as excellent complements to your piece.

**Figure 11-1:**
Sometimes
"everyday
backgrounds"
are best.

*Photo courtesy of Angela Mahoney (www.swede13.etsy.com)*

✔ **Reflective surfaces can really shine.** This advice is especially true if your items are delicate or finely made. Placing them on a mildly reflective surface, such as a sterling platter or a white ceramic plate, enables you to add interest, as well as improve lighting.

✔ **Avoid basic black.** Although black is indisputably the color of choice if you're attempting to hide those 10 extra pounds or, say, you're Catherine of Aragon, it's not so great as a background color when you're photographing goodies destined for your Etsy shop. Why? Because darker pieces get lost. Instead, opt for an almost-black background — charcoal works well — preferably with a bit of texture to add visual interest.

✔ **Add pop with color.** Pieces can really pop with a contrasting-color paper or fabric background. Subtle patterns that complement your piece also work well as backgrounds.

For inexpensive colorful backgrounds, check out your local craft store's scrapbook section. There you'll find 12-by-12-inch sheets of paper in more colors and patterns than you ever dreamed possible. These papers make perfect backgrounds for smaller pieces. Just steer clear of patterns that are super busy.

✔ **Create a seamless background.** Tape one end of a long sheet of thick paper — the kind you cut from a roll — to your wall, letting it drape down onto a table, where you can clamp the other end. You get a seamless "runway" effect that's especially useful for extreme close-ups or times when you don't want anything distracting from your piece (see Figure 11-2).

**Figure 11-2:**
Call attention to your item with a seamless background.

*Photo courtesy of Mark Poulin*

✔ **Avoid the "accidental" background.** Heavens to Etsy! The last thing you want potential buyers to see is all your dirty dishes or that pile of newspapers you keep forgetting to recycle! Don't taint your item by photographing it amid all your daily detritus. Make sure that any background you include in your product shots is there *on purpose* and complements your piece.

✔ **Don't give your background star billing.** If your background is more noticeable than the piece you slaved over for days, don't use it.

## Prop it like it's hot: Working with props

Props are a great way to add interest to your shot or convey something about the item you're selling. The trick to using them is making sure they don't detract from the piece you want to sell or otherwise confuse potential buyers. A prop must enhance your piece, conveying to buyers its possibilities. Props also must reflect your brand (see Chapter 16). That is, if your brand is elegant, you want to steer clear of props that scream "Behold my quirkiness!" (and vice versa).

The swell thing about props is that they're everywhere! You can find potential props in your garden shed, your craft closet, your grandmother's attic, your nephew's toy chest, or your uncle's garage. Experiment with lots of different props to see what works best. For example, you can use props as follows:

✔ **To convey the scale of your piece:** Using a universal prop — something everyone recognizes, like a coin, a book, a pencil, a chair, a toy, food, or whatnot — is a great way to show potential buyers the size of your piece. (Figure 11-3 shows a necklace on a pile of beans.)

**Figure 11-3:**
Using a universal prop can convey the scale of your piece.

*Photo courtesy of Jonathan Wilson*

✔ **To show how your piece can be used:** By putting your piece in its "natural environment," you give potential buyers an idea of how they can use it. For example, if you make USB drives shaped like R2-D2, you may insert one into your laptop's USB port. Or maybe you craft gorgeous place cards; in that case, you may position one atop a lovely vintage plate, to reinforce what your item is and does. (Figure 11-4 shows a colorful handmade pillow on a little girl's bed.)

**Figure 11-4:**
You can feature a prop that suggests how to use your piece.

*Photo courtesy of Elizabeth Wallberg, e photography*

✔ **To reflect how your piece was made:** Do you use special tools to construct your item? If so, consider using those implements as props. Knitting needles, embroidery hoops, pliers, cutters, paintbrushes, pencils, scissors, blowtorches — all these constitute excellent props; they add interest by conveying how the piece was made.

✔ **To suggest what inspired your piece:** Did the idea for your piece come to you while you were walking in the woods? Then a leaf, branch, or pine cone may make an excellent prop. Or if you had the epiphany for your piece while strolling along the seashore, a bit of sand or a seashell may serve as a prop. (As another example, Figure 11-5 shows an orange soap set with a group of oranges.)

✔ **To complement your piece:** A great way to create interest in your product shots is to place your piece alongside an object that complements it visually. Maybe the object you use as a prop is a complementary color — for example, the object is violet, and your piece is yellow. Or maybe the object reflects the genre of your piece in some way — say, the object is a vintage bowling pin, and your piece is a hand-sewn bowling shirt.

**Figure 11-5:**
Try using a prop that suggests what inspired your piece.

*Photo courtesy of Belle Terre (belleterre.etsy.com)*

# Model citizens: Using live models

Yes, models can be terrible divas. But the fact is, when they're not busy flinging cellphones at your head, models — whether they're babies, kids, adults, or your pet hamster — can do wonders for your product photos. Why? For two reasons:

✔ **Using a live model helps you convey the scale or fit of your piece.**
If you shoot your gorgeous necklace with a simple white background, potential buyers may not be able to get a handle on its length. Photographing that same necklace on a model, however, enables buyers to deduce at a glance how long it is, as well as how it rests on the décolletage (see Figure 11-6). Likewise, if you sell hand-sewn clothes in your Etsy shop, photographing your pieces on a live model shows potential buyers how they'll fit.

✔ **Using a live model makes your piece more relatable.** Models humanize your piece. When potential buyers see a model wearing your item, they inevitably imagine it looking just as fantastic on themselves or their loved ones. The same is true when you show a model using your item; potential buyers naturally imagine themselves or their loved ones using it in the same way.

**Figure 11-6:**
Using a live model can really bring your piece to, er, life.

*Photo courtesy of Rae Aldrich-Keisling*

If your pieces are of an intimate nature — think panties or earrings — be sure to note that the ones worn by the model are samples. You'll send an unworn pair to the buyer.

Of course, you can't use just any model. You want to choose models that enhance, not detract from, your piece. You must also select models that reflect your brand and your target audience. For example, if your brand and your target audience are on the edgy or punk end of the spectrum, then your models need to be, too (think tattoos, piercings, mohawks, and so on). However, if your aesthetic is more romantic, your models need to look that way as well.

Who should you enlist to model your pieces? Friends and family are obvious (and inexpensive) choices — assuming that they're appropriate for your brand and aesthetic. If you're selling a premium item, consider investing in a pro.

# Lighting Bug: Lighting Your Shot

If you've ever seen Cybill Shepherd in *Moonlighting,* you know the importance of flattering lighting! No doubt about it, whether you're photographing an aging actress or a tea towel on which you've embroidered the periodic table, good lighting is essential. Without it, your camera simply can't capture the color and texture of your piece. The following sections note a few lighting-related points to keep in mind when photographing your pieces.

## She's a natural! Using natural light

You don't need to start selling your plasma to afford an expensive lighting rig. The fact is, when it comes to photographing the goodies you've made for your Etsy shop, natural lighting — say, from a north-facing window or even when outside on an overcast day — is best. It's by far the most flattering light source. In addition, it enables you to capture the colors and texture of your piece.

## Dark matter: Avoiding the dark

Unless you live with the Inuits and it's that season when the sun never sets, shooting at night is a bad idea — most notably because simply not much natural light is available.

Instead, you want to photograph during the "golden hours." No, we're not recommending that you shoot during reruns of *The Golden Girls.* We're encouraging you to use the natural light available in the early morning, right after the sun rises, or near sunset, when the sun is low in the sky. You'll find the natural light during these periods to be as flattering as 4-inch heels.

## SPF 50: Avoiding direct sunlight

Direct sunlight can overexpose your photo, washing it out. If you can't avoid direct sunlight (people in Nevada, we're talking to you), try diffusing the light — for example, positioning a sheer curtain between the sun and the piece you're photographing.

Figures 11-7 and 11-8 show the difference between an object photographed in full sun and one photographed in diffused light. Notice how the diffused light in the second image softens the whole shot.

Another option you can try when you can't avoid direct sunlight is positioning your piece so that the sun is behind it. This technique creates a warm glow around the edges. (In this scenario, you may need to use reflectors or, as a last resort, your flash. If you must use your flash, diffuse it to avoid casting harsh shadows on your piece. See the next section for more information.)

**Figure 11-7:** Notice how shooting in full sun washes out an image.

*Photo courtesy of Angela at Teeny Bunny (www.TeenyBunny.etsy.com)*

**Figure 11-8:**
Diffusing the
light softens
an image,
making it
much more
appealing.

## Time to reflect: Using reflectors

For the love of all that's holy, if you can avoid it, don't use your flash when photographing items for your Etsy shop — unless harsh shadows, glare, reflections, and a generally flat appearance will somehow enhance your item's salability.

If you simply cannot achieve the necessary exposure without using your flash, consider covering the flash with tracing paper, white facial tissue, or some other sheer material to diffuse it (we introduce the idea of diffused light in the previous section).

Instead of using your flash, you can put reflectors to work. Use white walls or other home-grown reflective items (think white poster board, a hanging bed sheet, or, for a brighter reflection, a mirror) to "bounce" light onto your piece. Figures 11-9 and 11-10 show the difference between a shoot that didn't use reflectors and a shoot that did. Notice that the first image, for which a reflector wasn't used, is darker and a wee bit muddy; its colors just don't stand out. In contrast, the face of the angel in the second image pops a bit more, for an overall brighter, happier look.

**Figure 11-9:**
The photographer didn't use a reflector for this shot.

**Figure 11-10:**
Notice how using a reflector really lights up the piece.

Especially if you craft wee things — jewelry, personalized guitar picks, pet portraits on grains of rice — you may want to consider using a light tent. A *light tent,* sometimes called a *light box,* is a small structure made of transparent white fabric or plastic in which you place your item to photograph it. Light tents, which can be used with natural light or a simple lighting kit, come in a variety of shapes and sizes. Alternatively, you can build your own for a song. For help, visit www.etsy.com/storque/seller-handbook/fortys-foto-tips-2-make-a-light-box-244.

# Compose Yourself: Composing Your Shot

Suppose you found yourself at the Statue of Liberty with Annie Leibovitz. And suppose further that both of you were photographing Lady Liberty. No offense, but her pictures would probably be way better than yours — more captivating, more vital, more powerful, more interesting. Why? Well, lots of reasons. One, Leibovitz probably has a camera that's so good, it practically has super powers. But more than that, Leibovitz has a keen eye for composition — that is, the arrangement of visual elements in an image.

Just because you're no Annie Leibovitz doesn't mean you can't compose some really swell photos of your own for your Etsy shop. The pointers in the following sections can help.

## For starters: Trying basic composition principles

As you shoot your pieces, keep these basic compositional points in mind:

- ✔ **Angle the camera.** Angling, or tilting, the camera puts the subject slightly off center and creates movement and flow. The result: a more dynamic, intriguing image, as you can see in Figure 11-11.

- ✔ **Shoot tight.** Filling the frame with your subject not only adds visual impact, but enables potential buyers to see how well made your piece is (see for yourself in Figure 11-12).

**Figure 11-11:**
Angling the camera produces interesting results.

Photo courtesy of Colette Urquhart

**Figure 11-12:**
Shoot tight,
for added
impact.

Photo courtesy of Kristen Timmers

✔ **Blur the background.** Remember that photographic mullet we mention in the earlier section "Feature story: Considering extra features"? It's such a good idea, we're bringing it up again. By using a shallow depth of field (read: a low f-stop setting), you can blur the background to dramatically highlight your piece, as shown in Figure 11-13.

When the background is blurred, you can shoot in almost any setting; just make sure that the background colors don't clash with your subject. (For more on depth of field, see the later section "Focus, People! Focusing Your Image.")

✔ **Remember that less is more.** Don't crowd the scene with extraneous objects. Otherwise, potential buyers may not understand exactly which item in your photo is for sale.

✔ **Frame your subject.** One way to draw the viewer's eye to your piece is to frame it — that is, place some darker element in the perimeter. This technique helps prevent the viewer's eye from straying from your item.

✔ **Group pieces.** Especially if you make itsy-bitsy goodies, you can try grouping them, to catch a buyer's eye. Not only does this strategy make for a more eye-catching photograph, but it also shows potential buyers how pieces in your collection work together. Just be sure to note in your listing description which one of the items in the group is actually up for grabs. Also, avoid groups that are too large; using three to five pieces does the trick.

*Photo courtesy of Betsy and Bess (Christopher and Adrienne Scott; www.betsyandbess.etsy.com)*

**Figure 11-13:**
Blur the background to emphasize your item.

## Third's-eye view: Applying the rule of thirds

To be perfectly honest, we're not big on rules. (This fact may explain why we're both self-employed.) But one rule we can absolutely get behind is the rule of thirds. In addition to conveying a sense of tension and energy, the rule of thirds helps pique the viewer's interest. According to this rule, you want to do the following:

1. **Use two horizontal lines and two vertical lines to divide the scene you're photographing into nine equal parts (think of a tic tac toe grid, as shown in Figure 11-14).**

2. **Place key elements at any of the four points where the vertical and horizontal lines intersect (see Figure 11-15), or use the lines themselves as guides as you compose your image.**

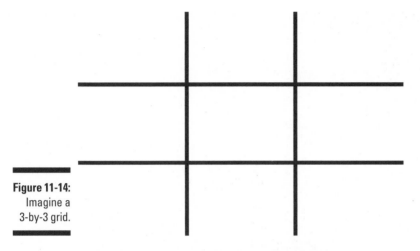

**Figure 11-14:**
Imagine a
3-by-3 grid.

**Figure 11-15:**
Use the grid
to compose
your image.

*Photo courtesy of Heather Torre (myselvagedlife.etsy.com)*

*Note:* With some digital cameras, you can display a grid on the LCD viewfinder, enabling you to organize your image around the lines and cross points.

# Focus, People! Focusing Your Image

A surefire way to turn off buyers is to include blurry images in your Etsy shop, especially if they're close-ups. How's a potential buyer supposed to view your piece in all its detailed splendor if your photos are as hazy as a Lindsay Lohan alibi? It's imperative that your product photos be crisp and clear, as in Figure 11-16.

**Figure 11-16:**
Notice how
crisp and
clear this
in-focus
photo is.

Photo courtesy of Becca Balistreri

To ensure excellent focus if you're shooting a close-up, use your camera's macro setting. This setting (which, as mentioned in the earlier section "Key club: Identifying key camera features," is usually indicated with a flower icon) ensures that your focus is sharp.

If you're using a slower shutter speed or you just drank a quadruple espresso, you need to take special care to keep your camera still as you photograph your piece. Using a tripod is one way to go; alternatively, you can rest your camera on a table or a stack of books.

We mention it a few times in this chapter: the so-called "photographic mullet," in which you keep your item in focus while blurring other parts of the scene. The way to achieve that look is to use a low f-stop setting to yield a shallow depth of field. However, this tip begs the question: What is depth of field? *Depth of field* refers to how much of the area in front of and behind the subject will appear in focus.

- ✔ In an image with a shallow depth of field, you get that blurred background we talk so much about, and the subject is in focus. You achieve a shallow depth of field by using a low f-stop setting.

- ✔ Images with a deep depth of field have the background, the subject, and the foreground in focus. A high f-stop setting yields a deep depth of field.

# Shoot, Shoot, and Shoot Some More: Taking Lots of Pictures

Back when film put you back a pretty penny — not to mention the cost of developing it — you may have been justified in being stingy with your shots. But these days, it's digital, Dawg! You can — and should — shoot lots of shots. And by lots, we mean *lots*. Like, a whole bunch. A gazillion should do the trick.

The point is, your product photos have to be *great* — like, Muhammed Ali, Audrey Hepburn, Paul Newman great. As we say earlier in this chapter, they need to convey the shape, size, color, and texture of your piece, as well as reflect you and your broader brand identity. On top of all that, they need to be easy on the eyes. Unless you're Helmut Newton, you're just not going to capture all that with a single click of the shutter button.

One more tip: As you shoot, make it a point to experiment. Swap out props and backgrounds. Try different angles, lighting, and depths of field. It's the only way to ensure that you wind up with a winning picture.

Before you start, make sure your camera's batteries are charged. The only problem worse than setting up your shoot and then discovering that you're out of juice is having to entertain your live model while you recharge.

# Clean-up on Image Five: Tidying Up Your Photos with Image-Editing Software

Even the best photos can use a little tidying up. For example, you may want to adjust the image's brightness or contrast, tweak the color in an image to make it really pop, or crop the image to make your subject stand out.

Please, we beg you: Don't use image-editing software to try to "fix" a bad photo. Some photos — photos that are dark, blurry, or otherwise foul — are simply beyond repair. Image-editing programs are for enhancement purposes only.

Fortunately, as you find out in Chapter 8, any number of image-editing programs are available to you, ranging in price from free to the cost of your arm and your leg. These programs include the following (if you want to read more about each one, flip to Chapter 8):

✔ Photoshop (www.photoshop.com)

✔ GIMP (www.gimp.org)

✔ Picasa (www.picasa.com)

✔ Picnik (www.picnik.com)

As we mention in Chapter 8, if you use a Windows PC, you can also use the Paint program, which came free with your computer. Yet another option is to use the software that came with your digital camera.

Unfortunately, we can't cover the ins and outs of using all these programs. But to give you a basic idea of how it's done, in the following sections, we step you through the process using Picnik, a free online photo-editing service, to fix your photos.

## Get the upload-down: Uploading your photo

Before you can tidy up your images, you must upload them to Picnik. Here's how:

1. **Copy your photos from your camera to your computer.**

   See your camera's manual for details on how to do this.

2. **Type www.picnik.com in your Web browser's address bar.**

   The main Picnik page opens (see Figure 11-17).

3. **Click the Get Started Now button.**

   Picnik directs you to a page where you can upload a photo (see Figure 11-18).

   You can create an account with Picnik on this page — either a free one or a fee-based one, which gives you access to additional site features — but you don't have to.

4. **Click the Upload a Photo button.**

   A dialog box appears; you use it to find the photo you want to upload.

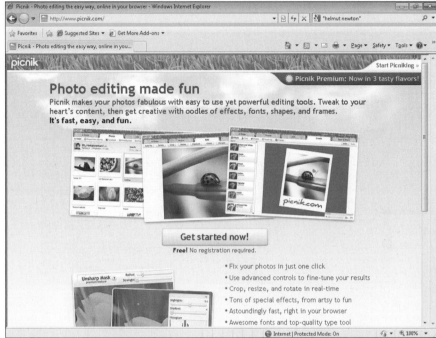

**Figure 11-17:**
Direct
your Web
browser to
the main
Picnik page.

**Figure 11-18:**
Upload
photos from
this page.

5. **Locate and select the photo you want to upload; then click the Open button.**

Picnik opens the photo and displays it in an Edit page in your Web browser (see Figure 11-19).

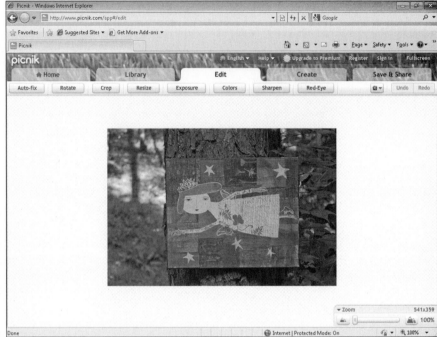

**Figure 11-19:**
Picnik
uploads
your photo,
displaying it
in a special
Edit page.

# Expose yourself: Adjusting your photo's exposure

Suppose that your photo is a little bit dark. Or maybe your subject is slightly washed out. In either case, you can adjust its exposure. Here's how:

1. **Click the Exposure button.**

   Picnik displays several exposure-related settings.

2. **Click the Auto-Fix button; alternatively, drag the Exposure and Contrast sliders to adjust the image manually (see Figure 11-20).**

   If you don't like how the image looks with the new settings applied, click the Reset button. Otherwise, click OK to see the controls shown in Figure 11-19.

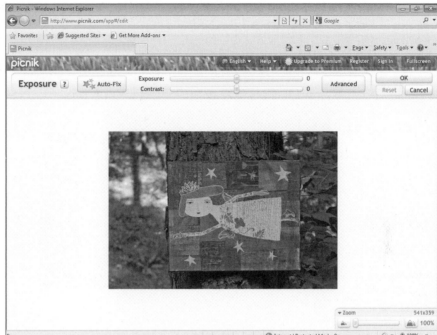

**Figure 11-20:**
Adjust
exposure
settings.

## Tweakly Reader: Tweaking your photo's colors

Tweaking the colors in your photo can add a touch of vibrancy. Here's how it's done:

1. **Click the Colors button.**

   Picnik displays several color-related settings.

2. **Click the Auto Colors button; alternatively, drag the Saturation and Temperature sliders to adjust the image manually (see Figure 11-21).**

   If you don't like how the image looks with the new settings applied, click the Reset button. Otherwise, click OK to see the controls shown in Figure 11-19.

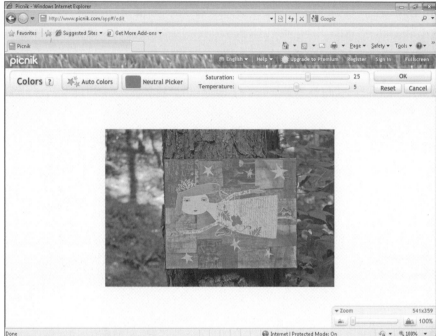

Figure 11-21:
Adjust color
settings.

# Crop circles: Cropping your photo

If you've captured some extraneous items in your image, or you simply want to focus it more tightly on your piece, you can crop it. Here's the drill:

1. **Click the Crop button.**

   A movable, resizable box appears over your image, and various crop-related settings display.

2. **The area of the image outside the box will be cropped from the image (see Figure 11-22). To move the box, click inside it and drag it until it covers the part of the image you want to keep. To resize the box, click any of its four edges and drag inward or outward; to resize the box but keep its proportions intact, click any of its four corners and drag inward or outward.**

   If you don't like how the image looks with the new settings applied, click the Reset button. Otherwise, click OK to see the controls shown in Figure 11-19.

Product images bound for your Etsy shop must be at least 430 pixels wide. If they aren't, Etsy stretches them to fit, which makes them look blurry. Note that we said *at least* 430 pixels wide; for best results, opt for an image that's between 800 and 1,000 pixels wide.

**Figure 11-22:**
Crop your
image.

# *Save yourselves! Saving your edited photo*

To ensure that all your hard work doesn't go to waste, you must save your edited photo. Follow these steps:

1. **Click the Save and Share tab.**

   Settings for saving your image appear.

2. **In the File Name field, type a descriptive name for the image file; then double-check the photo's size and format. (More on size and format in a jiff.) When you're satisfied with the settings, click the Save Photo button (see Figure 11-23).**

   A dialog box opens where you can indicate where you want to save your image.

If your image file is too large, you'll have a hard time uploading it to Etsy when you create the item listing in which the photo will appear (see Chapter 13 for details). For this reason, when you save your image in Picnik, you must ensure that it's no larger than 250KB and doesn't exceed 1,000 pixels by 1,000 pixels. One more pointer: Your image needs to be a JPG, GIF, or PNG file; Etsy doesn't support other file types.

**Figure 11-23:**
Save your
image.

3. **Locate and select the folder where you want to save your image; then click the Save button.**

   Picnik saves your image in the folder you chose.

---

# Watermark, watermark everywhere: Watermarking your photos

If you want, you can apply a watermark to your photos — that is, you can superimpose text over your image to prevent others from using it without your permission. Watermarks are especially useful if you're a photographer, painter, or some other type of graphic artist, and you sell prints of your images. If you do watermark your image, keep it subtle; otherwise, the watermark may overpower your image.

To apply a watermark using Picnik, click the Create tab (refer to Figure 11-19), click the Text button, click a font, type your text, and click the Add button. Picnik adds the text to your image; move it and resize it as needed, and use the Text Properties settings to change the watermark's intensity. (*Tip:* Try opening the Advanced Blend Modes drop-down list and choosing the Overlay option; that way, your watermark will be visible but slightly transparent.)

# Chapter 12

# Word Up: Composing Engaging Titles and Descriptions

**T**rue, a gorgeous photo of your piece may catch a buyer's eye. But the way you write about your piece in your item title and description can keep your buyer's attention. With these textual elements, you have an opportunity to engage buyers with a story about you and your piece. You can also answer questions about your piece, such as what it's made of, what it does, and why someone should buy it. Indeed, well-written and interesting titles and descriptions may just persuade a buyer to add your piece to her cart.

If your talents lie more in crafting and less in writing ("I'm a candy-wrapper handbag maker, not a writer!"), don't freak out. As you discover in this chapter, writing engaging item titles and descriptions is plenty doable. You also find out how to optimize your item titles, descriptions, and tags for searching, making it easier for prospective buyers to find your piece.

## Headline Muse: Writing Titillating Item Titles

Any newspaper writer will tell you that a first-rate headline is critical in grabbing readers' attention. A strong headline both hints at what the story that follows contains and coaxes the audience to read on. Superlative headlines — which, almost by definition, are brief — may use humor, puns, alliteration, rhymes, or other types of word play and often include clever double entendres. "Headless Body in Topless Bar," the headline of a *New York Post* piece on a local murder, is one example of an excellent (albeit disturbing) headline; another is "Super Cagey Go Ballistic Celtics Are Atrocious," the headline for a piece in *The Sun* (the United Kingdom's biggest-selling newspaper) about the Inverness Caledonian Thistle football club trouncing its Celtic rivals in the Scottish Cup.

As you've probably guessed, your item title acts a lot like a good headline. It's designed to grab a buyer's attention and entice her to read more about you and your item. Not surprisingly, then, many headline-writing principles apply when it comes to composing stand-out item titles:

- ✔ **Keep it short.** Your item title must be brief — no more than 155 characters (including spaces).
- ✔ **Be clever.** Use humor, puns, alliteration, rhymes, or other types of word play.
- ✔ **Use strong, concise words.** Avoid vague verbiage! Some words and phrases are just better than others. For example, don't call your piece "small"; call it "tiny" or "wee" or "diminutive" or "pea-size."
- ✔ **Use a mix of uppercase and lowercase letters.** Too many all-uppercase words, and it seems like you're shouting. Too many lowercase words, and it seems like you're e. e. cummings.

Your item title also needs to broadcast key information about your piece — most notably, what it is, what it's made of, and perhaps a few choice details about the piece, such as its color, size, or other personal touches.

You also want to include some strong keywords in your item title, to optimize it for search. You find out more about search engine optimization (SEO) later in this chapter.

To give you a good jumping-off point with your own item titles, Table 12-1 has a few examples.

| Table 12-1 | Examples of Strong and Weak Item Titles |
|---|---|
| *Don't* | *Do* |
| Thank-You Card | Give Thanks! Handmade Black-and-White Landscape Photo Print Thank-You Card |
| Men's Silver Bracelet | Cuff Guy: Rugged Handmade Sterling Silver Cuff for Men |
| Vintage Apron | Flouncy Floral Apron: Vintage Ruffled Cotton Apron with Pink and Purple Flowers |
| Purse Made of Candy Wrappers | Bon-Bon Bag: Handmade Eco-Friendly Candy-Wrapper Purse |

# Story Time: Telling a Story with Your Item Description

People who buy on Etsy aren't interested in meaningless, mass-produced goods. They want pieces with a past — something that has a story. Etsy allows sellers to enter an item description so they can tell the story behind their product. In the following sections, we explain how to uncover an item's story, answer questions about the item, and compose a thoughtful description.

## Likely story: Uncovering your item's story

Not sure what your piece's story is — or whether it even has one? Fear not. Start spinning your yarn (figuratively speaking) by answering a few questions:

- ✔ **What inspired you to create the piece?** Mentioning your source of inspiration is a great way to get the ball rolling. If you're a candy-wrapper handbag maker, maybe you got the idea to make candy-wrapper handbags while traveling in Mexico, where women's cooperatives craft all manner of items out of candy wrappers, including clutches, totes, and placemats.

- ✔ **How was the piece made?** Indicating the skills involved in making an item can be an excellent way to forge a connection with buyers. Was it woven? Sewn? Assembled by magical hamsters?

- ✔ **Who taught you the skills you use to create your piece?** Sharing how you learned the techniques you use to craft your pieces can be a great way to bond with prospective buyers. Maybe your great-grandmother learned the fine art of candy-wrapper handbag making while in prison and passed her skills down to you. Or maybe your uncle was a Mayan studies scholar and taught you their paper-weaving techniques — techniques that you then put to use making candy-wrapper handbags to justify your prodigious candy-eating habit.

Even if you choose not to focus on the story behind your item, don't hesitate to let your own personality shine through in your item description. If you tend toward quirky, then your item descriptions should, too. Ditto if you have a darker bent.

# Description prescription: Describing your item

It probably goes without saying that, in addition to including the "story" behind you and your piece, your item description must contain, well, a description of your item. But we believe in being thorough, so we're saying it. Think about what questions buyers are likely to have about your piece. Then answer all those questions in your item description. The description may cover the following points:

- **What is your piece?** Although it may seem obvious to you that your item is a handbag made of Snickers wrappers, to others, it may be less apparent.

- **What does your piece do?** Does your piece have a function? Or is it for decoration only? Be sure to note this info in your item description.

- **Who is your piece for?** Dogs? Babies? Men? On the flip side, who is it *not* for? For example, if it contains pieces on which an infant may choke, note that in your item description.

- **How does your piece work?** Does it have a clasp? Or buttons? Or a zipper? Do you tie it? Does it need batteries, or do you power it by driving a DeLorean equipped with a lightning rod past the town clock tower during a thunderstorm?

- **What color is your piece?** Colors may translate differently on different computer monitors. Including detailed color information in your item description is a good way to bridge that gap.

  Be specific here. Don't say that your piece is red when it's actually scarlet, brick, ruby, cherry, crimson, or burgundy.

- **How big is your piece?** Remember in *Spinal Tap* when Nigel Tufnel sketched out specs for a Stonehenge stage set but accidentally used a double-prime mark (for inches) instead of a prime mark (for feet)? The result was an 18-inch Stonehenge monument that was, as David St. Hubbins observed, "in danger of being crushed by a dwarf." To save your buyer from experiencing similar disappointment, include detailed and accurate sizing information about your piece. Avoid vague terms like "small" or "large," and instead opt for precise measurements, especially if you sell clothing. By the way, it doesn't hurt to include both systems of measurement — metric and old-school — in your item descriptions.

- **What materials did you use?** Do you use organic cotton? Hand-dyed wool? Swarovski crystals? Wrappers from Reese's Peanut Butter Cups? Whatever materials you use, they need to appear in your item description.

✔ **What techniques did you use to construct your piece?** Did you knit it? Weave it? Sew it? This info helps tell the story of your piece and reinforces to buyer that you made it by hand. It also helps attract buyers who are partial to a particular crafting technique.

Especially if you've priced your item on the higher side, be sure to indicate why in your item description. Whether your item is on the expensive side because you used high-end materials or because you crafted it using a particularly difficult technique, you need to share this info with your buyer. (Flip to Chapter 10 for more information on pricing your items.)

✔ **What does your piece feel like?** Is it soft? Smooth? Slick? Rough? Nubby? Scaly? Prickly? Stubbly? Indicate your item's tactile qualities in your item description.

✔ **What does your piece smell like?** Does it have a scent, such as lavender or ylang-ylang? If it's a vintage piece, does it have a musty odor? Does it come from a smoker's home?

Having a sale in your shop? Be sure to mention it in your item description and your shop announcement. (See Chapter 10 for the full scoop on having a sale.)

## Write away: Composing your item description

You have a handle on the story behind your item, and you know what information your item listing needs to contain. Now it's time to put the proverbial pen to paper and write your item description.

To make your item description as effective as possible, put the most important information about your item first. Putting important items first not only makes it easier for shoppers to quickly get the information they need about your piece, but also enables you to optimize your shop for search. (We talk more about search engine optimization later in this chapter.) Of course, what constitutes "the most important information" may differ from piece to piece; in general, however, this info likely includes what your item is, what it does, what it looks like, and what it's made of. From there, you can get into more "nice to know" information, such as what your item smells like (unless, of course, the whole point of your item is its smell, as is the case with soap, perfume, and the like), as well as the story behind your item or your work.

To keep your prospective buyer reading, use short paragraphs and bullet points. That construction is easier on the eyes than a gigantic block of text. Another way to break things up is to use subtitles — for example, one above the item description, one on top of any measurements information, and so on. You can set these subtitles apart from regular text by using all caps or boldface font.

Consider this example of an item description that falls short:

Bag made of candy wrappers.

Size: Medium

We don't know about you, but nothing in this description makes us want to buy the bag. Yes, the seller was brief — score one for her. But this description almost completely lacks any useful information! Worse, it's as though the seller just can't be bothered to tell anyone about her item.

Following is an example of a much more effective item description:

If you're bonkers for bon-bons, this candy-wrapper handbag is for you. This colorful, eco-friendly handbag, carefully hand-woven using Kit Kat, Nestle Crunch, and Snickers candy wrappers, is just the right size to carry a phone, wallet, and candy bar (of course).

I crafted this handbag, which can double as a makeup bag, using a technique I learned from my candy-crazy aunt. The handbag, which measures 22 centimeters (8.7 inches) across and 14 centimeters (5.5 inches) high, features a zipper along the top, as well as a color-coordinated wristlet for easy carrying. The use of candy wrappers gives the handbag a slightly shiny, reflective quality and a mild, chocolate-y aroma.

This candy-wrapper handbag is perfect for anyone with a sweet tooth!

Now *this* description makes us want to buy this handbag, pronto (and also to pound a Kit Kat).

# SEO Speedwagon: Using Search Engine Optimization to Drive Traffic

Remember *Field of Dreams*? The whole "If you build it, they will come" thing, when Kevin Costner's DIY baseball diamond attracted the 1919 roster for the Chicago Black Sox and, subsequently, a large enough crowd to save his family farm? Don't get us wrong — it's a nice story and all. But unless you specialize in hand-crafting redemption for disgraced baseball players from another dimension, the odds of the same thing happening with your Etsy shop are as slim as Kate Moss.

You have to do more than just build your Etsy shop to entice people to visit it. As you find out in this book, you need to supply gorgeous photos and intriguing descriptions of your wares. In addition, you need to engage in a little something called *search engine optimization* — SEO, for short. By using SEO, you can increase the likelihood that people who use search engines such as Google, Yahoo!, or Bing to search for certain keywords will see — and click on — a link to your Etsy shop in their list of results.

How can you harness the power of SEO for your Etsy shop? One way is to plant relevant keywords in your shop title, shop announcement, shop sections, and user profile (see Chapter 8 for details on these items). That way, people searching for those keywords will see your Etsy shop in their search results. Another way is to include these keywords in your shop item titles, descriptions, and tags, which is the focus of this section.

## *Keyword to your mother: Choosing the best keywords*

All this talk of keywords and SEO begs one obvious question: What keywords do you want to use?

Suppose that you hand-craft bracelets out of bottle caps. Sure, you can use keywords like "bracelet," or even "jewelry" in your item listings — in fact, you should. The problem is, you're not the only one using those terms. A recent search for the term "jewelry" yielded roughly 336,000,000 matches. Adding "bracelet" to the search string narrowed the list somewhat, but it still yielded almost 80,000,000 hits. Including "bottle cap" helped and got us down to about half a million.

---

### In-bound and determined: Garnering in-bound links

In addition to the keywords and phrases you plant in your item title and item description (as well as in your shop title, shop announcement, and other Etsy areas), you can optimize your Etsy shop or item for search through in-bound links. An *in-bound link* is a link from another page to your Etsy shop or item. Google and other search engines rate pages on how interesting they are, which they gauge in part by determining how many in-bound links a page has, as well as how credible the pages containing those links are. So the more pages link to your Etsy shop or item listing, and the more credible those pages are, the higher your shop or listing appears in search results.

So how can you garner more in-bound links? One way is to ask friends and family members who maintain blogs or social media accounts (for example, on Facebook or Twitter) to link to your shop. (You can also use your own blog and social media accounts for the same purpose.) In addition, you can build in-bound links by participating in the Etsy forums (see Chapter 19) and commenting on Etsy Storque articles (see Chapter 20). You can even include links to pages in your shop *within your shop* to build in-bound links, even though that may seem kind of like cheating. And, of course, you can encourage others to link to your Etsy shop and items by linking to their Etsy shops and items. What comes around, goes around!

No doubt about it, 500,000 is better than 336,000,000 — but not if your shop is buried in the bottom 499,999 matches. Why? Because when most people use a search engine, they don't dig deeper than the first few pages of search results (if they even go that far) to find what they're looking for. To increase traffic to your Etsy storefront, you must ensure that links to your items or shop appear in those first few pages — preferably on page one.

Short of purchasing Google or Yahoo! outright, how can you improve your search results? By doing a little research to determine whether the keywords you're using are appropriate or whether other keywords may serve you better. To aid you, Google offers its handy, dandy Keyword Tool. You use it like so:

1. **Launch your Web browser and type `https://adwords.google.com/ select/KeywordToolExternal` in its address bar.**

   The page for the Google AdWords Keyword Tool opens (see Figure 12-1).

2. **Type any keywords or phrases that you use in the Word or Phrase box.**

   Include one keyword or phrase per line.

3. **Fill out the CAPTCHA form — that is, type the characters that appear in the picture.**

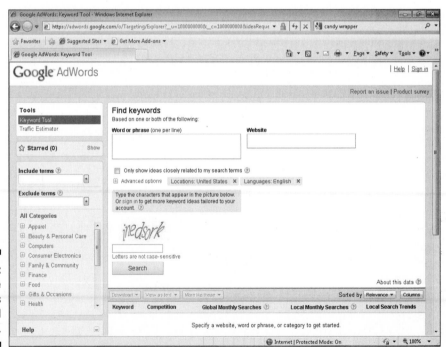

**Figure 12-1:**
The Google
AdWords
Keyword
Tool.

### 4. Click the Search button.

The Keyword Tool shows how often the keywords you typed are searched, as well as other keywords you may want to consider. In Figure 12-2, more than 1,000 local searches focused on the phrase "bottle cap bracelet." That is, over a 12-month period, 1,000 people in the United States searched for the phrase "bottle cap bracelet." Also notice that, in the same period, nearly 7,500,000 people searched for the term "jewelry."

Now, you may think that you need to focus on the higher-volume keywords or phrases — that is, keywords like "jewelry" rather than phrases such as "bottle cap bracelet." After all, more people are searching with those. But given how many matches are in that category, the chances of your shop or item ranking near the top are essentially nil. You have a much better chance of appearing near the top of the results for a narrow search, like "bottle cap bracelet."

What about finding keywords that may work better than the ones you're using? Simple. Just read through the list of keywords that the Keyword Tool spits out to find ideas for keywords or phrases you can use. This list contains actual search terms that people have entered into search engines to find items like yours. In this example, you may add "bottle cap jewelry" or "bottle cap crafts" as keywords.

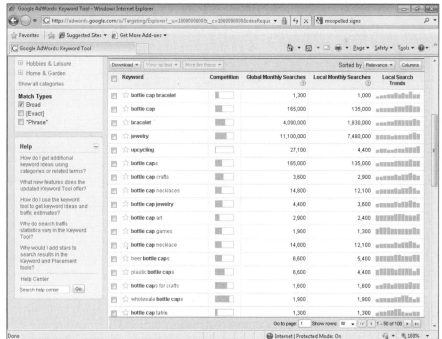

**Figure 12-2:**
Note how often your key-words are searched.

You can use Etsy Web Analytics to see which keywords visitors used to find you on Etsy. For more on Etsy Web Analytics, flip to Chapter 18.

## What you key is what you get: Using SEO with your item title and description

You find out how to write catchy item titles earlier in this chapter. But you also need to ensure that those titles are optimized for search. Keep a few points in mind:

- **Include keywords . . .** Every item title that you write needs to contain at least one keyword or phrase (more, if possible).

- **. . . But not too many.** Yes, you want to make sure that your title contains as many keywords as possible. But stuffing your title with too many keywords for the sake of SEO may render it terribly boring, if not completely unreadable. The idea is to write titles that are catchy for both people *and* PCs.

- **Put keywords first.** Place keywords at or near the beginning of your item title. Although search engines search your entire title for keyword matches, they display only the first 66 characters (including spaces) of it in the list of results. To increase the chances that anyone searching for that keyword will visit your shop, you want to make sure that the keyword shows up in that results list.

The same points apply to your item description — except one: Search engines display more characters from your item description in search results (160 in all, including spaces). But again, even though you have a little more wiggle room, you want to make sure that your keywords appear toward the beginning. You also want to repeat any keywords at least once (but preferably two or three times) in your item description, to boost your Etsy shop in the search rankings.

Here's an example of an item listing that makes good use of keywords:

> Grape Expectations: Nehi Grape Bottle Cap Bracelet
>
> Quench your thirst for handmade jewelry with this bottle cap bracelet! This eco-friendly bracelet represents the finest in bottle cap crafts. Constructed from vintage Nehi Grape bottle caps from my grandfather's attic, sterling silver findings, and purple Swarovski crystal beads, the bracelet measures 7 inches (17.7 centimeters) across but can be adjusted to accommodate a more diminutive wrist.

As you type your item title and description in Etsy, you can view how it will appear in Google search results, as shown in Figure 12-3. Simply click the Show Preview link under the Description text box. (For more on entering titles and descriptions as you list items, see Chapter 13.)

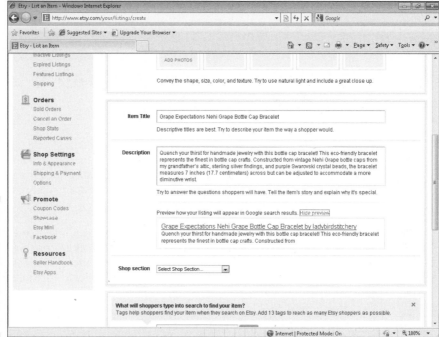

**Figure 12-3:**
Preview
how your
listing will
appear
in Google
search
results.

# Tag, you're it! Understanding tags

In addition to incorporating keywords into your Etsy item listings, you must add tags. Etsy uses these tags to help shoppers locate your item in categories besides using the site's search tool. Think of a tag as being the yin to a keyword's yang. For example, suppose that you've tagged your item with the word "fluffy." If someone types "fluffy" as a keyword on an Etsy search, your item will be among the results.

Because tagging is so critical to Etsy's search functionality, it's crucial for you to apply strong tags to your listing. When deciding what tags to apply, ask yourself what keywords you would enter if you were searching for your item. Start with the most obvious terms first. For example, suppose that you're selling a hand-sewn handbag. You may apply tags such as "purse" and "handbag." Next, you may apply tags that indicate the style of the handbag — say, "formal," "casual," "goth," "hippie," "frilly," or whatever. Then you may add tags to convey the bag's size (for example, "large"), texture (such as "quilted," "shiny," "matte," or what have you), and color ("ochre," "navy," and so on). You may also add tags to indicate any motifs used in the purse (think "Bettie Boop," "owls," or "race car"). Finally, you may apply tags that reflect materials used ("twill," "satin," "wool," "leather," and so on) and who the item is for ("women").

One more tip: If your piece is for a mature audience, you must tag it with the word "mature."

# Proofread, Please! Proofreading Your Item Title and Listing

Years ago, a neighborhood nursery posted a lovely yellow sign. It had been painted with care, its green letters tidy and even. The problem? Those green letters spelled out the following word: SHURBS. Presumably, the nursery, known for its fine selection of plants, had intended to advertise its lovely collection of shrubs. Instead, it broadcast its carelessness and lack of attention to detail.

As an Etsy shop owner, it's imperative that you (or someone you trust) proofread everything you post in your shop — item titles and descriptions included. Failing to do so may well lead potential buyers to conclude that you're sloppy, that you don't take pride in your work, or that you're incompetent. And *that* conclusion will likely prompt them to shop elsewhere!

Use a word-processing program to compose your item titles and descriptions instead of composing them while you're creating your listing on Etsy (discussed in Chapter 13). That way, you can take advantage of word-processing tools like spell check. You can then copy and paste the item title and description from your word-processing document to Etsy.

In addition to proofreading for spelling and grammatical errors, peruse your posts for other problems, such as redundant information. Big, pretentious words and fancy, genre-specific terms are other no-nos. For best results, stick with the common vernacular.

Also keep in mind that not everyone on Etsy speaks English as their first language. Don't include words or phrases in your listings that are likely to cause problems for these shoppers.

# Chapter 13

# Selling Like (Burning Hot) Hotcakes: Listing Your Items

- - - - - - - - - - - - - - - - - - - - - - - - - - - - - - - - - - - - - - - - - - - - - - - - - - - - - -

*In This Chapter*

▶ Listing an item

▶ Modifying a listing

▶ Duplicating a listing

▶ Relisting an item

▶ Removing a listing

▶ Tidying up your Etsy shop

- - - - - - - - - - - - - - - - - - - - - - - - - - - - - - - - - - - - - - - - - - - - - - - - - - - - - -

*F*ish gotta swim. Birds gotta fly. Camels gotta spit. And an Etsy seller . . . well, she's gotta sell. The first step to selling on Etsy — after setting up your Etsy store (and crafting the piece you want to sell) — is to create an item listing.

Simply put, an item listing is a page in your Etsy store that contains information about an item you have for sale. This item listing contains an item title and description, a list of materials you used to create your piece, a category and tags to help buyers find your item, images of your piece (you can include as many as five), pricing information, shipping details, and more.

In Chapter 11, you discover how to photograph your items. Chapter 12 is devoted to the ins and outs of composing item titles and descriptions. In this chapter, you put it all together and create your first Etsy listing!

## *Lister, Lister: Listing a New Item*

Listing a piece in your Etsy shop is surprisingly painless — provided that you've done all the necessary legwork first. (You've composed your item title and description, captured a few gorgeous pictures of your piece, set its price, established your shop policies, and so on.) Etsy steps you through the whole process, which we cover in the following sections.

As you toodle around Etsy, you may notice the occasional listing whose title contains the word *reserve*. A reserve listing is simply a listing that a seller has posted for a specific buyer — someone with whom she's communicated previously. For example, if a buyer contacts a seller to create a custom piece, the seller posts the piece as a reserve listing.

## Ready, set, go! Starting the listing process

You begin the listing process from the Your Account page. After you log in to your Etsy account, follow these steps:

1. **Click the Your Account link along the top of any Etsy page.**

   The Your Account page opens; Figure 13-1 shows what it looks like without any listings.

2. **If it's visible, click the List an Item Now button (you can see it in Figure 13-1); alternatively, click the Add New Item link, under Items, on the left side of the page.**

   The List an Item page opens (Figure 13-2a shows the top of the page, Figure 13-2b shows the middle, and Figure 13-2c shows the bottom).

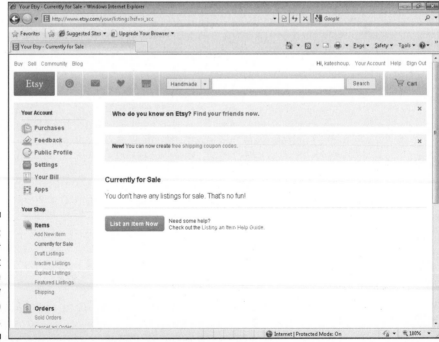

**Figure 13-1:** The Your Account page without any shop listings.

**Figure 13-2:**
Use this page to create a listing.

## About face: Filling in item information

Your first step is to enter some basic info about the item — who made it, what it is, and when it was made, as well as under which category it should appear (see Figure 13-3). Follow these steps:

1. **In the About This Item section, click the Who Made It? drop-down list and select the option that best reflects who made the item.**

2. **Click the What Is It? drop-down list and indicate whether the item is a finished product or a supply or tool to make things.**

3. **Click the When Was It Made? drop-down list and choose the option that best describes when the item was made.**

4. **In the Categories section, click the What Is It? drop-down list and choose a category for your item.**

5. **Click the What Type? drop-down list and choose a subcategory.**

6. **Choose as many subcategories in the What Type? drop-down lists as necessary to categorize your item.**

**Figure 13-3:**
Add basic
item info
here.

| About this Item | Who made it? | What is it? | When was it made? |
| --- | --- | --- | --- |
| | I did | A supply or tool to make things | 2010 - 2011 |
| Categories | What is it? | What type? optional | What type? optional |
| | Needlecraft | Cross Stitch | Select a category... |

## Picture this: Uploading images of your item

Next up after you fill in item information is adding photos to your listing. Here's the drill:

1. **In the Photos section, click the Add Photos button.**

   The Choose File to Upload (PC) or File Upload (Mac) dialog box opens.

2. **Locate and select the first image you want to upload, and click the Open button.**

   Any images that you upload must be at least 570 pixels wide (the height can vary) and no more than 1,000 pixels wide or high. Note, too, that image files must be of the JPG, GIF, or PNG variety.

3. **Repeat Steps 1 and 2 to add more images to your listing (see Figure 13-4).**

**Figure 13-4:**
Upload your product photos.

Convey the shape, size, color, and texture. Try to use natural light and include a great close up.

Your listing can feature as many as five images — and that's how many you want to include!

4. **To change the order in which the images appear in your listing, click on the image that you want to move and drag it either left to move it up in the order or right to move it down in the order.**

The first image in the list will be the thumbnail image that appears in search results. Make it a good one!

# Description prescription: Describing your item

To help convey your item's fabulousness, you must include an item title and description, as shown in Figure 13-5. (Refer to Chapter 12 for help with composing your item title and description.) And if you've created sections for your shop, which Chapter 8 covers, you can specify the section in which this item should appear. Here's how:

1. **In the Item Title field, type a title for your item.**

2. **In the Description field, enter a description of your item.**

   Notice that a preview of how your listing will show up in Google search results appears below the Description field (see Chapter 12 for details).

3. **If you've created sections for your shop, click the Shop Section drop-down list and choose the section in which you want the listing to appear.**

**Item Title** | Original LadyBird Design Cross Stitch Kit

Descriptive titles are best. Try to describe your item the way a shopper would.

**Description** | This LadyBird cross-stitch kit contains everything you need to stitch up an original LadyBird design, including white, 18-count Aida fabric; all necessary DMC threads; and a full-color pattern. The finished stitched piece measures 10 x 13 inches. If you're sweet on tweeters, or know someone who is, then this kit is for you!

Try to answer the questions shoppers will have. Tell the item's story and explain why it's special.

Preview how your listing will appear in Google search results. Hide preview

Original LadyBird Design Cross Stitch Kit by ladybirdstitchery
This LadyBird cross-stitch kit contains everything you need to stitch up an original LadyBird design, including white, 18-count Aida fabric; all necessary DMC

**Figure 13-5:**
Enter a title and description for your item.

**Shop section** | Cross Stitch Kits

## It's in the tag: Tagging your item

As you know, tagging is critical to Etsy's search functionality. To tag your listing, follow these steps (see Figure 13-6):

1. **Type a tag for your item in the Tags field and click the Add button.**

2. **Repeat Step 1 until you've added all appropriate tags.**

   You can apply as many as 14 tags to your listing. (Notice that the first tag automatically is the top-level category you've applied; any sublevel categories also automatically appear as tags.) To maximize the chances of buyers finding your item, you want to use as many tags as you're allowed. If you run out of ideas for tags, turn to your trusty thesaurus for help. (Chapter 12 has the full scoop on tagging.)

3. **To indicate the materials used in your piece, type a material in the Materials field and click the Add button.**

4. **Repeat Step 3 until you've added all appropriate materials.**

   You can apply as many as 13 materials to your listing. To maximize exposure, enter as many materials as you can.

**Figure 13-6:**
You tag your item in this section.

## Sales figures: Adding selling information for your item

Follow these steps to spread the word about the item's price, quantity, and other important info (see Figure 13-7):

1. **Enter the item's price in the Price field.**

   An Apply Shop Tax Rates check box appears.

2. **If you don't wish to apply your shop's tax rate to this listing, uncheck the Apply Shop Tax Rates check box; otherwise, leave it as is.**

   Find out how to establish your tax settings in Chapter 9.

3. **Type the item's quantity in — you guessed it — the Quantity field.**

Notice the message next to the Quantity field: "Etsy charges costs $0.20 USD per item." This fee is your one-time listing fee, for which Etsy will bill you. (Note that this fee is nonrefundable, even if you unlist your item.) In addition to this listing fee, you're charged a transaction fee when your item sells (not *if* — let's be optimistic!). This transaction fee amounts to 3.5 percent of your total sale price (not including shipping). These fees are assessed at the end of each month; you can pay them either using the credit card you have on file with Etsy or via PayPal. For more info on paying your Etsy bill, see Chapter 18.

4. **In the Shipping section, click the Load a Shipping Profile drop-down list and choose the shipping profile you want to use.**

   Etsy updates the shipping information to reflect the selected profile. (For help with creating shipping profiles, refer to Chapter 9.)

   Using a shipping profile isn't mandatory. If you want to enter the shipping information on a case-by-case basis, you're free to do so. But if you have a lot of listings to upload, you'll find that using shipping profiles makes your work go a lot faster!

| Price | $ 40.00 | USD | ☑ Apply shop tax rates | | |
|---|---|---|---|---|---|
| Quantity | 1 | Etsy charges $0.20 USD per item | | | |
| Shipping | Cross Stitch Kits ▼ | | | | |

Where does it ship from?
United States ▼

| Ships to | Cost | With another item ? | |
|---|---|---|---|
| European Union | $ 15.00 | $ 5.00 | ✕ |
| United States | $ 5.00 | $ 2.50 | ✕ |
| Mexico | $ 7.50 | $ 2.50 | ✕ |
| Canada | $ 7.50 | $ 2.50 | ✕ |
| Brazil | $ 15.00 | $ 5.00 | ✕ |
| Everywhere else ? | $ 20.00 | $ 5.00 | ✕ |

Add location

**Figure 13-7:** Enter the item's price, quantity, shipping info, and other details here.

# The reviews are in! Reviewing your listing

You're almost done! Follow these steps to review your listing one last time:

1. **Click the Preview Listing button at the bottom of the List an Item page.**

   Etsy displays a preview of your listing. (Figure 13-8a shows the top of the page, Figure 13-8b shows the middle, and Figure 13-8c shows the bottom.)

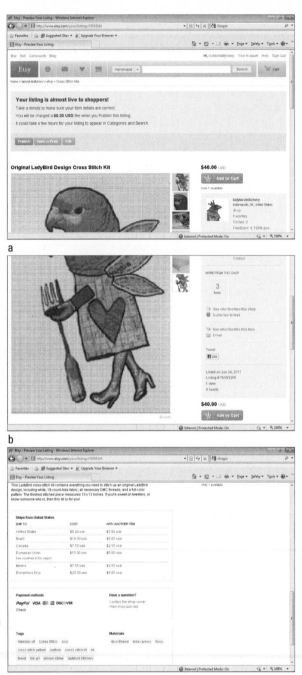

**Figure 13-8:**
Review your
listing.

2. **Review your listing; if you notice something that you need to change, click the Edit button at the top of the page, make your change, and click the Preview Listing button again.**

3. **To submit your listing, click the Publish button at the top of the page.**

   The listing is submitted to Etsy and appears in the Currently for Sale page in Your Account (see Figure 13-9).

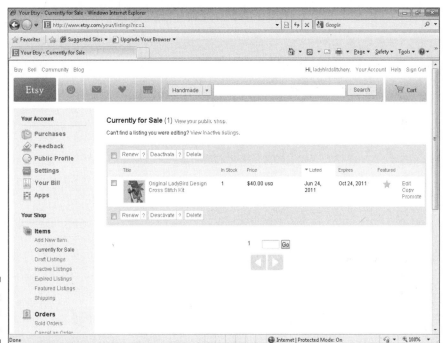

**Figure 13-9:** Your listing is posted.

# Timing Is Everything: Timing Your Listing (and Knowing When It Expires)

When you post your listing, it likely will appear within a few seconds (albeit briefly) on the main Etsy page under Recently Listed Items. To ensure that the maximum number of potential buyers see it during that brief, shining moment, you may want to consider submitting your listings at certain times — say, at 9:30 p.m. EST, after mommies on the East Coast have put their wee ones to bed, or at 12:15 PST, when everyone in California is on their lunch break. (Of course, Etsy is an international enterprise, meaning that whenever you post, odds are it's peak time *somewhere*.)

If your schedule doesn't allow you to create listings at peak times, don't sweat it. You can enter your listing details but wait to submit your listing until the time is right. To do so, simply complete the steps in the preceding section, but instead of clicking the Publish button to post the listing, click the Save as Draft button. Then when you're ready to post the listing, simply go to Your Account, click the Draft Listings link under Items on the left side of the page, click the check box next to the listing you want to post, and click the Publish button to upload the listing.

Any listing that you post on Etsy remains active for 120 days (unless, of course, you sell the item or deactivate the listing, as we describe later in this chapter). To find out when a listing expires, log in to your Etsy account and follow these steps:

1. **Click the Your Account link along the top of any Etsy page.**

   The Your Account page opens.

2. **Click the Currently for Sale link, under Items, on the left side of the page.**

   The Currently for Sale page opens.

3. **Locate the listing whose expiration date you want to determine.**

   The expiration date appears in the Expires column (refer to Figure 13-9).

   If your Etsy shop boasts multiple listings, you can sort them by expiration date on the Currently for Sale page. To do so, click the Expires column header.

# Ch-Ch-Ch-Ch-Changes: Editing a Listing

Look, nobody's perfect (although, obviously, you're pretty close). You may make a mistake when creating your listing and need to change it. Or maybe a potential buyer asks a question about the item you have for sale, and you want to update the item's listing to reflect your answer. Or you may want to add or change a listing photo.

Fortunately, regardless of why you need to change a listing, editing Etsy listings is a breeze (and free). You can edit any part of your item listing — the item title, item description, price, images, tags, materials, shipping information, you name it. To edit a listing, log in to your Etsy account and follow these steps:

1. **Click the Shop icon in your Etsy header bar.**

   Your Etsy shop opens (see Figure 13-10).

2. **Click the listing that you want to edit in your Etsy shop.**

   The listing opens (see Figure 13-11).

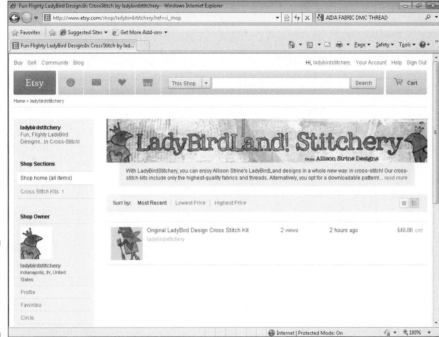

**Figure 13-10:**
View the listing in your Etsy shop.

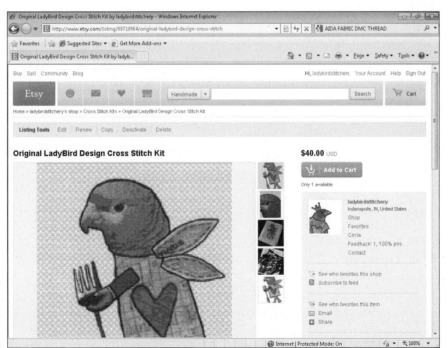

**Figure 13-11:**
Your listing opens.

3. **Click the Edit link in the Listing Tools toolbar along the top of the listing.**

   The Edit Listing page opens (see Figure 13-12). This page is nearly identical to the List an Item page shown earlier in this chapter.

4. **Edit the listing using the same techniques you employed to create it.**

5. **Click the Preview Listing button to preview the listing.**

6. **Click the Publish button to publish the edited listing.**

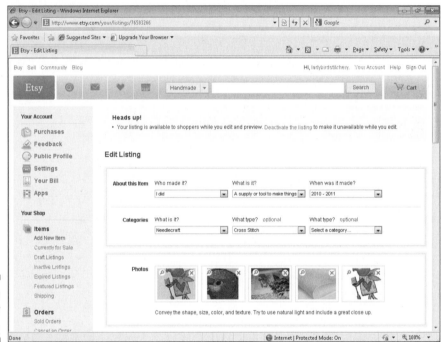

**Figure 13-12:**
Edit your
listing.

Another way to launch the edit operation is to open the Currently for Sale page in Your Account and click the Edit link on the right side of the listing that you want to edit (you can see this link in Figure 13-9). The Edit Listing page opens; repeat Steps 4 through 6 to edit your listing.

# Copycat: Copying a Listing

Suppose that you've created multiple items that are the same. In this case, instead of building a new listing for each item from scratch, you can create one listing and then copy it. Here's how you do so (after you log in to your Etsy account):

1. **Click the Shop icon in your Etsy header bar.**

   Your Etsy shop opens (refer to Figure 13-10).

2. **Click the listing that you want to copy in your Etsy shop.**

   The listing opens (refer to Figure 13-11).

3. **Click the Copy link in the Listing Tools toolbar along the top of the listing.**

   The List an Item page opens.

4. **Step through the listing-creation process, as we describe earlier in this chapter.**

   As you do, notice that the information in each section is entered for you, based on the listing you copied; you can change this information as needed.

5. **Click the Preview Listing button to review your listing.**

6. **To post the listing, click the Publish button.**

   A new listing based on the one you copied is posted (see Figure 13-13).

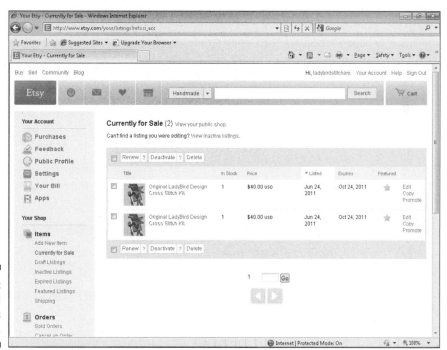

**Figure 13-13:**
Your copied listing is posted.

Another way to launch the copy operation is to open the Currently for Sale page in Your Account and click the Copy link on the right side of the listing that you want to copy. The Item Info page that you saw when you created your listing opens; follow Steps 4 through 6 to copy your listing.

# Renewable Resources: Renewing a Listing

In addition to copying listings (as we explain in the previous section), you can renew them. For example, you may renew a listing if it has expired, or if the item has sold and you want to restock your shop by offering a new, identical item.

You can also renew an active listing. When you do, the listing gets a new listing date and a new expiration date (120 days from the date of renewal). A renewal can breathe new life into the listing, placing it closer to the top of item searches and briefly in the Recently Listed Items section.

When you renew a listing, even an active listing, you're assessed a 20¢ listing fee.

## Don't be a sellout: Renewing a sold listing

To restock your shop by renewing a listing for a sold item, log in to your Etsy account and follow these steps:

1. **Click the Your Account link along the top of any Etsy page.**

   The Your Account page opens.

2. **Click the Sold Orders link, under Orders, on the left side of the page.**

   The Orders page opens.

3. **Click the All tab to view all sold orders (see Figure 13-14).**

4. **Find the listing that you want to renew and click its Renew Sold link.**

   An Edit Listing page appears (refer to Figure 13-13).

5. **Edit the listing using the same techniques you employed to create it.**

6. **Click the Renew button to renew your listing.**

   Etsy posts a new listing and directs you to the Currently for Sale page.

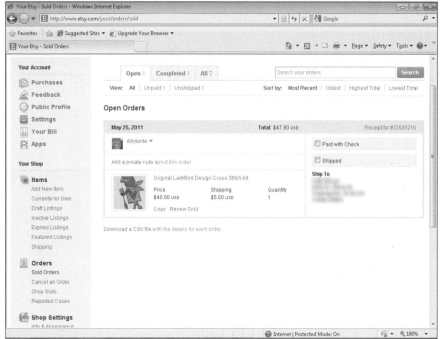

# Stay active: Renewing an active listing

Here's how you renew an active listing while you're logged in to your Etsy account (it's a cinch!):

1. **Click the Your Account link along the top of any Etsy page.**

   The Your Account page opens.

2. **Click the Currently for Sale link, under Items, on the left side of the page.**

   The Currently for Sale page opens (refer to Figure 13-9 for an example).

3. **Click the check box next to the listing that you want to renew.**

   To renew more than one active item at a time, click the check box next to each active listing that you want to renew. To select all your listings, click the check box just above or below the list. This same trick applies when you renew expired listings, covered in the next section.

4. **Click the Renew button (there's one at the top of the list of active listings and another one at the bottom of the list).**

   Etsy prompts you to confirm the renewal.

5. **Click Renew again.**

   Etsy renews the listing and directs you to the Currently for Sale page.

You can also renew an active item from within your Etsy shop. To do so, log in to your account, click the link to your shop in the Etsy header bar, open the listing that you want to renew, and click the Renew link in the Listing Tools toolbar along the top of the listing (refer to Figure 13-9 to see this link). When prompted to confirm the renewal, click the Renew button.

## Expiration mark: Renewing an expired listing

Renewing an expired listing is a lot like renewing an active listing:

1. **Click the Your Account link along the top of any Etsy page.**

   The Your Account page opens.

2. **Click the Expired Listings link, under Items, on the left side of the page.**

   The Expired Listings page opens. This page looks a lot like the Currently for Sale page, shown in Figure 13-9.

3. **Click the check box next to the expired listing that you want to renew.**

4. **Click the Renew button (there's one at the top of the list of expired listings and another one at the bottom of the list).**

   Etsy prompts you to confirm the renewal.

5. **Click Renew again.**

   Etsy renews the listing and directs you to the Currently for Sale page.

# Pull the Plug: Deactivating a Listing

Suppose that, after you crafted an item and listed it in your Etsy shop, your dog ate it. While you construct a replacement, you can deactivate the listing. You can deactivate listings in your Etsy shop for any reason, free of charge. When you deactivate a listing, it disappears from your Etsy shop. Note, however, that deactivating a listing doesn't change its expiration date.

To deactivate a listing, log in to your Etsy account and follow these steps:

1. **Click the Your Account link along the top of any Etsy page.**

   The Your Account page opens.

**2. Click the Currently for Sale link, under Items, on the left side of the page.**

The Currently for Sale page opens (refer to Figure 13-9 for an example).

**3. Click the check box next to the listing that you want to deactivate.**

To deactivate more than one active item at a time, click the check box next to each active listing that you want to deactivate. To select all your listings, click the check box just above or below the list.

**4. Click the Deactivate button (there's one at the top of the list of active listings and another one at the bottom of the list).**

Etsy deactivates the listing and directs you to the Currently for Sale page.

When you're ready to reactivate the listing, again making it visible to people who visit your Etsy shop, here's what you do:

**1. Click the Your Account link along the top of any Etsy page.**

The Your Account page opens.

**2. Click the Inactive Listings link, under Items, on the left side of the page.**

The Inactive Listings page opens (see Figure 13-15).

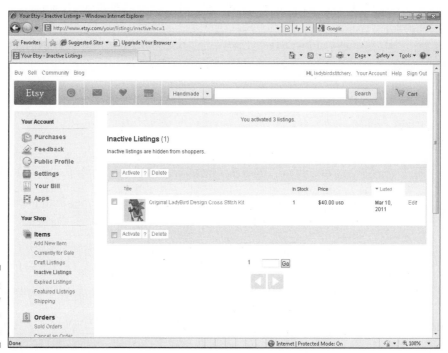

**Figure 13-15:**
Renew an active listing.

3. **Click the check box next to the listing that you want to reactivate.**

   To reactivate more than one deactivated item at a time, click the check box next to each listing that you want to reactivate. To select all your listings, click the check box just above or below the list.

4. **Click the Activate button (there's one at the top of the list of deactivated listings and another one at the bottom of the list).**

   Etsy reactivates the listing, removing it from the Inactive Listings page.

# Rearrange Your Face: Rearranging Your Etsy Shop

As you add more listings to your Etsy shop, you may decide that you want to rearrange the order in which they appear. For example, instead of having your items listed in the order you added them to your shop, with older items appearing farther down in the list (the default), maybe you want to group together all items of a certain color. Or put all items of a single type on one page. Or move all the most expensive items to the top of your store's main page. Or move an older listing to the top of your list.

Lucky you — rearranging your shop is simple, as you find out in the following sections.

## Be an enabler: Enabling the Rearrange Your Shop feature

Before you make a move, you have to log in to your Etsy account and enable Etsy's Rearrange Your Shop feature. Here's how:

1. **Click the Your Account link along the top of any Etsy page.**

   The Your Account page opens.

2. **Click the Options link, under Shop Settings, on the left side of the page.**

   The Shop Options page opens (see Figure 13-16).

3. **Under Rearrange Your Shop, click the Enabled option button.**

4. **Click the Save button.**

   Etsy saves your changes.

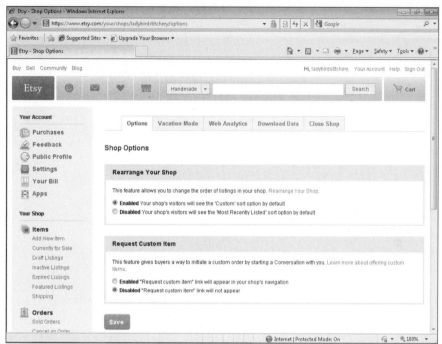

**Figure 13-16:**
The Shop
Options
page.

# Get moving! Moving your listings

Now you're ready to get down to business rearranging your goodies. Here's what you do:

1. **Click the Shop icon in your Etsy header bar.**

   Your Etsy shop opens.

2. **Click the Rearrange Your Shop link, under Your Shop, on the left side of the page.**

   Your shop changes to Rearrange mode.

3. **To change the order of a listing, click the listing, drag it to the desired spot in the order, and release your mouse button (see Figure 13-17).**

   The listing is moved.

   To move a listing to a different page in your Etsy shop, hover your mouse pointer over the item that you want to move. Then click the page you want to move it to.

4. **Repeat Step 3 until the items in your shop are in the order you want.**

5. **Click the Save Changes button to save your arrangement.**

**Figure 13-17:**
Drag a
listing to
change its
place in the
order.

## Feature comforts: Featuring an item in your Etsy shop

When it comes to rearranging your Etsy shop, another option is to feature certain item listings. When you do, those listings appear in a special "Featured" section on your shop's main page. You can feature as many as four item listings at a time.

To feature an item listing in your shop, follow these steps:

1. **Click the Your Account link that appears along the top of any Etsy page.**

   The Your Account page opens.

2. **In the Items section on the left side of the Your Account page, click the Currently for Sale link.**

   The Currently for Sale page opens (refer to Figure 13-9 for an example of this page).

3. **Click the star in an item listing's Featured column to feature that list-ing in your shop.**

   Voilà! As you can see in Figure 13-18, the item listings that you selected appear at the top of your shop's main page, with extra-large thumbnails to make them really pop.

To change the order in which featured items appear on your shop page, follow these steps:

1. **Click the Your Account link that appears along the top of any Etsy page.**

   The Your Account page opens.

2. **In the Items section on the left side of the Your Account page, click the Featured Listings link.**

   The Featured Listings page opens (see Figure 13-19).

3. **To move an item up in the order, click its Up button; to move it down, click its down button.**

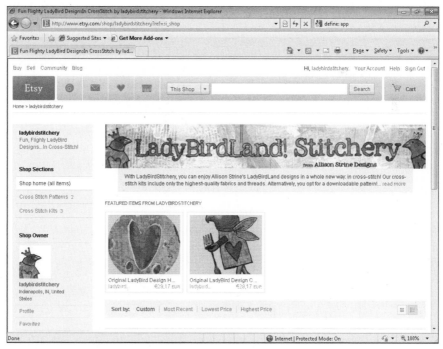

**Figure 13-18:** Feature an item listing to really make it pop.

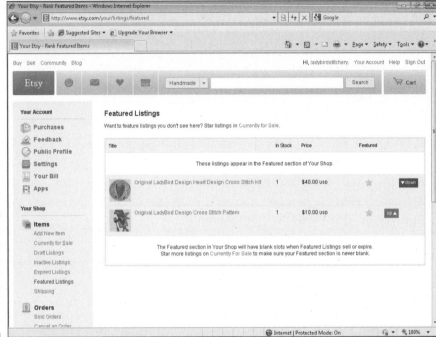

**Figure 13-19:**
Change
the order
of your
featured
listings
here.

# Chapter 14

# Wrap It Up: Closing the Deal

---

---

*H*allelujah! You've made a sale! It's time for some rejoicing — and possibly some invoicing. In this chapter, you get the scoop on how to deal with such end-of-sale matters as finding out when you've sold something, tracking your sales, invoicing, and receiving payment.

## You've Got Sale: Finding Out You Have a Sale

When you sell an item in your Etsy shop, Etsy notifies you via e-mail straight away. As you can see in Figure 14-1, this e-mail contains loads of important information, including the following:

✔ Which item sold

✔ The price and quantity of the item that sold

✔ The payment method used

✔ The buyer's details, including her shipping address and e-mail address

✔ Any notes the buyer left

✔ A link to the sales invoice (we discuss invoices in more detail later in this chapter)

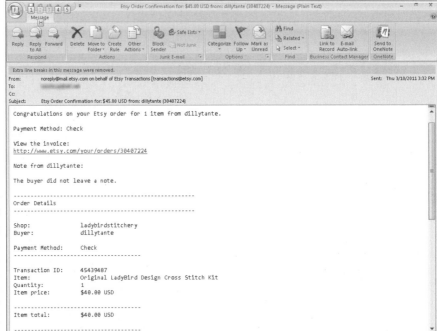

**Figure 14-1:**
Etsy e-mails
you when-
ever you
sell an item
in your Etsy
shop.

To make sure that your e-mail program's spam filter doesn't come between you and these notification e-mails, consider adding the e-mail address transactions@etsy.com to your list of safe senders. For details on how to perform this task, see your e-mail program's help information.

One way to stay on top of sales is to set up your e-mail program to send a text message to your phone whenever you receive e-mails with the word *Etsy* in the subject line. For details on taking care of this task, see your e-mail program's help information. Alternatively, you can use EtsyText, a free Etsy app that sends you a text message anytime something in your shop sells (standard text-messaging rates apply). For more info, visit etsytext.com.

# Baby Got Track: Keeping Track of Sales in Your Account

When you know you've sold an item, you can view it in Your Account. You can keep track of what sales you've made, which items the buyers have paid for, and whether you've shipped the items. To view a sale in Your Account, log in to your Etsy account and follow these steps:

1. **Click the Your Account link along the top of any Etsy page.**

   The Your Account page opens.

2. **Click the Sold Orders link, under Orders, on the left side of the page.**

3. **Click the Open tab.**

   The Open Orders page opens, displaying a list of items that you've sold but not yet shipped (see Figure 14-2). We talk about shipping in detail in Chapter 15.

Note that you can view orders you've shipped by clicking the Completed tab. To see all orders — ones that are open and ones that have shipped — click the All tab.

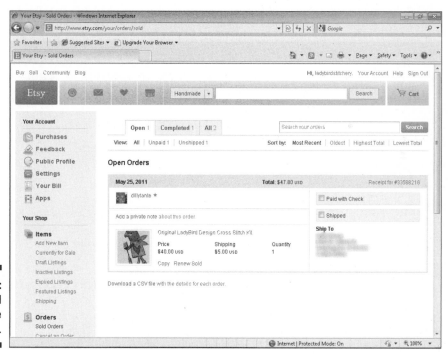

**Figure 14-2:**
View sold items in the Open tab.

# Guided by Invoices: Handling Invoices

When someone buys something from your Etsy shop, one of two things happens:

- ✔ If the buyer paid for the item via PayPal, PayPal sends her a receipt for the item via e-mail.

- ✔ If the buyer chose a different payment method — personal check, money order, frankincense — Etsy e-mails the buyer a link to the invoice (see Figure 14-3).

In other words, when it comes to invoicing, you have to do pretty much nothing. Etsy handles everything for you!

Even though Etsy handles invoicing for you, you should still reach out to your buyer to express your thanks. As you find out in Chapter 17, this is an important part of customer service — and it's essential to the success of your shop.

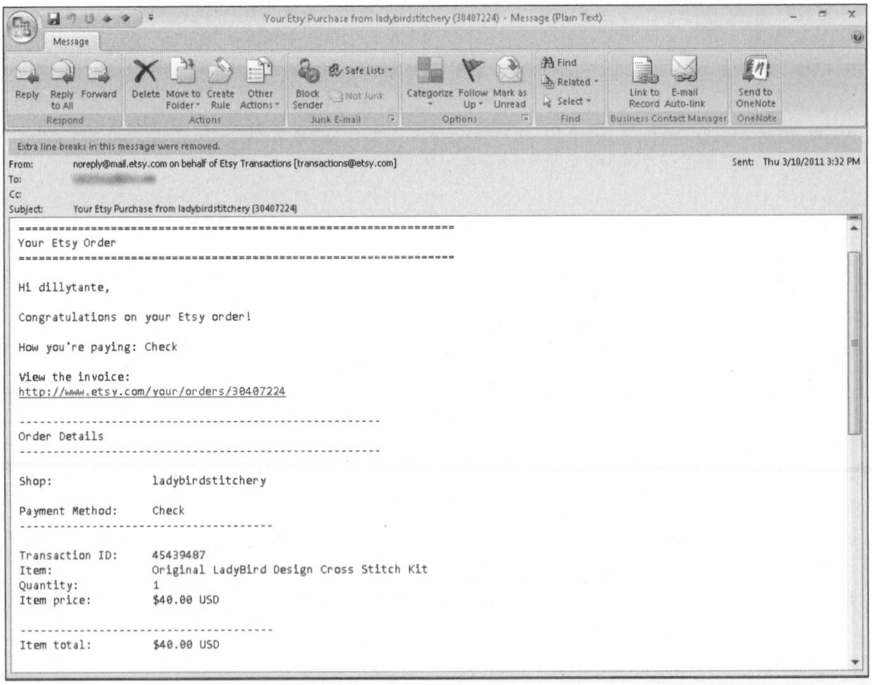

**Figure 14-3:** Buyers receive invoices automatically.

However, sometimes you need to view an invoice for a sale — say, to check the buyer's shipping address. Additionally, you may at times need to send a revised invoice to your buyer. You find out how to do both in this section.

## See for yourself: Viewing a sales invoice on Etsy

One way to access that invoice is to click the View the Invoice link found at the top of your notification e-mail message (refer to Figure 14-1). Alternatively, log in to your Etsy account and try the following:

1. **Click the Your Account link along the top of any Etsy page.**

   The Your Account page opens.

2. **Click the Sold Orders link, under Orders, on the left side of the page.**

3. **Click the Open tab.**

   The Open Orders page appears (refer to Figure 14-2).

4. **Click the listing in the Open Orders page to view it (see Figure 14-4).**

**Figure 14-4:** Open the listing for the sold item.

**5. Click the View Invoice link.**

Etsy displays the invoice for the transaction (see Figure 14-5). It contains key info about the transaction — whether the buyer has paid for the item, whether you've shipped the piece, the buyer's shipping address, how much the item cost, and more. It also features a Print Order button; click it to print the invoice for your records.

## Invoice coach: Sending a revised invoice to the buyer

What if you need to send a buyer a revised invoice — for example, to upgrade shipping? Unfortunately, Etsy doesn't offer any tools to handle this task. You can, however, use PayPal to send an updated invoice (assuming that you have an account), regardless of whether your buyer intends to use that service to pay for the item. First, you need to gather the following info:

**Figure 14-5:**
View the invoice.

✔ The buyer's e-mail address

✔ The item name

✔ The transaction ID number

✔ The date of purchase

✔ The quantity purchased

✔ The price of the item

✔ The tax rate (if applicable)

✔ The cost of shipping

Fortunately, Etsy puts all this information right at your fingertips, in the sales invoice. You can also see some of this info in the e-mail Etsy sent when the item sold, shown in Figure 14-1. Armed with this data, you're ready to create your new invoice on PayPal. Here's what you do:

1. **Type `www.paypal.com` in your Web browser's address bar and log in to your PayPal account (see Figure 14-6).**

**Figure 14-6:**
Log in to
PayPal.

2. **Click the Request Money tab.**

   The Request Money page opens (see Figure 14-7).

3. **Click the Create an Invoice button.**

   The Create a New Invoice page opens (see Figure 14-8). Notice that it contains several key pieces of information, including your contact information and a pregenerated invoice number and invoice date (as shown in Figure 14-8a).

4. **Fill out the necessary information in the appropriate fields.**

   This information includes the following (see Figure 14-8b):

   - The buyer's e-mail address
   - The item name and the transaction ID number
   - The date of purchase
   - The quantity purchased
   - The item price
   - Any tax information
   - Your shipping fees

   You can also include terms and conditions and a note to your buyer, if you want.

   If the buyer purchased multiple items from you, you can include each one in a single invoice. Just click the + button to the right of the item information to add a new row of item-related fields.

5. **To send your invoice, click the Send button.**

   If you want, you can preview your invoice first by clicking the Preview button.

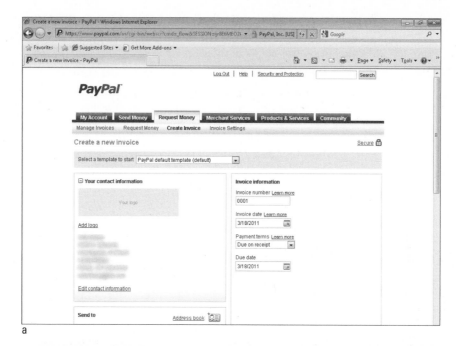

**Figure 14-8:**
Create a
new invoice.

PayPal sends the invoice to your buyer, with a link back to PayPal to render payment. A link to the invoice appears in the Manage Invoices screen, accessible from the Request Money tab (see Figure 14-9).

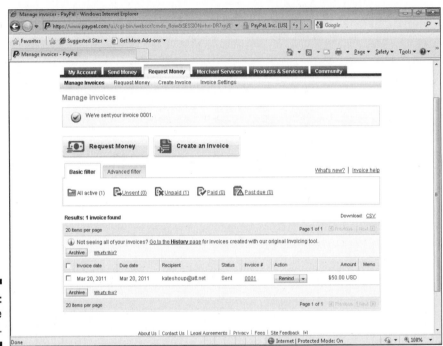

**Figure 14-9:**
The invoice is sent.

# Show Me the Money: Receiving Payment

As you've probably deduced, exactly how you receive payment depends on the method of payment used. For example, if the buyer opted to pay by check, you'll receive said check in the mail. Ditto for cashier's checks, money orders, and the like.

Note, however, that there's a Godzilla-size difference between when a check's funds are released to you and when the check actually clears. Make sure that you ship your item only after the check clears; it can take a week or more. Otherwise, you'll be on the hook for those funds if the check bounces. (Note that the same goes for cashier's checks and money orders.)

When you receive a payment via PayPal, you'll receive an e-mail indicating that the payment has been deposited in your PayPal account. Be aware that although your PayPal account is linked to your bank account, they're not one and the same: Dough deposited into your PayPal account doesn't automatically appear in your bank account's balance — you have to transfer the funds. (You find out how in Chapter 18.)

After you receive your payment — and, if the payment is a check, cashier's check, or money order, the funds have cleared — you need to do one more thing (apart from shipping the item to your buyer, of course): Mark the item as Paid on Etsy. Here's how (after you log in to your Etsy account, of course):

1. **Click the Your Account link along the top of any Etsy page.**

   The Your Account page opens.

2. **Click the Sold Orders link, under Orders, on the left side of the page.**

3. **Click the Open tab.**

   The Open Orders page appears (refer to Figure 14-2).

4. **Click the Paid with *X* check box to indicate that you received the payment.**

   Etsy updates the listing to indicate that you received payment (see Figure 14-10).

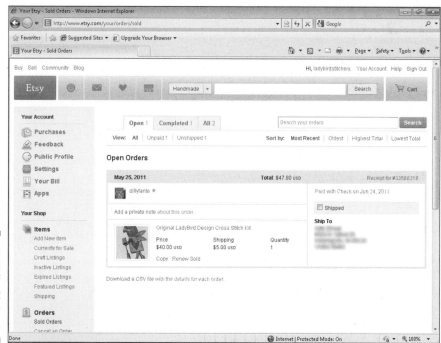

**Figure 14-10:** Track receipt of payment in Your Account.

# Chapter 15

# The Ship Hits the Fan: Shipping Your Items

### In This Chapter

▶ Buying shipping supplies

▶ Packaging your item with care

▶ Finding a shipper (both domestic and international)

▶ Choosing delivery confirmation and insurance

▶ Using PayPal to ship

▶ Closing the order in Etsy

*T*he moment you receive payment for your piece (and, if applicable, the check, cashier's check, or money order has cleared), it's time to begin the difficult process of letting your piece go. As hard as it may be to say goodbye — after all, you slaved over its creation and gave it the best care possible — the time has come to send it on its way. In this chapter, you discover everything you need to know to pack and ship your item to its new happy home.

 If you're worried about protecting your privacy during the shipping process, consider obtaining a post office box and using that to send and receive Etsy-related packages. For information, see the following page on the USPS Web site: `https://poboxes.usps.com`.

## The Right (Packaging) Stuff: Obtaining Shipping Supplies

Imagine a Venn diagram with one circle representing Etsy users and another representing people who love the environment. Odds are, the part where those circles intersect is pretty huge. This duality no doubt explains why so many Etsy sellers prefer to use recycled shipping materials — boxes, bubble wrap, envelopes, packing paper, and the like. Some even go the DIY route, crafting their own mailers and packaging materials from their or others' detritus — for example, running old wrapping paper and magazine sheets through a shredder to create cushioning for fragile items.

Here's another option for no-cost materials: If you mail via the United States Postal Service, you can obtain Priority Mail flat-rate boxes free of charge. Visit the USPS Web site (www.usps.com) for more info, and see the later section "Stay First Classy: Surveying Shipping Options" for details on Priority Mail and flat rates.

Of course, you can also purchase shipping supplies for your Etsy shop. Even the most devoted recyclers may need to buy some shipping supplies, such as packing tape or the occasional mailer. Whether you seek boxes or bubble wrap, or ribbon or tissue, you can find what you need at these sites:

- ✔ ULINE (www.uline.com)
- ✔ Paper Mart (www.papermart.com)
- ✔ Nashville Wraps (www.nashvillewraps.com)

Of course, you can also visit your local office-supply store (think Office Max, Office Depot, Staples, and the like) to stock up on shipping supplies. Note, however, that higher prices may somewhat offset the convenience of shopping for supplies at these brick-and-mortar retailers.

One more piece of advice: Invest in a postal scale. You'll need it to weigh your packages if you plan to ship from home. Also keep a flexible tape measure on hand, in case your carrier charges by box size instead of weight. (See the section "Stay First Classy: Surveying Shipping Options," later in this chapter, for more information.)

If you have space in your home or studio, set up a shipping station and stock it with all your shipping supplies. Trust us, it'll make the task of packaging your pieces easy, peasy!

# Package Deal: Showing Your Love and Care with Packaging

Yes, everyone knows that it's what's on the inside that counts. But that truism doesn't mean that what's on the outside isn't also important. Translation: When shipping your piece to your buyer, be sure to package it with care. In the following sections, we discuss wrapping different sorts of items, using attractive and brand-friendly packaging, and including goodies.

How you package your items says something about you and your Etsy shop. Make sure it doesn't say, "I'm lazy and careless!"

## Wrapper's delight: Wrapping any kind of item safely

Of course, it goes without saying that you must take steps to ensure that your piece will arrive in one, er, piece. When it enters your buyer's home, it needs to be in excellent shape (think Jillian Michaels). To that end, consider the following guidelines:

- ✔ Be sure to pack fragile items carefully. Use cushioning materials such as bubble wrap or shredded paper to prevent breakage, and employ plenty of sturdy packing tape to ensure that your package isn't shredded en route. (We talk about supplies in more detail earlier in this chapter.)
- ✔ Pack bendable booty, such as art prints and the like, with a firm, flat backing.
- ✔ If, like the Wicked Witch of the West, your item is moisture averse, slip it into a sealed plastic bag before sending it on its way.

Although it's critical to package your items carefully to prevent damage, don't take things too far. Excessive packaging — especially if it doesn't involve recycled materials — is wasteful and sad.

## Nice package! Using attractive, brand-friendly packaging

Strive to delight your buyer not only with your piece, but also with your packaging. Don't just toss your lovingly crafted item in an envelope and plop it in the post; instead, develop packaging that, in addition to protecting your item, looks good. You don't have to wrap your packages in expensive gift paper with hand-curled ribbon (although some Etsy sellers do); most buyers are perfectly satisfied with a package that has been carefully and securely wrapped with clean, plain, environmentally friendly paper.

Smoking: It's not just bad for your health — it's also bad for your Etsy shop! Never smoke around your inventory, craft stash, or packaging materials. Inevitably, that stale ciggy smell will permeate your stock — and you'll asphyxiate your buyer when she opens your parcel!

In addition, make sure that your packaging reflects your brand. For example, if your brand is frou-frou, your packaging needs to be, too. On the flip side, if your brand is all modern minimalism, you want to ensure that your packaging is similarly under-the-top. Also, invest in stickers or a stamp with your shop's logo for use in your packaging. (You find out more about developing your brand in Chapter 16.)

One way to reflect your brand in your packaging is to use colored tissue paper. For example, if your logo is green and red, you may wrap your items in green and red tissue. If you go this route, be sure to moisture-proof your package by wrapping it in plastic; otherwise, the dye from the paper may bleed onto your piece.

## Goody-goody: Including extras in your parcel

It goes without saying that your package needs to include the item your buyer purchased. (Like, duh.) Beyond that, you may include any or all of the following:

✔ **A handwritten note:** If you want to make your buyer's day, include a handwritten note in your packaging. It doesn't have to be a 40-page opus; just a few lines thanking the buyer for her purchase and wishing her well will do. (Be sure to address her by name — it's so much more personal.) You also may ask her to leave feedback about you on Etsy, and include any special instructions for using or caring for the item.

Consider investing in special note cards or postcards that reflect your brand — or, better yet, make your own! For example, you may design a note card that includes your shop logo. Alternatively, if you sell art prints, you may design a postcard with one of your best-selling images.

✔ **Business cards:** To make sure that your buyer remembers you and your store, slip two business cards into your package — one for your buyer and one for her millionaire best friend.

✔ **An invoice:** Unless the package is a gift and it's being sent directly to the recipient, be sure to include a printout of the invoice in your package. Including the invoice is especially important if your buyer lives abroad; it'll keep the package from being held up clearing Customs. To print an invoice, open it as described in Chapter 14 (make sure you've marked the item as paid); then click the Print Order button (see Figure 15-1) and choose your print settings as normal.

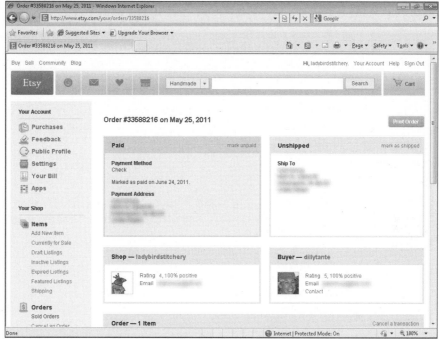

**Figure 15-1:**
Print a
copy of the
invoice to
include
in any
package.

✔ **A coupon:** Including a coupon — or, more specifically, a coupon code — in your packaging is a great way to generate sales. For help with creating coupon codes, see Chapter 16.

✔ **A freebie:** Some Etsy sellers include freebies in their packaging — small, lightweight items tossed in at no additional cost. The best freebies reflect your brand or your inventory in some way — for example, buttons, bookmarks, stickers, or magnets with your shop logo, or samples of new or favorite products in your line. Another approach is to include freebies that complement the item purchased. For instance, if you specialize in hand-sewn dog collars, you may toss in some Scooby Snacks. Or if you spin yarn, you may include a printout of a simple pattern.

Although some Etsy sellers like to include candy or other treats in their packages, it's not always a great idea. For one thing, some buyers may be diabetic or may suffer from nut allergies, and receiving sweets via post may constitute torture (or death!) for them. For another thing, many buyers live in hot climates, meaning that any candy you send may melt, thereby ruining your piece.

# Ship Shop: Choosing a Shipping Carrier

When it comes to shipping carriers, you have loads of options — truth be told, an overwhelming number. To figure out which carrier is right for you, you need to do a bit of legwork. Here are a few places to start:

- ✔ **United States Postal Service (USPS):** www.usps.com
- ✔ **United Parcel Service (UPS):** www.ups.com
- ✔ **FedEx:** www.fedex.com
- ✔ **DHL:** www.dhl.com

We're talking domestic shipping in the United States here. For information about shipping internationally, see the later section "Crafters without Borders: Shipping Internationally."

As you research carriers, assess the following:

- ✔ How long they take to deliver
- ✔ What shipping options they offer
- ✔ How much the various shipping options cost
- ✔ Whether such services as insurance and delivery confirmation are included (see the later section "Insure Thing: Insuring Your Parcel" for details)
- ✔ Whether they pick up outgoing packages from your place
- ✔ What they do if a package gets lost

Most Etsy users (at least, ones in the United States) opt for the United States Postal Service.

# Stay First Classy: Surveying Shipping Options

After you've selected a carrier, you need to give more thought to various shipping options based on speed and price. For example, if you've opted for USPS, you need to decide whether you want to go with First Class or Priority Mail. In general, First Class, which is the less expensive option, is handled in the same way as Priority Mail, but it's put on the truck last — meaning that if the truck is full, the First Class mail has to wait for the next one, which may affect delivery time. Unless it's a particularly busy time of year (Christmas, we're talking about you) or your packages typically weigh more than 13 ounces each (the First Class cutoff), First Class may suffice for your needs.

You also need to decide whether you're willing to offer expedited shipping — for example, USPS Express Mail for overnight delivery (for an added charge, of course).

If you decide to offer expedited shipping, be sure to indicate in your shop policies (see Chapter 9) and item listings (see Chapter 13) how buyers can take advantage of that option. For example, you may instruct buyers to convo you, and mention that you'll send them an updated invoice from PayPal that includes the correct shipping price. (For help with sending invoices from PayPal, refer to Chapter 14.)

If you've opted to use the USPS, you can determine which shipping option is right for you using the USPS Postage Price Calculator. Here's how:

1. **Type ircalc.usps.com in your Web browser's address bar.**

   The Postage Price Calculator page opens.

2. **Click the Select a Destination drop-down list and choose the country to which you want to ship the item.**

3. **Type your zip code in the From Zip Code field; then type the recipient's zip code in the To Zip Code field.**

4. **Note the flat-rate price that applies to your package.**

   To see whether a different option is cheaper, select the shape that best matches that of your package.

5. **Enter the package's weight in the Pounds and Ounces fields.**

6. **Click Continue.**

   A list of delivery options appears.

7. **To view all delivery options together, click the Display All Options check box.**

Depending on what option you choose, you may be able to purchase and print the postage online, right from the Postage Price Calculator. To find out, click the desired postage option; if a Print Postage button appears in the Product Selected area, it means that you can purchase and print your postage online. (Simply click the Print Postage button to do so.)

## Flat and rate plus weight: Figuring out which way to go

The USPS offers flat-rate pricing for Priority Mail in addition to weight-based rates. Which option you choose depends on how heavy your item is:

✔ If your piece fits in the small flat-rate box or envelope and it weighs more than 1 pound, the flat-rate route is for you. Simply put, the more you can cram into the flat-rate box, the better the deal.

✔ If your piece weighs more than 1 pound or requires a medium or large box, run the numbers before you commit to the flat rate. If the item is light or is shipping to a zone near you, the weight-based rate may be better.

These tips also apply to UPS, which offers flat-rate shipping on medium and large packages.

# Crafters without Borders: Shipping Internationally

Although you can certainly limit your Etsy business to domestic buyers, part of the fun of selling on Etsy is connecting with international customers. First, however, you need to get a feel for the ins and outs of shipping internationally. Keep a few points in mind:

✔ Items shipped to some countries, such as Canada and countries in the E.U., may be subject to duties or taxes. Make sure that the buyer knows she'll be responsible for these. A good way to do so is to include language to that effect in your shop's Policies page.

✔ If your package contains "potentially dutiable contents" (that's post-office-speak for items subject to duties or taxes), you need to include a Customs form — period, end of story. (If you're not sure whether your item is "potentially dutiable," read the next bullet.) To figure out what type of form you need, check with your carrier or check out this page on the USPS site: webapps.usps.com/customsforms/helppickaform. htm. Be sure you fill out the form thoroughly, to keep it from being held up at Customs.

✔ Shipping certain items — think food products, plant and animal products, precious jewelry, and so on — is prohibited in some countries. To find out whether your item is prohibited, check out the Index of Countries and Localities page on the USPS Web site (pe.usps.com/ text/imm/immetry.htm). Here you'll find a list of countries; click the link next to the country in question to view a list of restricted and prohibited items. (Note that these prohibitions and restrictions apply regardless of the carrier you use.)

> Don't indicate that the item is a gift, even if your buyer asks you to. It's not cricket, and it can get you into trouble. Besides, even gifts may be subject to duties and taxes.

Be sure to warn international customers that you can't be responsible for delays if your package gets stuck in Customs. Also be aware that, unless you opt for a courier service like FedEx or DHL, tracking a package beyond your country's borders is nigh impossible.

If you're just getting started, consider shipping to just a few countries — say, Canada, Mexico, Japan, Australia, and E.U. countries. Then when you're more comfortable with the procedures involved, you can expand to ship everywhere. Just don't indicate that you're willing to ship anywhere on earth unless you've done the research to find out how much that will cost!

If you've chosen to ship via USPS, a great place to start is the aforementioned Index of Countries and Localities page on the USPS Web site (pe.usps.com/text/imm/immctry.htm). You can also check out the First-Class Mail International Prices page (www.usps.com/prices/first-class-mail-international-prices.htm#cz) and the Priority Mail International Prices page (www.usps.com/prices/priority-mail-international-prices.htm). Except with flat-rate Priority Mail, the USPS divides countries into groups based on their locations and then assesses pricing by group. To determine which group a country is in, click a View Price Groups by Country link. (You'll see several of these links in the First-Class Mail International Prices and Priority Mail International Prices pages.)

If you find yourself shipping internationally regularly, look into using Endicia (www.endicia.com). In addition to enabling you to print labels for domestic packages, Endicia allows you to print international shipping labels that integrate the necessary Customs forms — and with a discount, to boot! Plus, Endicia's International Mail Advisor feature helps you navigate the complexity of shipping internationally by spelling out which items are prohibited where, and more.

# Insure Thing: Insuring Your Parcel

Remember that movie *Castaway* with Tom Hanks? He plays a FedEx employee who hitches a ride on a cargo plane stuffed with packages, which crashes, marooning him on a desert island with only a volleyball for company. This storyline just goes to show you that sometimes FedEx planes crash, jettisoning their cargo to the bottom of the sea. If the piece you so lovingly crafted and packaged is on board, chances are, it won't reach your buyer — unless she's the Little Mermaid.

To ensure that you're covered in case your package goes astray, you may want to opt for insurance from your shipping carrier — especially if your item is on the pricey side. Unfortunately, insuring packages containing less expensive pieces may be prohibitively expensive; you have to decide whether it's worth it to you. You can also opt for delivery confirmation — it's free with USPS Priority shipping. That way, if your package goes AWOL, you can track its location.

Your carrier may not offer insurance for certain items, especially if you're shipping internationally. In that case, you may opt to go with a third-party provider, such as Shipsurance (www.shipsurance.com) or U-Pic (www.u-pic.com).

# PayPal Rationale: Shipping through PayPal

If you use USPS as your shipping carrier, you can ship through PayPal, even if your buyer paid using another method. Not only does PayPal not charge extra for this service, but it's cheaper than going through the USPS. Plus, as always, if you ship Priority Mail, delivery confirmation is free! (If you opt for First Class, you're automatically charged 19¢ for delivery confirmation. You can't opt out of this charge, but you can take comfort in knowing that it's cheaper than buying it directly from the USPS.) If you're shipping internationally, you'll appreciate PayPal's premade Customs forms. As an added bonus, you can bypass the post office completely: PayPal enables you to print your postage right from your computer and offers free package pickup.

In the following sections, we describe the whole quick 'n' easy process of shipping your parcels through PayPal.

You know, you don't have to use PayPal to buy postage and print shipping labels online. If you're shipping via USPS, you can also use Endicia (www.endicia.com) or the USPS Web site's Click-N-Ship feature (direct your Web browser to www.usps.com and then click the Print a Shipping Label button along the top of the page).

## Designated driver: Designating your preferred carrier

To ship through PayPal, first indicate your preferred shipping carrier:

1. **Type www.paypal.com in your Web browser's address bar and log in to your PayPal account.**

   The My Account page opens.

2. **Click the Merchant Services tab.**

   The Merchant Services page opens.

3. **Under Shipping & Tax, click the Shipping Preferences link.**

   The PayPal Shipping Information page opens (see Figure 15-2).

4. **Under Default Shipping Carrier, click either U.S. Postal Service or UPS; then click the Save button.**

   PayPal updates your profile.

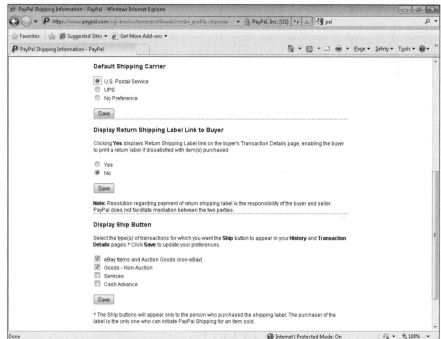

**Figure 15-2:** Specify your preferred shipping provider.

# *Just deet it: Providing the necessary details*

To use PayPal to ship an item you've sold, follow these steps:

1. **Type www.paypal.com in your Web browser's address bar and log in to your PayPal account.**

   The My Account page opens.

2. **If your buyer purchased the item using PayPal, click the Payments Received link; then click the Print Shipping Label that appears alongside the transaction entry for the item that you want to ship.**

   If your buyer used a different method of payment, type the following URL into your Web browser's address bar: `www.paypal.com/us/cgi-bin/webscr?cmd=_ship-now`. The Create Your Shipping Label page opens (see Figure 15-3).

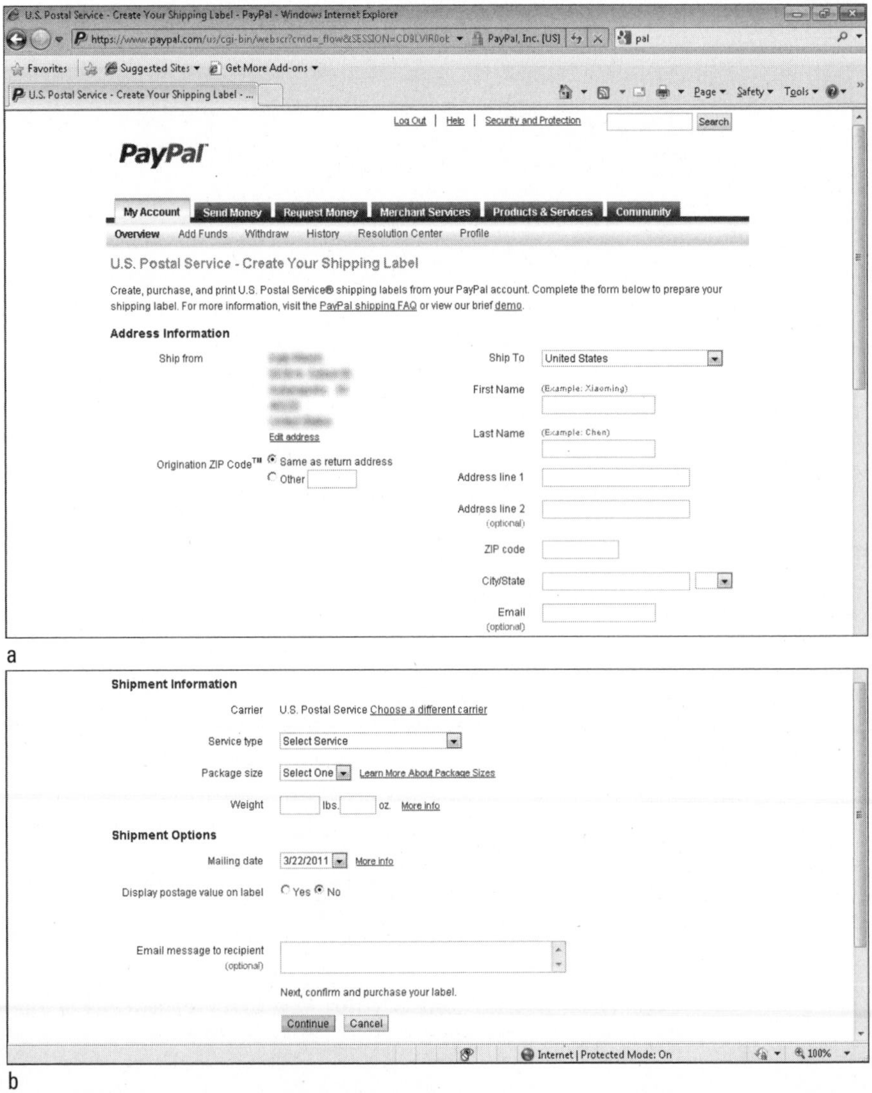

a

b

**Figure 15-3:** Enter the necessary details for your shipping label in PayPal.

3. **If the recipient paid via PayPal, her details — first name, last name, mailing address, and, optionally, e-mail address — are added automatically; if not, enter them in the appropriate fields (refer to Figure 15-3a).**

   To make sure that you don't enter any of the buyer's info incorrectly, consider copying and pasting it from the invoice (Chapter 14 explains how to work with invoices).

   If the buyer's shipping address on Etsy differs from the one on PayPal, check with the buyer to see which one is correct.

4. **Choose the desired service type (Priority Mail, First Class, or what have you) and enter the package size and weight in the Shipment Information section (refer to Figure 15-3b).**

   The page expands to include mailing options, such as signature confirmation, insurance, and the like.

5. **Choose mailing options, such as signature confirmation, insurance, and so on.**

6. **Click the Continue button.**

   PayPal displays a confirmation page (Figure 15-4a shows the top of the page, and Figure 15-4b shows the bottom).

7. **Verify that the information is correct; then click the Pay and Continue button.**

   PayPal creates your label.

8. **To print the label, click the Print Label button.**

   Although you can use regular paper, it's better to use paper with adhesive backing; that way, you don't have to use tape to attach the label to your package.

## Deliverance: Sending your package on its merry way

After you affix the label to your package, you're ready to send it. One option is to request a free carrier pickup from the USPS Web site (www.usps.com/pickup/welcome.htm); alternatively, you can hand it off to your regular carrier, take it to your local post office, or drop it in a collection box.

To track the package, click the Track button that appears where the Print Shipping Label button was on the My Account page in PayPal. (You and the buyer will also receive a tracking number via e-mail.)

While we're on the subject of your regular mail carrier: Make it a point to buddy up to yours. That way, if you have any shipping-related questions, your carrier will be happy to answer them!

a

**Figure 15-4:**
Review your
shipping
details on
the con-
firmation
page.

b

# Marky Mark: Marking the Item As Sent in Etsy

After you ship your item, you have one more step to complete: marking the item as Sent in Your Account on Etsy. Here's what you do after you log in to your Etsy account:

1. **Click the Your Account link along the top of any Etsy page.**

   The Your Account page opens.

2. **Click the Sold Orders link, under Orders, on the left side of the page.**

3. **Click the Open tab.**

   The Open Orders page appears.

4. **Click the Shipped check box in the listing for the item you just shipped.**

   Etsy updates the listing to show that it has been shipped (see Figure 15-5). The item also appears on the Completed Orders page, which you access by clicking the Completed tab.

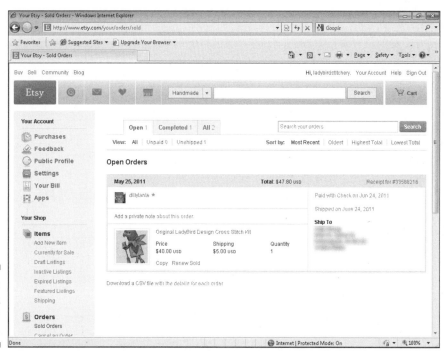

**Figure 15-5:** Mark the item Shipped.

# Part IV
# All Up in Your Bidness: Handling Business Matters

The 5th Wave                    By Rich Tennant

"He saw your laptop and wants to know
if he can check his feedback ratings."

# In this part . . .

You're not just opening an Etsy shop; you're launching your very own small business. To ensure that it succeeds, you need to approach it seriously. In this part, you'll enlarge your skill set, evolving from an artisan to a proper entrepreneur. We include such topics as marketing and branding your Etsy shop, providing unrivaled customer service, and handling financial matters such as taxes and whatnot. Armed with the information in this part, you'll be takin' care of business in no time flat.

# Chapter 16

# High Exposure: Marketing Your Etsy Business

*In This Chapter*

▶ Defining your brand

▶ Promoting your shop using Etsy tools

▶ Building an e-mail list

*A*lthough marketing as a discipline is relatively new, in practice, marketing is as old as Joan Rivers. Indeed, the first Cro-Magnon to convince a fellow knuckle-dragger to barter for *his* mastodon-fur cape instead of the one offered in the next cave was the earliest marketer. ("But this mastodon-fur cape 100-percent stench free. Og's not.") Naturally, if you want to evolve your Etsy shop into a thriving enterprise, you need to do the same. This chapter is devoted to the ins and outs of marketing your Etsy business so that it doesn't go the way of the Neanderthal.

Let's be honest: This chapter constitutes a very basic primer on the subject of marketing. If you're serious about your Etsy business, you'll want to study this subject in greater depth. *Small Business Marketing For Dummies,* by Barbara Findlay Schenck (published by John Wiley & Sons, Inc.), is a great jumping-off point!

## Brandy, You're a Fine Girl: Building Your Brand

An important part of any business — whether it's a multinational widget-making corporation with more employees than Lichtenstein has citizens, a small mom-and-pop pizzeria that serves the surrounding neighborhood, or your Etsy shop — is its brand.

So what, exactly, is a brand? Although many people believe that the word *brand* is synonymous with the word *logo,* it's not. Yes, your logo is part of your brand (more on that in a moment), but the brand itself is a much broader concept. You can think of your *brand* as the image you want to project for your business. Your brand is what you're known for.

Before you begin building your brand, you need to pin down a few key pieces of information:

- ✔ **The brand promise:** Was it Kierkegaard or Dick Van Patten who said, "People don't buy drill bits — they buy holes"? Pinpointing your brand promise means determining what you're *really* selling. What does your brand promise to do? You're not selling handmade aromatherapy candles; you're selling unparalleled relaxation. *That's* your brand promise.

- ✔ **The target market:** You want to have some idea of who's likely to be interested in your product so that you can tailor your brand accordingly. Who is your customer? Is your audience male or female? Young or old? Single or smug married? Where does your target market live? How much disposable income does your customer have? What level of education has your target market obtained?

- ✔ **The competition:** In addition to recognizing your target market, you need to identify your competition. Who are they? What do they offer? How are their brands or products similar to yours? How are they different? Do your target markets overlap? This assessment can help you position your own brand in such a way that you gain an advantage.

- ✔ **The brand personality:** Think of your brand as being like a person (preferably not your mother-in-law). Is it quirky? Refined? Silly? Wise? This personality creates an emotional connection with your target market. You convey your brand's personality through visual elements, such as your logo, and through its voice — that is, your tagline (discussed momentarily), your item descriptions (see Chapter 12), your shop announcement (see Chapter 8), and even your Etsy convos (see Chapter 17).

- ✔ **The unique selling proposition (USP):** Every good brand has at least one characteristic that makes it different from everything else on the market. Using the aromatherapy candle example, maybe your candles burn longer than other candles on the market, or smell different, or come in super-pretty jars. Whatever special quality your candles have, that's their USP.

With that information in hand, you're ready to start building your brand. In the following sections, we explain how to create taglines and logos, and we discuss the importance of infusing your brand into everything related to your Etsy shop.

## Tag lady: Composing a tagline

Do you recognize the phrase "You deserve a break today"? What about "Just do it," "Don't leave home without it," "The quicker picker-upper," or "Time to make the doughnuts"? If so, then you know the power of a tagline. A *tagline* is a memorable phrase that expresses who your brand is and what it does. It serves as a marketing slogan and reflects the brand it seeks to promote.

Part of building your brand is composing a tagline of your own. As you do, consider that a good tagline

- **Is short, concise, specific, and, ideally, clever:** The longer the tagline, the more likely people are to lose interest in it.

- **Speaks to your target market:** If your target market is 20-something hipsters, your tagline shouldn't use language that your grandmother favors.

- **Reflects your brand's personality:** If your brand is quirky, you don't want a stuffy tagline!

- **Hints at your brand promise and its USP:** Take the tagline for M&M's, for example: "Melts in your mouth, not in your hands" suggests that M&M's are not only super tasty, but also not messy.

A great place for your tagline is your shop title or your shop's banner. For help with changing your shop title and banner, refer to Chapter 8.

## Loco for logos: Creating a logo

As we mention earlier in this chapter, many people confuse a brand's logo with the brand itself. And it's easy to see why; after all, the logo — along with the tagline — represents the brand. It's critical, then, that the logo (as well as other visual elements, such as the colors and fonts you use in marketing materials such as business cards and whatnot) reflect the brand's personality and speak to your audience.

Keep some points in mind as you develop your logo:

- **Consider your colors.** Different colors evoke different emotions and convey different ideas. For example, if you specialize in custom motorcycle gear, a baby-pink logo may not be the way to go.

- **Make sure you're sending the right message.** Your logo's visual style communicates something about your brand. For example, if your logo has a minimalist style, it suggests that your brand does, too. Be sure that your logo sends the message you want.

✔ **Be original.** Although it's certainly fine to look to other brands and logos for inspiration, don't try to copy — especially if the logo in question is a competitor's.

If you're not comfortable developing your logo, don't hesitate to get help. If you're on a strict budget, why not ask a friend with an artistic bent for help? Alternatively, try bartering with a professional designer.

Consider using your logo as your Etsy avatar. That way, anytime you comment in a forum or send a convo, other Etsyites see your logo. For help with changing your avatar, refer to Chapter 8.

## Integrate expectations: Working your brand into all you do

The key to branding is infusing it in everything you do. Express your brand by using your tagline and logo in your business cards, letterhead, envelopes, postcards, packaging, and other promotional materials. Your brand also needs to permeate your Etsy shop by appearing in your shop banner and avatar. You can even communicate your brand by using your tagline and logo on your Facebook page and Twitter profile. In this way, you increase the chances of your customers identifying *your* brand among the flotsam and jetsam of Etsy.

A great resource for promotional print items — think business cards, postcards, sticker books, and so on — is Moo (www.moo.com). Why? With Moo, you can upload images right from your Etsy shop for use in your print materials. Moo also prints special MiniCards — mini business cards that display photos of your work. These cards can work as price tags, coupon cards, luggage tags, and more.

## Poetry in Promotion: Using Etsy Tools to Promote Your Shop

Etsy recognizes the importance of marketing your shop and offers several built-in promotional tools. Specifically, Etsy enables you to create coupon codes for your shop, buy a spot in a special showcase to boost your shop's visibility, create a special widget for your blog or other Web site to advertise your Etsy shop, and promote your shop on Facebook.

## Coupon d'état: Creating coupons

Coupons have come a long way since their invention in 1887, when Asa Candler, an early investor in the Coca-Cola company, devised a plan to distribute millions of coupons for free servings of the now-famous tonic. In fact, these days, coupons are *everywhere,* including on Etsy.

Yes, that's right: You can channel your own inner Asa Candler and offer your Etsy customers discounts on merchandise or free shipping through coupons — or, more specifically, coupon codes. Buyers can then apply these codes to purchases during the checkout process. For example, you may offer a coupon to celebrate your store's anniversary or an upcoming holiday, to reward repeat customers, or to share with your Facebook fans or Twitter followers.

To spread the word about your coupon code, you can simply include the code in the packaging with any items you sell — say, by tucking a business card in with your piece. Alternatively, if you maintain a newsletter, you may want to include a coupon code there to drive sales in your Etsy shop. (You find out more about newsletters later in this chapter.)

To create a coupon code, log in to your Etsy account and follow these steps:

1. **Click the Your Account link along the top of any Etsy page.**

   The Your Account page opens.

2. **Click the Coupon Codes link, under Promote, on the left side of the page.**

   The Reward Customers with Coupons page opens (see Figure 16-1).

3. **Click the Create New Coupon button.**

   The Create New Coupon dialog box opens (see Figure 16-2).

4. **In the Coupon Code field, type the code you want to use for the coupon.**

   Note that this code must contain between 5 and 20 alphanumeric characters (no punctuation), with no spaces.

5. **Click the Discount Type drop-down arrow and choose the type of discount you want to offer — Percent Discount or Free Shipping.**

   If you choose Percent Discount, type the discount amount in the % Off field. If you choose Free Shipping, optionally check the Only for Domestic Shipping Addresses check box.

   When a customer redeems a coupon, Etsy's 3.5% transaction fee applies to the discounted price. (Flip to Chapter 1 for more about Etsy fees.)

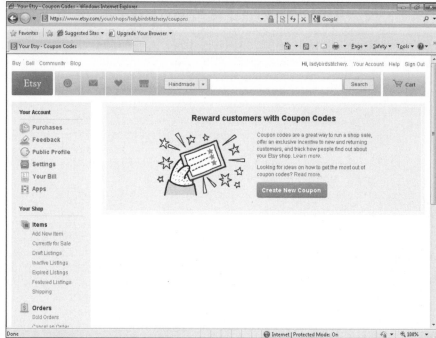

**Figure 16-1:**
Create a
coupon
code.

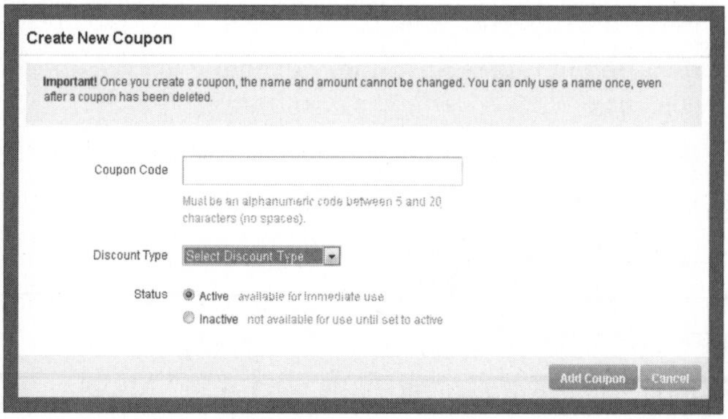

**Figure 16-2:**
Enter the
coupon
details.

6. **Click the Active option button to activate the coupon code.**

7. **Click the Add Coupon button.**

   Etsy creates the coupon code and lists it on the Coupon Codes page (see Figure 16-3).

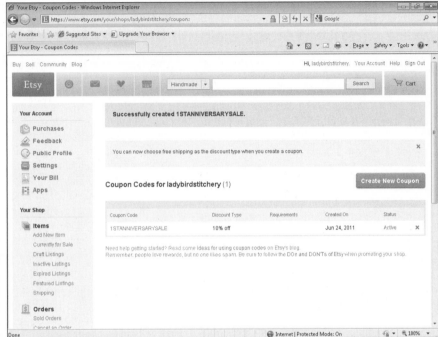

**Figure 16-3:**
Etsy creates the coupon code.

If you want to deactivate a coupon code — for example, if the holiday for which the code was created has passed — you can easily do so. Simply click the code's Active link in the screen shown in Figure 16-3. Then, in the dialog box that appears, click the Inactive option button and click Save Changes. Etsy deactivates the code for you. If you want, you can reactivate the code later by clicking the code's Inactive link and clicking Active in the dialog box that appears.

## Showcase showdown: Buying a spot in an Etsy showcase

If you're looking to up your exposure on Etsy, considering featuring your shop in an Etsy showcase. If you purchase a showcase slot — it costs $7 for a 24-hour run — you're sure to experience an uptick in the number of people who view and heart your shop and listings! (Not familiar with hearting? Check out Chapter 21.)

## Gifted child: Issuing gift certificates

In addition to offering coupons, you can sell gift certificates to your Etsy shop. A gift certificate must be a tangible item — say, a paper certificate or a postcard that's mailed to the recipient, or even a digital PDF file, which can be e-mailed. (If you go the digital route, be sure to select a file type that the recipient can't alter.)

In addition to touting your shop's name and Etsy address — say, www.ladybirdstitchery.etsy.com — the gift certificate must include a unique, secret code (this can be anything you want), with instructions for the person redeeming the gift certificate to both choose the Other payment method when checking out and enter that code in the Message to Seller section. (Note that you may need to enable the Other payment method; to do so, click the Your Account link that appears along the top of every Etsy page, click the Shipping & Payment link under Shop Settings, click the Payment Methods tab, click the Other check box under Payment Methods You Accept to select it, and then click the Save button. See Chapter 9 for more about setting payment methods.)

To sell a gift certificate, you create an item listing for the gift certificate, just as you would for any other item in your shop (see Chapter 13 for details on listings). This item listing must contain the phrase "gift certificate" both in the title and description and as a tag, and must include all the same information as the gift certificate itself (minus the unique, secret code). The listing also needs to clearly state that the gift certificate is valid only in your Etsy shop. Be aware that Etsy will assess a fee both when you sell a gift certificate and when your buyer uses the gift certificate to purchase another item in your shop.

When it comes to issuing gift certificates, you'll want to be crazy organized: Keep track of the unique code applied to each gift certificate, the amount each gift certificate is for, and when each gift certificate is redeemed. Note that if a customer applies a gift certificate to an item that costs more than the gift certificate's value, you need to send that person a revised PayPal invoice for the difference. (Refer to Chapter 14 for help with sending PayPal invoices.)

Several Etsy showcases exist, one for each category and certain subcategories on the site (Chapter 3 has the full scoop on categories). Items in a showcase appear at the top of the page when someone clicks its category link on Etsy's home page. For example, if you purchase a spot in the Needlecraft showcase, Etsy rotates item listings from your shop among listings from 24 other sellers at the top of the Needlecraft page.

To buy a spot in an Etsy showcase, log in to your Etsy account and follow these steps:

1. **Click the Your Account link along the top of any Etsy page.**

   The Your Account page opens.

2. **Click the Showcase link, under Promote, on the left side of the page.**

   The Your Showcase Reservations page opens (see Figure 16-4).

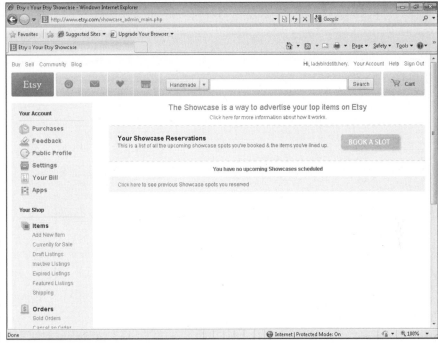

**Figure 16-4:**
Reserve
a spot in
an Etsy
showcase.

3. **Click the Book a Slot button.**

   The Purchase a Showcase Spot page opens (see Figure 16-5).

4. **Click the category in which you want your item listing to be featured.**

   The Purchase Showcase Spot page for the category opens (Figure 16-6 shows the page for the Needlecraft category).

   You must showcase an item in its own category. For example, if you've categorized an item as Needlecraft, you must showcase it in the Needlecraft category.

5. **Click the Pick an Available Day drop-down arrow and choose the day when you want to feature your item.**

   Your item listings will appear in the showcase for 24 hours on the date you selected, starting at midnight Eastern Standard Time.

6. **Click the Purchase Spot button to purchase the showcase spot.**

   A record of the purchase appears in the Your Showcase Reservations page (see Figure 16-7).

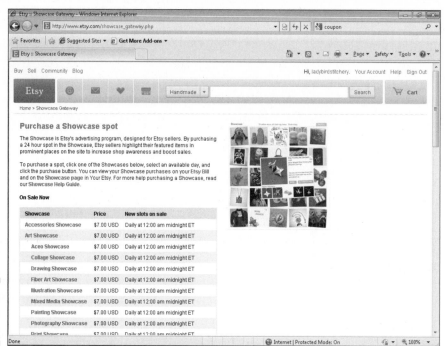

**Figure 16-5:**
Choose a
category.

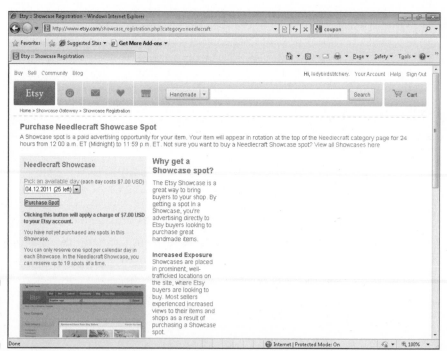

**Figure 16-6:**
Choose your
time slot.

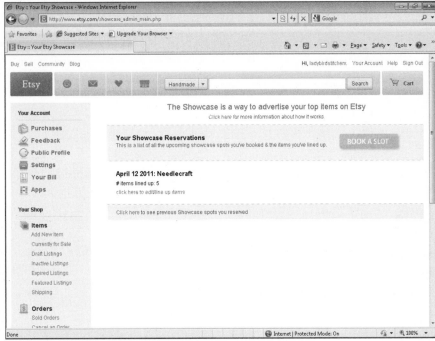

**Figure 16-7:**
Etsy
reserves
your spot
in the
showcase.

By default, Etsy showcases the first ten items in your Etsy shop. To change which items appear, click the reservation's Click Here to Edit/Line Up Items link, shown in Figure 16-7. The showcase page opens (see Figure 16-8).

If the list doesn't show an item that you want to feature, type its listing ID in the Listing ID field and click Add. The item that you added then appears at the top of the list, and the item that was formerly at the bottom of the list is bumped off. Repeat as many times as needed until the showcase contains only the items that you want to include.

## Mini me: Creating an Etsy Mini

Do you maintain a blog or some other type of personal Web site? If so, you can use it to host an Etsy Mini, a wee widget that displays items in your Etsy store. People who visit your site can click an item in the Etsy Mini to view it on Etsy. After you install an Etsy Mini on your site, it updates automatically when you list new items.

To add an Etsy Mini to your site, log in to your Etsy account and follow these steps:

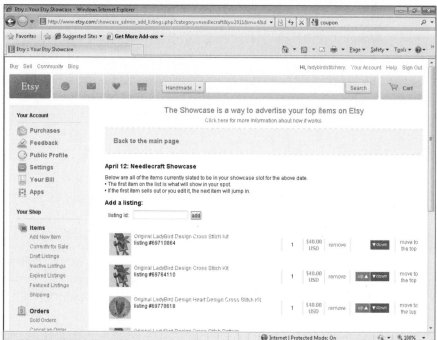

**Figure 16-8:**
Rearrange
your
showcase.

1. **Click the Your Account link along the top of any Etsy page.**

   The Your Account page opens.

2. **Click the Etsy Mini link, under Promote, on the left side of the page.**

   The Build Your Own Etsy Mini page opens (see Figure 16-9a and 16-9b).

3. **Click the Items from My Shop option button under Items to Show.**

4. **Click the option button for the desired image size — Thumbnail or Gallery — under Choose Image Size.**

5. **Under Choose Layout, click the Columns drop-down arrow and select the number of columns you want to display.**

6. **Under Choose Layout, click the Rows drop-down arrow and choose the number of rows you want to display.**

   Etsy displays a preview of the Etsy Mini.

7. **Select the code in the Copy This Code for the JavaScript Version field and copy it.**

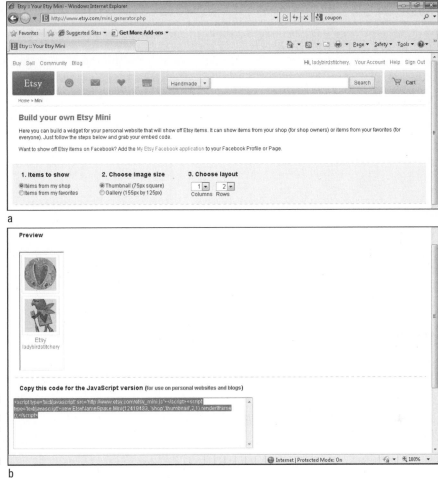

**8. Paste the code that you copied into your own Web site's code.**

Your Web page updates to include the Etsy Mini (see Figure 16-10).

Yes, you're right. We skipped a few steps — namely, the ones that cover figuring out how to access your Web page's code and where in that code to paste the code you just copied. Why? Because those steps vary, depending on what kind of site you maintain (a blog or some other type of Web site). For help, troll the help files that your site host provided.

**Figure 16-10:**
Paste the
Etsy Mini
code into
the HTML
in your own
Web page.

## *Save Facebook: Promoting your Etsy shop on Facebook*

With more than a half billion members, Facebook is a great place to promote your Etsy shop. In fact, Facebook supports a special Etsy app, called My Etsy, for just that purpose. When you install My Etsy on your Facebook page, users who "Like" your page will see news about your Etsy shop in their own Facebook News Feed.

Before you can use My Etsy, you must create a Facebook page for your Etsy shop. Note that we said *page,* not *profile.* The My Etsy app works only on Facebook pages designed for businesses, not on the personal profile you probably maintain to keep up with friends. For help with creating a Facebook page, see Facebook's help info.

After you've created a Facebook page for your business, log in to your Etsy account and follow these steps:

1. **Click the Your Account link along the top of any Etsy page.**

   The Your Account page opens.

2. **Click the Facebook link, under Promote, on the left side of the page.**

   Etsy directs you to a Facebook page that explains what the My Etsy application does.

3. **Click Add to My Page.**

   Facebook requests your permission to proceed.

4. **Click Allow.**

   The Add My Etsy page opens.

5. **Click the Add My Etsy button.**

   Facebook adds a My Etsy tab to your Facebook page.

6. **Click the My Etsy tab.**

   The My Etsy for Facebook page opens.

7. **Type your Etsy user name in the Enter Your Etsy User Name field.**

8. **Click the Submit button.**

9. **To share your favorite items and shops on your My Etsy tab, click the Yes option button.**

10. **Click the Create My Etsy Tab button.**

    The My Etsy tab displays your Etsy shop listings.

---

## Tweety bird: Using Twitter to promote your Etsy shop

Twitter is a great tool for promoting your Etsy shop. For example, you can use Twitter to share a quote from a happy customer, promote upcoming sales, or announce that you've posted new items in your shop. If you do use Twitter, just be sure you mix your promotional tweets with ones that aren't overtly geared toward generating sales. Otherwise, you'll find yourself with few followers!

# Go Postal: Sending an E-mail Newsletter

A great way to keep in touch with your customers is to send periodic e-mail newsletters. For example, you may send an e-mail newsletter to announce an upcoming sale or contest, to spread the news about a new product, or to share a coupon.

Who should receive your e-mail newsletter? If your answer is "anyone and everyone who has ever ordered from my Etsy shop," simmer down. The fact is, Etsy considers that behavior spamful, noting in its Terms of Use that "without express consent from the user, you are not licensed to add any Etsy user to your e-mail or physical mail list." (Check out www.etsy.com/policy/terms for the complete Terms of Use.) You can, however, add someone's name to your e-mail list if that person gives consent. Naturally, you don't want to convo all your past customers to see if they want a seat on your bandwagon — *that's* a violation of Etsy's Terms of Use, too.

The only way to build your mailing list without honking off Etsy is to simply ask customers if they want to opt in at the same time you e-mail them to thank them for their order and confirm their shipping address (as we explain in Chapter 17).

When it comes to composing and distributing your newsletter, you have a few ways to go.

- **Use your word-processing software.** Compose your letter, paste it into your e-mail program, enter your customers' addresses, and send it on its way.

- **Look to an e-mail newsletter service.** As your list grows, you may opt to use an e-mail newsletter service, such as MailChimp (www.mailchimp.com). Not only does MailChimp enable you to manage subscribers and employ different templates to add some visual spice to your newsletter campaign, but you can use it to send up to 12,000 e-mails per month free. Other e-mail newsletter services include Constant Contact (www.constantcontact.com) and Vertical Response (www.verticalresponse.com).

Whatever route you go, make it a point to send your newsletters regularly — say, biweekly, monthly, or quarterly. If you're planning a sale or launching a new product line, you may pepper in a few extra missives.

# Chapter 17

# You've Been Served: Providing Excellent Customer Service

. . . . . . . . . . . . . . . . . . . . . . . . . . . . . . . . . . . . . . . . . . . . .

*In This Chapter*

▶ Communicating clearly with customers

▶ Shipping packages as fast as you can

▶ Leaving feedback for (and asking for feedback from) your buyers

▶ Handling a bungled transaction

. . . . . . . . . . . . . . . . . . . . . . . . . . . . . . . . . . . . . . . . . . . . .

**R**unning your own Etsy shop is a little like being the Wizard of Oz: You preside over your own Emerald City from behind a curtain of sorts, working the wheels and levers of your online craft business while hidden from view.

If you truly want to be a great and powerful Etsy seller, however, you must pull back the curtain and interact with your Ozmites — er, customers. It's not enough to craft gorgeous items and list them in your shop; you must also provide excellent customer service — before, during, and after each sale. In this chapter, we stress the importance of clear communication, prompt shipping, and fast feedback. We also provide guidance on how to gracefully deal with bungled transactions.

# Let's Talk: Communicating with a Buyer Before, During, and After a Transaction

Communication is *the* single most critical factor to ensuring the success of your Etsy business. After your fabulous inventory catches your buyers' attention, your prompt and friendly communication — whether it's via e-mail or an Etsy convo — will keep them coming back for more (not to mention recommending your shop to their friends).

A *convo* — short for "conversation" — is a communication with another member using Etsy's internal messaging system. You can use convos to communicate with any other Etsy member. To access your convos, click the Conversations icon that appears in the Etsy header bar (assuming that you're signed in to the site); the Conversations page appears (see Figure 17-1).

You can also set up Etsy to send you an e-mail anytime you receive a message via convo. Here's how:

1. **Click the Conversations icon.**

   The Conversations page opens.

2. **Click the Notification Preferences link.**

   The E-mails page opens (see Figure 17-2).

3. **Click the Edit link in the General Notifications area.**

   Two check boxes appear in the General Notifications area.

4. **Click the Someone Sends Me a Convo check box to select it.**

5. **Click the Save button.**

   Etsy saves your settings.

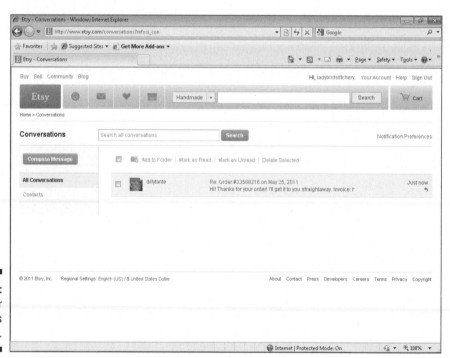

**Figure 17-1:**
Access your
Etsy convos
here.

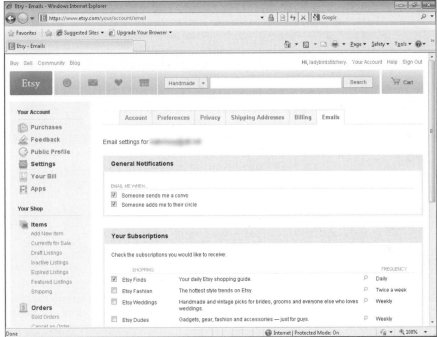

**Figure 17-2:**
The E-mails page is where you change various settings related to e-mail.

When it comes to communicating with buyers, you must strike a balance. Communicate too little, and your buyers may conclude that you don't care about your customers. Communicate too much, and your buyers may perceive you to be a nuisance. So when, exactly, do you want to reach out to buyers? And what, exactly, do you want to say? For guidance, read on.

It's a good idea to set up a separate e-mail address for correspondence on Etsy. That way, you can keep all your business-related messages in one place. Also set up Etsy to forward convos to your dedicated shop e-mail address.

## Questionable behavior: Answering customer questions

Even if you upload five spectacular photos of your item and compose a listing description with enough detail to satisfy Tolstoy himself, prospective buyers will still have questions about your piece. Queries may range from "How big is it?" to "What does it smell like?" to "How fuzzy is it?" to "Um, what is that thing?" to "Can you make this in puce?"

Whatever the question, it's critical that you answer it — and the sooner, the better. Unless you've been stranded on a desert island or you're, say, in labor, try to respond to all questions within 24 hours. Quickly replying to e-mails and convos containing queries from potential buyers does more than just help them determine whether your item is right for them; it reassures them that you're a seller they can count on.

When communicating with customers, keep things simple. Providing too much information may confuse them. Focus on communicating the information that will be most helpful to the customer. For example, if a customer asks how quickly you can put an item in the post, simply respond by telling her, "Tomorrow." Don't say, "Well, I'd do it today, but my dog just ate my cactus, and I have to take her to the vet, so it will have to be tomorrow." TMI.

## Mind your manners: Giving thanks

As you may know, Etsy sends you a notification e-mail when someone purchases an item from your Etsy shop. When you receive this e-mail, you need to contact the buyer to thank her for her purchase and to confirm that you've received payment for it (assuming that you have). While you're at it, give the buyer some idea of when she can expect to receive the item and invite her to drop you a line if she has any questions. (We provide a sample note covering this and additional info later in this chapter.)

On Etsy, as in life, simple courtesy goes a long way! Saying thank you is key to keeping your customers happy.

You can contact the buyer in one of two ways (the method you choose depends simply on which one you prefer):

- ✔ **E-mail:** As shown in Figure 17-3, Etsy includes the buyer's e-mail address in its notification e-mail.

- ✔ **Convo:** You can use Etsy to hold a convo with a buyer (or any other Etsy user) right on the site. To initiate a convo with your buyer, visit Your Account, click the Sold Orders link on the left side of the page, click the buyer's name, and click Contact, as shown in Figure 17-4. When the New Conversation box, shown in Figure 17-5, opens, type your message and click Send.

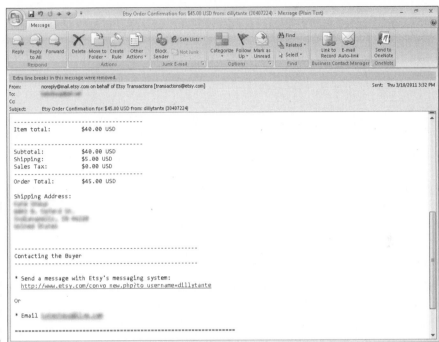

**Figure 17-3:** Locate the buyer's e-mail address on your notification e-mail.

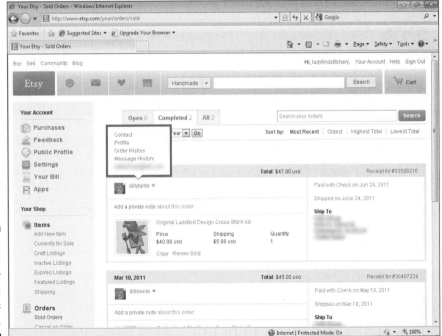

**Figure 17-4:** Find the buyer's user name on the Orders page.

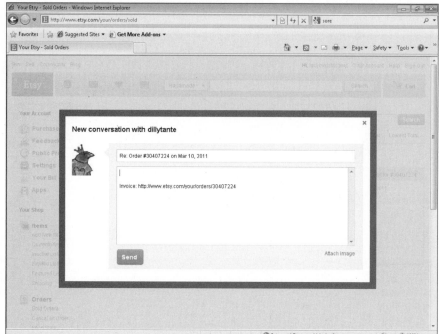

To launch an Etsy convo with any other Etsy member — read: not just some-one who has purchased something from your Etsy shop — open that person's Etsy page and click the Contact link under her name. The same box from Figure 17-5 appears.

If you want, you can configure Etsy to include some special text in the transac-tion notice that buyers receive when they purchase from your shop. For exam-ple, you may use this text, which Etsy calls your Message to Buyers, to thank your buyer, to convey your standard shipping practices, or to share some other useful tidbit. To set up your Message to Buyers, go to Your Account, click the Info & Appearance link under Shop Settings, type your message in the Message to Buyers area, and click the Save button (see Figure 17-6). Note that you don't want to use this autogenerated message in lieu of the one you send yourself; use it as one more point of contact.

**Figure 17-6:**
Enter your
Message
to Buyers
here.

## *Ship happens: Double-checking the shipping address*

Know what's a major drag? Placing a perfectly packaged parcel in the post — with the wrong delivery address. To avoid this postal pitfall, double-check with your buyer *before* you ship that the shipping address that appears on the transaction invoice is indeed correct. You can do this in your initial convo with the buyer — the one in which you thank her for her purchase. (Check out the later section "Sample shout-out: Covering all the bases in one short, pleasant message" for a sample note.)

Double-checking the shipping address is especially critical if the address that the buyer supplied to Etsy differs from the address that the buyer supplied to PayPal. (If the buyer pays using PayPal, you'll receive a notice from that site in addition to the one you receive from Etsy.)

Also make a point to touch base with your buyer after you ship her package, to let her know it's on its way. When you do, be sure to include the name of the shipping company and the package's tracking number (if applicable).

## Get a clue: Finding out how they found you

In the course of communicating with your buyers, whether it's in your initial convo or later in the process — for example, when you ship the item — ask how they found you. Did the buyer happen upon your store while browsing Etsy? Did she see your work on a blog? Or did an ad pique her interest? This info can help you determine how well your marketing strategy is working — which is critical to the long-term success of your Etsy shop. (Flip to Chapter 16 for the scoop on marketing your Etsy shop.) While you're at it, considering asking buyers if they want to opt into your mailing list (also discussed in Chapter 16).

## Lost in translation: Communicating with foreign buyers

Especially if you sell internationally, you must be prepared to correspond with buyers who are not native English speakers. Even if you sell only in the United States, you'll run across the occasional transplant. To ward off misunderstandings when communicating with foreign buyers, keep these points in mind:

- **Keep messages brief and simple.** Using long, complex words and sentences will almost certainly create confusion.
- **Steer clear of slang.** Including nonstandard English is just asking for trouble. At best, your customer may misunderstand you. At worst, you may inadvertently offend her.
- **Avoid abbreviations and jargon.** Spell out what you want to say using clear, standard language.

## Sample shout-out: Covering all the bases in one short, pleasant message

Still a bit stymied over what your message needs to contain? Here's a sample missive combining all the elements to cover:

Hi Murgatroyd!

Just a quick note to thank you so much for your purchase. You made me smile!

Payment has been received, and your treats will ship to the following address:

[Insert Address Here]

I'll send you an e-mail when your package is ready to ship.

Also, may I ask where you found my shop — from an ad maybe, or just browsing around Etsy? And while I have you, are you interested in signing up for my monthly newsletter?

Thanks again, and I hope you have a fabulous day!

Allison

# Speed Is of the Essence: Shipping It Quickly

If you've ever ordered anything on Etsy — and, let's face it, who hasn't? — you're no doubt familiar with the sweet torture of waiting for that prettily packaged parcel to roost in your mailbox. To keep your buyer from expiring from anticipation, and to improve your chances of getting excellent feedback, be a dear and ship her goodies as soon as is feasibly possible (read: after she has paid for them and, if applicable, the check, money order, or cashier's check has cleared). Of course, you'll want to double-check her shipping address first (as we explain earlier in this chapter).

For more information about shipping options and about packaging your parcel like a pro, refer to Chapter 15.

# Feedback Is Good: Leaving Feedback Promptly and Prompting for It

Etsy relies on feedback to facilitate trust among buyers and sellers. At the conclusion of a sale, both the buyer and the seller leave feedback about the transaction. Other Etsy users can then view this feedback to determine whether a particular buyer or seller is aboveboard.

To view another user's feedback score, click the Feedback link in that shop's home page or public profile.

You and your buyer have 120 days to leave feedback on your mutual transaction. That's plenty of time to receive payment and for your buyer to receive her item! So no excuses.

Leaving feedback isn't mandatory. If you opt out, Etsy doesn't send a gaggle of intimidating fellows to your door to harass you. But leaving feedback is a good idea because it helps ensure that buyers feel safe shopping on Etsy — and that's good for all of us. Just remember, any feedback that you leave affects your buyer's feedback score — and, by extension, her reputation on the site. It's super important that you issue feedback consistently, fairly, and honestly.

You can leave feedback for a buyer as soon as you receive payment, after you ship the package, or when you're certain that the buyer has received the item — whichever you prefer. Here's how:

1. **While signed in to your Etsy account, go to Your Account.**

2. **Click the Feedback link on the left side of the screen.**

   The Items Awaiting Feedback page appears (see Figure 17-7).

3. **Click the Positive, Neutral, or Negative option button under the transaction you want to rate.**

   Before leaving neutral or negative feedback, see if you can hammer out with the buyer whatever issue is bothering you, via e-mail or a convo. Often conflicts on Etsy are simply the result of a misunderstanding.

Figure 17-7:
Click the
Feedback
link on
the Your
Account
page to
access
the Items
Awaiting
Feedback
page.

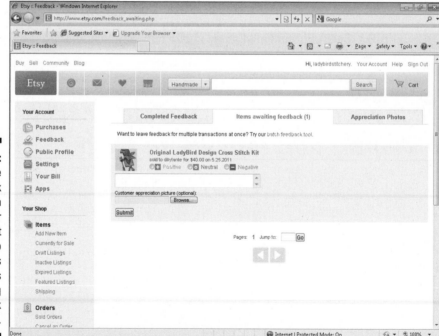

4. **Optionally, type a comment about the transaction or the buyer.**

5. **Click Submit.**

   Etsy posts your feedback on the site.

After the transaction is complete, you can politely ask the buyer to return the favor by leaving feedback for you. Why? Because buyers feel more comfortable purchasing from sellers who have received positive feedback. Keep in mind, though, that leaving feedback is optional. If your buyer opts out of leaving feedback, avoid the temptation to ask her a second time. It's annoying and spammy.

Consider including instructions for leaving feedback in your message — for example, "To leave feedback for me, log in to your account and click the Feedback option in Your Account."

# Bungle Fever: Handling a Bungled Transaction and Other Tough Issues

Despite our best efforts, transactions occasionally do go to heck in a hand basket. Payments get lost, parcels get lost, people get angry — it's enough to make you lose your mind, too! To prevent bungle fever–induced insanity, read on.

## Hand it over: Prompting a buyer to pay up

Most of the time, buyers pay right away when they purchase from an Etsy shop. In fact, if they opt to use PayPal, they *must* pay right away. But occasionally, you may encounter buyers who take their sweet time when it comes to tendering the Benjamins. If that happens, you must take matters into your own hands by issuing a polite reminder for them to pay up. Not sure what to write? Try something like the following:

Dear Loretta,

Just a quick note to thank you for your purchase. I'm so glad you found some goodies to love!

Whenever you get a chance, please send me your check (the total is $44.50) so that I can put your piece in the mail.

Thanks so much, Loretta! I can't wait until you see your treats. Happy day to you!

Allison

If your buyer fails to respond to your gentle nudge, you may relist the item and cancel the sale. For more information, see the upcoming section "Tropic of Cancel: Canceling an order."

## Lost Etsy: Dealing with lost shipments

"Neither snow nor rain nor heat nor gloom of night," my eye! It's an unfortunate fact that sometimes the postal service simply fails to deliver. If one of your packages has gone the way of Amelia Earhart, you have a few options:

- ✔ **Ask your buyer to give it a few days.** More often than not, "lost" packages are merely delayed. Shipping times vary depending on destination and time of year.

- ✔ **Use the tracking number to locate the package.** Assuming that you sprang for delivery confirmation with the United States Postal Service or opted for a higher-end carrier, such as UPS or FedEx, you can track the package. Visit your carrier's Web site for more information. (Flip to Chapter 9 for guidance on setting your shop's shipping policies.)

- ✔ **Report the missing package.** If you sent the package via USPS, you can report it missing — even if you didn't pony up to pay for delivery confirmation. If you're lucky, the Postal Service will find your package. (If not, at least you'll have done your part to improve the system.) To report a missing package, fill out the form on this Web page: `https://postal inspectors.uspis.gov/forms/MLNtRcvd.aspx`.

If all these efforts fail, you'll unfortunately have to send a replacement item or refund the buyer's money (or, if you're feeling especially customer friendly, both). Yes, it hurts — but it's part of running a legitimate Etsy shop. The exception? If you feel that you're being scammed. Although you can't know for sure whether your buyer is pulling a fast one, checking her feedback rating may give you some insight. If she's received 1,298 glowing reviews, she's probably on the up and up. If, on the other hand, she's garnered multiple negative marks, she may be honestically challenged. Our advice? Trust your gut.

Even if you suspect that you're being taken, it may be worth it to refund a buyer's dough for the sake of your own feedback rating. It's your call.

One more pointer: If you do refund a buyer's money for an item lost in the mail, you need to cancel the order. That way, you'll at least receive a refund from Etsy for your transaction fee. For help with canceling the order, see the section "Tropic of Cancel: Canceling an order."

## Case study: Dealing with a reported case

Although Etsy urges buyers and sellers to work through problems related to nondelivery themselves via civilized means (such as with convos or e-mails), buyers sometimes feel compelled to report nondelivery cases to Etsy. If this situation happens to you, you'll receive an e-mail from Etsy outlining the details of the case and instructions for resolving it. The case will also appear on the Reported Cases page in Your Account. (Click the Reported Cases link under Orders to view the reported case.)

After you've taken the appropriate steps to resolve the case, as outlined in the e-mail Etsy sent you, you can request that the case be closed by clicking it on the Reported Cases page, checking the Request Closure check box, and leaving a comment that explains why you're requesting that the case be closed. Unless the buyer responds to your closure request within seven days, the case will be closed automatically. If the buyer does respond to the closure request, the case remains open and unresolved — which can lead to the suspension or termination of your Etsy account. To avoid these egregious outcomes, you must quickly take the necessary steps to resolve the dispute. (If you need Etsy's help in resolving the issue, contact `cancellations@etsy.com`.)

## *Refundsal, Refundsal, give back your fare: Issuing refunds*

When it comes to refunds, different sellers have different policies. Some sellers are happy to issue full refunds for any reason, other sellers allow buyers to exchange for other goods in their shop, and still others hold a firm "all sales final" stance.

Whatever position you adopt on this matter, be certain that your shop policies explain it clearly. Flip to Chapter 9 for more about setting up shop policies.

If you do decide to allow refunds, how you process them depends on which payment option your buyer chose. For example, if she sent a check, you'll likely refund her money by sending her a check back. If she paid using PayPal, you'll use the site to reimburse her.

For help with using PayPal to reimburse a buyer, visit PayPal's Help Center page. You can find it at `www.paypal.com/help`. Clicking the Returns and Refunds link under Filing Disputes and Claims reveals a list of help articles that relate to issuing refunds.

# Tropic of Cancel: Canceling an Order

In certain circumstances, you, as a shop owner, can cancel an order. For example, you may cancel an order if the buyer fails to pay, if both you and the buyer agree to cancel the transaction prior to shipment, if you cannot complete the transaction (for example, due to inventory problems), if the item was lost in the mail, or if the buyer returned the item to you. When you cancel an order, Etsy refunds your transaction fee.

If you want to renew the listing for the item in question, do so before you cancel the order. Otherwise, you'll lose the listing description, images, and other information — and losing all that would be a drag. For help with relisting an item, refer to Chapter 13.

If you want to leave feedback for the order, you need to do so *before* canceling it. After an order is canceled, you can't leave feedback for it.

To cancel an order, follow these steps:

1. **While signed in to your Etsy account, go to Your Account.**

2. **Click the Sold Orders link under Orders.**

3. **Click the item's name in the Sold Orders page.**

   The listing opens (see Figure 17-8).

4. **Click the View Invoice link.**

   The order's Invoice page opens (see Figure 17-9).

5. **Click the Cancel an Order link in the page's Order section.**

   The Cancel an Order page opens (see Figure 17-10).

6. **Click the transaction that you want to cancel.**

7. **Click the Reason for Canceling Transaction drop-down list and choose the reason for the cancellation.**

8. **Answer the questions that appear.**

   The precise questions that appear depend on the reason you select in Step 6.

9. **If you want, type a message for the buyer in the Message to Buyer field.**

10. **Click the Submit Cancellation button.**

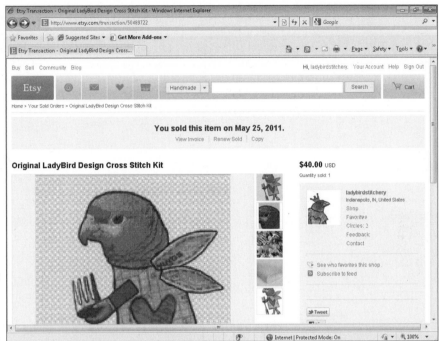

**Figure 17-8:**
Open the
listing.

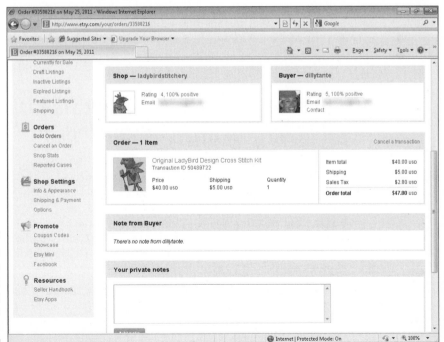

**Figure 17-9:**
Click the
Cancel an
Order link
to cancel a
transaction.

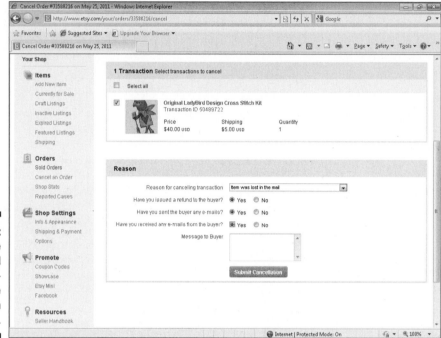

**Figure 17-10:**
Enter the requested information on the Cancel an Order page.

After you submit the form, Etsy finalizes the cancellation (it may take up to 48 hours), notifies you and the buyer that the cancellation has occurred, credits your account with any fees associated with the order, and removes all record of the order from the site.

## The customer is usually right (ish): Dealing with a difficult customer

Honestly, nearly everyone on Etsy is great. For real. But every so often, you're bound to run into someone who, well, *isn't*. Whether the offender is rude, demanding, or simply a pain in the patootie, keep these points in mind:

✔ **Polish your policies.** Clear, concise shop policies can go a long way toward heading off problems down the road. Be sure that your shop's policies are as comprehensive as possible. (For guidance on creating your shop's policies, refer to Chapter 9.)

✔ **Don't take it personally.** If, after receiving your beautiful baubles, your buyer doesn't appreciate their magnificence, that's on her, not on you.

- **Be professional.** However tempting it may be to uncork on a difficult buyer, don't — at least, not where buyers can hear you. Keep all communications firm, polite, and to the point. Oh, and resist the temptation to air your grievances on the Etsy forums. Everything that you write there is visible to anyone on the Internet — including your mother. And calling out a buyer by name is a violation of the site's policies, which can lead to your expulsion.

- **Extend the olive branch.** Most buyers aren't evil — really. They just want to feel like you're willing to work with them to achieve a happy, speedy transaction. Kindly communicate to them that you'll do everything possible to make that happen — and then do it.

If you feel that you've done all you reasonably can to rectify a problem with a buyer, to no avail, don't be afraid to cut your losses by refunding the buyer's money. Better to get a problem buyer out of your hair than to kill yourself trying to make her happy.

## No shirt, no shoes, no service: Refusing service to a buyer

Although Etsy asks that sellers do everything they can to honor a sale, on extremely rare occasions, you may feel that you must refuse service. For example, if you feel that you're being harassed by a buyer, or if a buyer becomes belligerent — or if, say, you're a Hatfield and the buyer is a McCoy — you do have the right to refuse service, no questions asked. You may also refuse service if your gut instinct tells you that the buyer isn't on the up and up — for example, if you sense that she has paid with a stolen credit card or is attempting to commit some other type of fraud.

Refusing service is a rare event, indeed. It's something you want to do only as a last resort.

To refuse service to a buyer, simply use an Etsy convo to politely inform the buyer that you won't be able to send the item she purchased. You need not explain yourself; in fact, the less you say, the better. Then take the necessary steps to cancel the sale and refund the buyer's money (as we describe earlier in this chapter).

After you refuse service to a buyer, if that person continues to contact you, you can report the problem to abuse@etsy.com. If Etsy agrees with you that the behavior constitutes harassment, Etsy may suspend the buyer's account.

## *In the end: Opting to Kiss and Make Up*

If the result of any mayhem is neutral or negative feedback, fear not. Thanks to an Etsy feature called Kiss and Make Up, buyers and sellers can, er, kiss and make up. To initiate Kiss and Make Up proceedings with a buyer-turned-baddie, go to Your Account, click the Feedback link, click the Completed Feedback tab, and click the red Kiss and Make Up link beneath the befouled feedback entry. Etsy displays a form where you can enter new, positive feedback for the buyer user. Etsy also sends the buyer a Kiss and Make Up proposal via a convo to urge her to leave positive feedback on you as well.

# Chapter 18

# Business as Usual: Managing Your Etsy Store

*I*f you're a fan of Chinese food, you're probably familiar with the pupu platter — you know, the appetizer that features a little bit of everything. This chapter is the literary equivalent. It covers an assortment of topics that relate to managing and growing your Etsy business. They include paying Etsy bills, transferring money from your shop to your bank account, handling taxes and keeping records, running your shop with Etsy tools, and turning your thriving shop into a legitimate business.

Please forgive us: We've tried to cram several books' worth of information into this one wee chapter. We strongly urge you to educate yourself further on all these business matters and more. A good place to start is *Small Business For Dummies,* 3rd Edition, by Eric Tyson and Jim Schell. Also try *Home-Based Business For Dummies,* 3rd Edition, by Paul Edwards, Sarah Edwards, and Peter Economy. (John Wiley & Sons, Inc., publishes both of these books.)

## I'm Just a Bill: Paying Your Etsy Bill

You're not the only baby who needs a new pair of shoes; the folks at Etsy have their own financial obligations. As you find out in Chapter 1, Etsy stays afloat by charging sellers a listing fee (currently 20¢) for each item listed on the site. In addition, Etsy collects a commission from the seller for each item sold — currently, 3.5 percent of the total price of the item (not counting shipping). These fees are assessed at the end of each month. Etsy lets you know when it's time to pay up by sending you a billing statement via e-mail.

To pay your bill, log in to your Etsy account and follow these steps:

1. **Click the link in the billing statement that Etsy sent via e-mail to open the Your Etsy Bill page on Etsy.**

   You can also access the Your Etsy Bill page, shown in Figure 18-1, by clicking the Your Account link that appears along the top of every Etsy page and clicking the Your Bill link on the left side of the page.

2. **Click the Make a Payment Now button.**

   The Make a Payment page opens (see Figure 18-2).

3. **Under Amount to Pay, indicate whether you want to pay your entire Etsy bill, the portion that's due at this time, or some amount in between.**

4. **Under Method of Payment, choose PayPal or the credit card that you have on file with Etsy.**

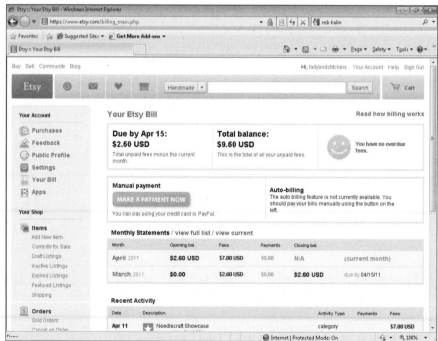

**Figure 18-1:**
View your
Etsy bill.

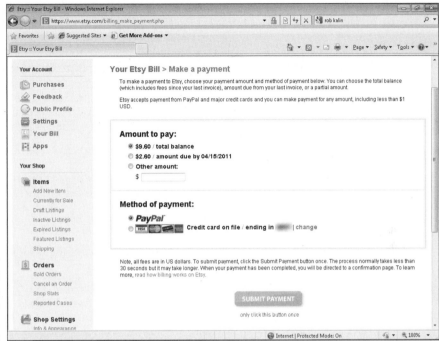

**Figure 18-2:**
Pay your
bill.

5. **Click the Submit Payment button.**

   If you opted to pay with a credit card, you'll see a screen that thanks you for your payment, with a link that you can click to return to your Etsy bill.

   If you opted to pay with PayPal, Etsy directs you to the PayPal site (www.paypal.com), where you're prompted to log in. After you do so, review the payment information. Assuming that it's correct, click the Continue button. PayPal processes your payment and directs you back to Etsy.

If you want to remain in good standing with Etsy, it's crucial that you pay your Etsy bill promptly. If you fail to do so, Etsy can suspend or even terminate your Etsy account.

# Bank Shot: Depositing PayPal Funds into Your Bank Account

Assuming that you configure your Etsy shop to accept PayPal, you'll likely find it to be the payment method of choice among many of your customers. When someone pays for an item using PayPal, the funds for that transaction land in your PayPal account. Although you're free to leave them there — for example, you may do so if you plan to use PayPal to make your own Etsy purchases — at some point, you'll likely want to transfer them to your bank account, especially as your Etsy business grows. Fortunately, doing so is easy. Plus, PayPal charges you zilch to process the transaction (although your bank may hit you for a charge).

To transfer money from your PayPal account to your bank account, log in to your PayPal account at www.paypal.com and follow these steps:

1. **If necessary, click the My Account tab.**

2. **Place your mouse pointer over the Withdraw link at the top of the page, and choose Transfer to Bank Account from the menu that appears.**

   The Withdraw Funds by Electronic Transfer page opens.

3. **In the Amount field, enter the amount of money that you want to transfer.**

4. **Click the To drop-down list and choose the account to which you want to transfer the funds, and then click the Continue button.**

   The Review Withdraw Funds page opens.

5. **Review the details of your transaction; assuming that everything is in order, click the Submit button.**

   PayPal processes the transaction.

It may take three to four business days for your funds to appear in your bank account.

---

## Separation anxiety: Separating your personal and business finances

Especially if you plan to grow your Etsy business into a full-time operation, do yourself a favor: Open a business bank account for your Etsy shop, preferably with a credit or debit card. Then use that account to handle all expenses related to your Etsy shop. At tax time, you won't have to cull your business transactions from your personal ones to report your business expenses. Plus, if you ever need to verify your income — say, if you're taking out a loan to make a major purchase — you'll be able to provide the lending authority with everything it needs.

**Note:** Depending on your location, you may need to show your business license to open a business account with your bank. We discuss business licenses later in this chapter.

# Taxing Matters: Appeasing Uncle Sam

A world with no taxes would be lovely indeed — except for the fact that it would also be a world with no roads, public school teachers, or firefighters. Indeed, without taxes, there would be no Internet — and, by extension, no Etsy! After all, taxes bankrolled the U.S. government's Advanced Research Projects Agency (ARPA), which, in 1969, created the network that would eventually become the Internet. (Thanks, Al Gore!) To make sure you're square with Uncle Sam, read on.

We're not licensed accountants or lawyers, nor do we play them on TV. To be absolutely certain that you're in compliance with local and federal tax laws, seek the advice of these experts.

## To tax or not to tax: Collecting sales tax

Odds are, you need to collect sales tax at least some of the time, unless you live in Alaska, Delaware, Montana, New Hampshire, or New Jersey, five states that don't impose a statewide sales tax. You also may not need to collect sales tax if you use your Etsy shop to sell prescription drugs (not recommended); agricultural products, such as animal feed or seed; groceries; or products for resale. So when do you need to collect sales tax?

Here's the short answer: You must collect sales tax — sometimes called a *franchise tax,* a *transaction privilege tax,* or a *use tax,* among other aliases — on most goods and some services delivered to a customer who lives in a U.S. state where your business maintains a physical presence, such as a store, office, or employee. So, for example, if you run your Etsy shop from your fifth-floor walkup in Brooklyn, and someone from the state of New York buys something from your shop, you need to hit that person with sales tax. But if your buyer lives in Cali, you're both off the hook (unless your shop is a collective and your partner lives in Long Beach).

In general terms, the sales tax process works like this:

1. **You get a sales tax ID number from your state (check your state government's Web site for details).**

2. **Each time you conduct a taxable transaction, you calculate the tax owed and collect it from the buyer.**

3. **You keep excellent records about the tax that you've collected through your Etsy business (as we advise later in this chapter).**

4. **Each month, quarter, or year (depending on your level of sales), you file a tax return and submit the sales tax that you've collected to your state.**

5. **You stay out of jail.**

So how much sales tax do you need to collect? Ay, there's the rub. Sales tax rates vary widely from state to state. Plus, some cities, counties, and jurisdictions impose sales tax above and beyond the state rate. To make sure that your Etsy shop complies, you absolutely want to research your local laws, and maybe even consult a fancy-pants accountant or attorney for guidance.

Here's the good news: You can set up your Etsy shop to calculate and collect sales tax automatically. That way, when a shopper from your neck of the woods ponies up for one of your items, she's charged the appropriate tax automatically. It's like magic! For help with setting up your shop to collect sales tax, refer to Chapter 9.

The sales tax ID number that you obtain from your state entitles you to buy supplies and other items for your Etsy business wholesale — which is typically at least half off the retail price. Holy bonus, Batman!

## Drawn and quartered: Paying quarterly income tax

If you run your business as a sole proprietorship (covered later in this chapter) and you live in the United States, you have the distinct pleasure of paying income taxes not once, not twice, not three times, but *four times* per year — on April 15, June 15, September 15, and January 15 (unless any of those days falls on a weekend or holiday, in which case you must pay up on the next business day).

Paying these quarterly taxes is a breeze. You can download the necessary form (called a 1040-ES) from the IRS's Web site, here: `www.irs.gov/pub/irs-pdf/f1040es.pdf`. You need to download a similar form from your state government's site. Then fill out the forms, cut your checks, and send them in to the appropriate office. (Check the form for details.)

Alternatively, you can pay your taxes online using the Electronic Federal Tax Payment System, or EFTPS, for short: `https://www.eftps.gov/eftps`. (*Note:* EFTPS is for federal taxes only; you need to check with your state to see what resources are available for paying taxes online.)

Figuring out how much you owe is a little more involved. One approach is to simply look at your prior-year tax return, figure out how much you paid in taxes, divide that number by four, and send that amount for each quarterly installment — but that strategy won't do if you expect your income to be vastly different. Our advice? Don't listen to us. Seek the guidance of a qualified accountant.

# Write this off: Determining tax deductions

If your Etsy shop is a proper business (rather than a hobby) and it's set up as a sole proprietorship (one of the arrangements we discuss later in this chapter), you're free to deduct shop-related expenses from your taxable income. Here are a few examples (again, for a complete list, hit up a qualified accountant):

- ✔ **Cost of goods sold:** This category is the cost of the materials that you purchased to craft your inventory. For example, if you make jewelry, your cost of goods sold (COGS, for short) may include the price that you paid for beads, thread, findings, and so on. The COGS may also include what you shelled out for your pretty packaging and your shipping costs.

- ✔ **Equipment:** Did you buy a kiln to fire the ceramic bowls that you list in your Etsy shop? Or a laptop to help run your Etsy business? Or a printer to print invoices for your Etsy customers? If so, you can deduct the cost of these items from your taxable income.

- ✔ **Selling expenses:** These expenses include Etsy fees, PayPal fees, banking fees — even phone calls related to your business.

- ✔ **Advertising fees:** Say that you bought an Etsy showcase. Or maybe you printed some snazzy business cards for your Etsy shop. These costs and other marketing expenses are fair game. (Chapter 16 provides a general introduction to marketing tasks.)

- ✔ **Office expenses:** These purchases include pens and pencils, paper, letterhead, printer supplies, and the like.

- ✔ **Mileage:** Do you regularly drive to your local craft store to stock up on supplies for your Etsy shop? Or to the post office, to ship items to Etsy buyers? If so, you can deduct your mileage for those outings; the current rate, at the time of this writing, is 50¢ per mile. Any tolls or parking fees that you incur en route are also deductible.

- ✔ **Home office:** If you use a portion of your home to run your Etsy shop — maybe you devote a special room to crafting the pieces that you sell or handling administrative tasks — you can claim a home-office deduction. (If you rent studio space, you can deduct that area instead.)

- ✔ **Legal or professional services:** If you follow our advice and hire an accountant, you can deduct his fee. Ditto for any fees associated with other professionals who serve your business — attorneys, graphic designers, and the like.

If you forked over more than $600 to a particular person for services rendered — for example, your attorney or graphic designer — you must send that person a 1099 form. Ask your tax consultant for more information.

If your Etsy shop earns a profit — that is, its gross income is higher than the deductions that you claim for it — in any three of five consecutive years, it's officially a "for-profit" business in the eyes of the IRS. That status means you're free to deduct away! Otherwise, the IRS places severe limitations on what expenses you can deduct. Put another way: Don't deduct the supplies that merely feed your craft addiction but don't support a business. The IRS will notice if your deductions dwarf your income. Avoid waving the proverbial red flag by ensuring a reasonable balance!

# Recording Artist: Keeping Accurate Records

Yes, we know. Record-keeping is for squares. But if you want to avoid getting sideways with the IRS — not to mention stay on top of your business — you'll want to be scrupulous about your record-keeping, however tedious it may be. Keep careful track of all your sales and expenses. And keep all receipts — even the little ones. All those road tolls and parking fees add up! You'll also want to hang on to invoices, bank statements, and any other financial-type documents that cross your desk.

It's smart to put all this information in one place. Consider some suggestions:

✔ An accordion file is a good way to go; it enables you to separate your receipts and other documents by month or by category.

✔ Another approach is to use a digital solution, such as QuickBooks (quickbooks.intuit.com), Outright.com (www.outright.com), or even a simple Excel spreadsheet. All three are great for keeping track of your sales and expenses.

To make it easier for you to manage your shop, Etsy enables you to download sales data in CSV form and save it on your hard drive. You can then view this data by opening the CSV file in a spreadsheet program such as Microsoft Excel. To download this data, log in to your Etsy account and follow these steps:

1. **Click the Your Account link that appears along the top of every Etsy page.**

   The Your Account page opens.

2. **Click the Sold Orders link under Orders on the left side of the page.**

3. **Click the Download a CSV File link to initiate the download.**

   The Download Shop Data screen appears; to download a CSV containing all listings currently for sale, click the Download CSV button under Currently for Sale Listings and follow the onscreen prompts to save the file to your hard drive. (The steps differ by operating system.)

To download a CSV with order information, select the desired month and year in the Orders area, click Download CSV, and again follow the onscreen prompts.

You can also download your monthly Etsy bill in CSV format. Again, log in to your Etsy account and click the Your Account link; then click the Your Bill link under Your Account. On the Your Etsy Bill page, click the desired month; then click the Download This Entire Monthly Statement as a CSV link on the page that appears and follow the onscreen prompts.

You'll also want to keep an eye on your inventory as part of your record-keeping so that you don't run low. One approach may be "one out, one in" — that is, as soon as you sell an item, you make and list a new one.

# Don't Be a Tool: Using Etsy Tools to Manage Your Shop

Anthropologists used to say that tool use differentiated humans from other animals — until a few observant researchers spotted chimpanzees modifying sticks and using them to fish termites from holes in the ground. Tool use does, however, differentiate the serious Etsy sellers from other shop owners on the site — specifically, the use of Etsy tools to manage a shop. This section covers a few of Etsy's more popular termite-fisher-outers.

## We need those numbers, STAT! Viewing sales stats

You can use Etsy's Shop Stats tool to assess your sales activity at a glance. This tool offers you a great way to quickly digest whether sales in your shop are up, down, or steady. To access the tool, log in to your Etsy account and follow these steps:

1. **Click the Your Account button that appears along the top of every Etsy page.**

   The Your Account page opens.

2. **Under Orders on the left side of the page, click the Shop Stats link.**

3. **To view your daily stats, click the Daily tab; to view your monthly stats, click the Monthly tab (see Figure 18-3).**

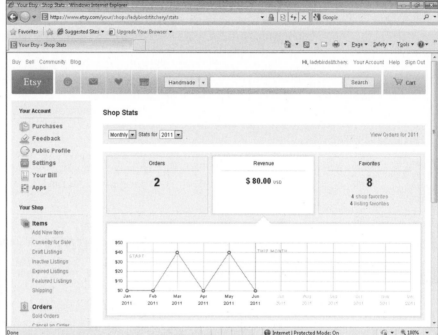

**Figure 18-3:**
Checking
your shop
sales stats
is a cinch.

## *The artist is out: Switching to vacation mode*

Although many people don't take near enough vacations, it's a well-known fact that they're as good for you as Brussels sprouts. Vacations do more than help you rest and relieve stress; they promote creativity — which is pretty important if your livelihood depends on your ability to be creative!

Of course, the key to getting the most out of any vacation is being able to put aside your work while you're away. Fortunately, Etsy enables you to put your Etsy shop in vacation mode. When your shop is in vacation mode, your listings aren't visible to anyone who visits your shop. In addition, you can add a special vacation mode notice, to appear along the top of your shop page. Anyone who attempts to convo you receives an autoreply containing the text that you specify. (Of course, you don't have to actually be "on vacation" to put your shop in vacation mode. You can use this feature anytime you need a break from your Etsy shop.)

It's not a bad idea to put your shop in vacation mode a day or two before you leave. That way, you have time to handle all your orders before your departure. You may also leave your shop in vacation mode for a day or two after you get back so that you can ease into things.

To put your shop in vacation mode, log in to your Etsy account and follow these steps:

1. **Click the Your Account button that appears along the top of every Etsy page.**

   The Your Account page opens.

2. **Under Shop Settings on the left side of the page, click the Options link.**

3. **Click the Vacation Mode tab.**

   The Vacation Mode page opens (see Figure 18-4).

4. **Click the On: Your Shop Is On Vacation option button under Vacation Mode (refer to Figure 18-4a).**

5. **Type the desired text — how long you'll be away, when you'll be back, and so on — in the Vacation Announcement field.**

   This text replaces your shop announcement.

6. **In the Conversation Auto-Reply field (refer to Figure 18-4b), type the message that you want prospective customers to receive if they convo you while you're away.**

7. **Click the Save button.**

   Etsy puts your shop in vacation mode.

It doesn't hurt to add a special "on vacation" shop banner to your shop anytime you put it in vacation mode. For help with swapping out your shop banner, refer to Chapter 8.

## Analyze this: Using Web Analytics to track your Etsy business

Ever wonder how many people have visited your Etsy shop? Or what keywords they used to find an item in your store? Thanks to Etsy Web Analytics, you can find out. With Etsy Web Analytics, a free service powered by Google Analytics, you can track such metrics as page views, site visits, popular content, and page referrals — helpful for, say, determining whether that ad you placed on that blog is actually directing readers to your Etsy shop like it's supposed to. Before you can use Etsy Web Analytics, you must have both a Google account and a Google Analytics account. (Both are free.) We walk you through the whole process in the following sections.

### *Great googly moogly! Creating a Google account*

To create a Google account, follow these steps:

1. **Type www.google.com your Web browser's address bar.**

   The main Google page opens.

2. **Click the Sign In link in the upper-right corner of the page.**

   The Google Accounts page opens.

3. **Click the Create an Account Now link (it's on the right side of the page).**

4. **Enter the requested information — e-mail address, password, location, and so on — and click the I Accept. Create My Account button.**

5. **To verify the account, Google sends an e-mail to the address that you entered; open the e-mail and click the link provided to verify the account.**

### *Going GA-GA: Creating a Google Analytics account*

When you have a Google account, you can create your Google Analytics account, like so:

1. **Type www.google.com/analytics in your Web browser's address bar.**

   The Google Analytics page opens.

2. **Click the Access Analytics button on the right side of the page.**

3. **If you're not signed in to your Google account, enter your e-mail address and password in the appropriate fields and click the Sign In button.**

4. **Click the Sign Up button in the page that appears.**

   A New Account Signup page opens.

5. **In the Web site's URL field, type www.etsy.com.**

6. **In the Account Name field, type your Etsy shop's URL — as in, *shopname*.etsy.com, where *shopname* is your shop's name.**

7. **Enter your country and time zone in the appropriate fields; then click the Continue button.**

8. **Type your last name and first name in the appropriate fields, select your country or territory, and click the Continue button.**

9. **Read the Google Analytics user agreement; then click the Yes, I Agree to the Above Terms and Conditions check box to select it.**

10. **Click the Create New Account button.**

    The Tracking Instructions page opens.

String of letters

11. **In the code that appears in the text box, locate the string of letters and numbers that appears in this format: UA-XXXXXXXX-X (see Figure 18-5); this string of letters and numbers is called a Web Property ID. Write down this Web Property ID.**

12. **Click the Save and Finish button.**

### Come together: Setting up Etsy to work with Google Analytics

After you create a Google Analytics account, you need to set up Etsy to work with Google Analytics. Log in to your Etsy account and follow these steps:

1. **Click the Your Account link that appears along the top of any Etsy page.**

   The Your Account page opens.

2. **Click the Options link under Shop Settings on the left side of the page.**

3. **Click the Web Analytics tab.**

   The Web Analytics page opens (see Figure 18-6).

4. **In the Web Property ID field, type the Web Property ID that you wrote down in the preceding section.**

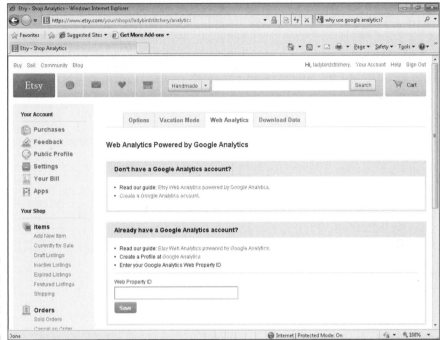

**Figure 18-6:**
Set up
Etsy Web
Analytics.

### *I spy with my little eye: Viewing your site activity*

After you connect Etsy to Google Analytics, you can view your Etsy activity on the Google Analytics site. To do so, simply log in to your Google Analytics account. (Type www.google.com/analytics in your Web browser's address bar, click the Access Analytics button, enter your e-mail address and password, and click the Sign In button.) The Overview page for your Etsy shop appears (see Figure 18-7).

On this page, you can pinpoint, among other key nuggets, how many people have visited your shop and how long they spent there. You can also access information such as where they came from (that is, which Web page they were on before they accessed your shop) and more.

Don't be surprised if you don't see any useful info right away. Google needs a bit of time to start tracking your site.

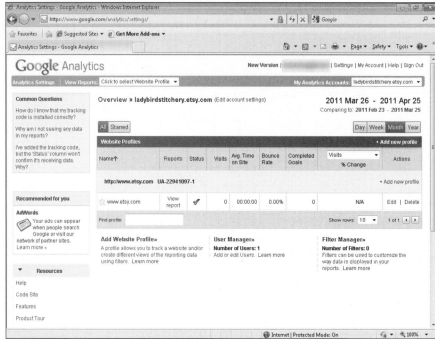

Figure 18-7:
View your
site info.

## *An app a day: Using Etsy apps to run your store*

Need some extra help running your Etsy shop? Try installing some Etsy applications, or *apps,* for short. Apps are available to handle all manner of jobs: minimizing the hassle of international shipping (ATS International Shipping), managing your inventory (RunInventory), handling taxes (TaxTime), renewing listings (Clockbot), and more.

Third-party vendors develop most apps. That's a tech-y way of saying that although you can access the apps from Etsy's Web site, Etsy didn't build them. And *that's* a polite way of saying that if you have a problem with an app, don't bug Etsy about it; bug the company that actually *made* the app.

You can find out what apps are available by browsing the App Gallery. To access it, log in to your Etsy account, click the Your Account link that appears along the top of any Etsy page, and click the Etsy Apps link under Resources on the left side of the page. To view shop-related apps, click the Shop Tools link on the left side of the page (see Figure 18-8).

Click an app's link to find out more about the app. To download it, click the Visit Web Site button that appears on the app's page (see Figure 18-9) and follow the onscreen instructions. (We'd walk you through the process, but the precise steps vary by app.)

Check out the Etsy Blog's "Handmade Code" series; it highlights the newest, coolest Etsy apps. To find it, simply click the Blog link along the top of any Etsy page and search for "Handmade Code."

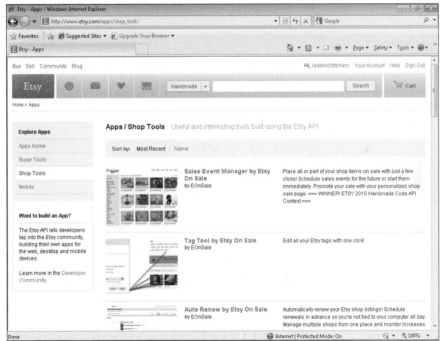

**Figure 18-8:**
The Etsy
App Gallery.

**Figure 18-9:**
Download
an Etsy app.

# Too Legit to Quit: Making Your Business Legit

If you're starting your Etsy shop as a hobby, you probably haven't given much thought to the structure of your Etsy business. It's just you, making stuff and putting it up for sale on Etsy. But if your Etsy shop has grown into a full-time operation — or you want it to — you'll want to consider what business structure is best for you. The structure that you choose affects both your personal liability if your business is sued and the taxes you have to pay.

You have a few main options to consider, as you find out in the following sections:

✔ Sole proprietorship

✔ General partnership

✔ Corporation

✔ Limited liability corporation

So how do you decide what type of business structure is right for you? That's an excellent question — and one that you want to direct to a lawyer or accountant. Also be sure to seek the help of a lawyer or accountant when it comes to actually setting up your company, because the precise steps for doing so differ depending on where you live.

Depending on your location, you may be required to obtain a business license to operate your Etsy shop in an aboveboard manner. You may also need a business license to open a business checking account. For information about business license requirements in your area, visit `www.sba.gov/local resources/index.html`.

## O sole mio: Understanding sole proprietorships

If you're just starting out with your Etsy business, odds are, you're running a sole proprietorship sort of by default. That is, you own your business outright and are solely responsible for all decisions and debts that pertain to it. This type of business is by far the easiest to start, but it's also the riskiest type to run. Why? Because you're held personally accountable if something goes wrong. For example, if someone using your product becomes sick or injured, that person could sue you, personally, placing your assets (and any assets that you hold jointly with a spouse) at risk. You're also personally accountable for any debt that the business assumes.

## Grab your partner, do-sell-do! Getting a handle on partnerships

A general partnership consists of two or more co-owners. Typically, the parties in a general partnership split the profits from the business equally, although that's not always the case. For example, if you and your friend go into business together, but you invest more in startup costs, you may agree to a different split of the profits — say, 60/40. General partnerships are similar to sole proprietorships, in that you and your partner(s) are personally responsible for any debt that the business incurs.

*Note:* In addition to general partnerships, limited partnerships exist. In that case, one partner contributes funds and shares in profits but assumes no role in the workings of the company.

## Collective soul: Checking out Etsy collectives

On Etsy, a shop run by multiple peeps is called a collective. A collective may consist of two or more friends or, say, members of a particular Etsy team.

A collective may be a collaboration, in which you and your partner combine skills to make and list items in your Etsy shop — for example, you spin yarn, and your partner knits it into scarves. Alternatively, you may set up a collective so that you and your partner can make your own pieces but sell them from the same storefront. Yet another type of collective is one in which you act as the artist but a partner handles shop-management tasks, such as listing or shipping items.

If you go the collective route, you need to know a few rules:

- The profile page for the collective's shop must list each person in the collective, each person's role in the shop, and each person's relationship to other members of the collective.

- The person who registers the account is responsible for all account-related activities, including paying the account's Etsy bill. That is, Etsy can't split responsibility for the bill (or other transactions) between partners. This person is also responsible for any action taken under the banner of that account in the Etsy forums and teams.

- If you and your partner have a falling-out about the account, Etsy can't mediate your dispute.

Although running your Etsy shop with a partner can be a great way to grow your business on the double, it can also double your headaches. Be sure to weigh the benefits of running your shop in tandem with someone else (an extra set of hands to build your inventory and an extra set of gray matter to bounce ideas off) with the drawbacks (profit sharing and potential conflicts). Choosing your partner carefully goes a long way toward minimizing problems. Although it may be tempting to leap into a collective with a friend or family member, be aware that doing so may strain the relationship. Be absolutely certain that you and your prospective partner share the same vision and work ethic, and that your relationship is strong enough to endure any bumps along the way.

## Go corporate: Considering corporations

A corporation is a legal entity all its own, separate from its founders (you), managers, and employees, and owned by its shareholders (again, you, along with anyone else you decide to bring into the fold). Operating as a corporation means, among other things, that your personal assets are protected in case the company is sued.

Two types of corporations exist: C-corporations and S-corporations. Although C-corporations provide the most financial protection to shareholders and offer other advantages, many small businesses go the S-corporation route because they're cheaper to start and easier to maintain.

To avoid running afoul of the IRS, speak to your accountant in detail about how to deal with profits if you opt to form a corporation.

## LLC Cool J: Looking at limited liability companies

A popular choice for many business owners, a limited liability company (LLC) is a sort of hybrid between a partnership and a corporation. It's a popular choice for business owners because an LLC not only limits your liability for business debt, but also allows you to choose whether you want to be treated as a partnership or as a corporation, depending on which has the lower tax burden.

# Part V

# Commune System: Exploring the Etsy Community

The 5th Wave                    By Rich Tennant

"The website's down? No problem. I'll stitch it together with some decorative patches and vintage code."

# In this part . . .

If you're looking to sell gorgeous handmade and vintage pieces, Etsy is unarguably the Best. Place. Ever. But Etsy is more than just an amazing online marketplace; it's also a vast and diverse community of super-special people. This part is devoted to covering all the ways you can hook into this amazing Net-based neighborhood.

# Chapter 19

# Community Building: Joining the Etsy Community

*A*nyone who has spent more than 30 seconds on Etsy knows that it's a bang-up place to buy and sell gorgeous handmade and vintage pieces. But Etsy is more than just an amazing online marketplace; it's also a vibrant community of interesting, creative people. On Etsy, connections are made, friendships are formed, love matches are made, and lives are enriched. In this chapter, you discover how you can participate in this lively Etsy community.

## Talk amongst Yourselves: Using Etsy Forums

The *Merriam-Webster Dictionary* defines *forum* as "a public meeting place for open discussion," derived from the marketplaces and public places found in ancient Roman cities across that great empire. Similarly, Etsy's forums serve as meeting places for Etsy members. In essence, Etsy forums are public message boards where members can discuss all manner of topics.

Etsy supports five main forums:

▸ **Announcements:** This forum is reserved for Etsy staff, for posting site-related announcements. Check this forum for news about upcoming site changes.

- ✔ **Site Help:** If you have general questions about how to use Etsy, questions about site features, or queries related to site policy, this forum is for you. Odds are, someone in the Etsy community or on the Etsy staff can — and will — answer your question!

- ✔ **Business Topics:** Are you looking for shop-related advice — for example, help running and marketing your Etsy shop, assistance with PayPal-related issues, info about shipping, or advice on navigating the ups and downs of running a small business? If so, visit the Business Topics forum.

- ✔ **Ideas:** Did you wake up at 3 a.m. with an idea that could revolutionize Etsy? Then post it in the Ideas forum. It acts like a suggestion box of sorts. You can also use this forum to discuss changes to the site or offer site-related constructive criticism.

- ✔ **Bugs:** If you come across some part of the site that's not working as intended, check the Bugs forum to see if anyone else has experienced the same glitch. If not, use the forum to report it.

In the following sections, we explain how to access these Etsy forums, view and respond to threads, and start your own thread.

None of Etsy's forums is meant to serve as a complaint desk. If you need to air a grievance, e-mail it to `community@etsy.com`.

## Forum letter: Accessing Etsy forums

To participate on an Etsy forum, log in to your Etsy account and follow these steps:

1. **Click the Community link along the top of any Etsy page.**

   The Community page opens (see Figure 19-1).

2. **Click the Forums link on the left side of the page.**

   The Forums page opens (see Figure 19-2).

3. **Click the title of the forum that you want to visit.**

   The forum page opens.

## Postess with the mostess: Viewing and responding to posts in a thread

Notice that posts in any Etsy forum are divided into threads (Figure 19-3 shows threads in the Business Topics forum). You can view and respond to any thread you want. Here's how:

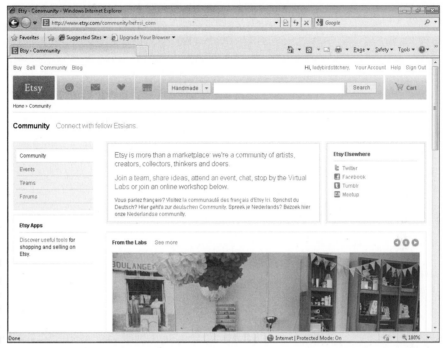

**Figure 19-1:**
The Etsy
Community
page.

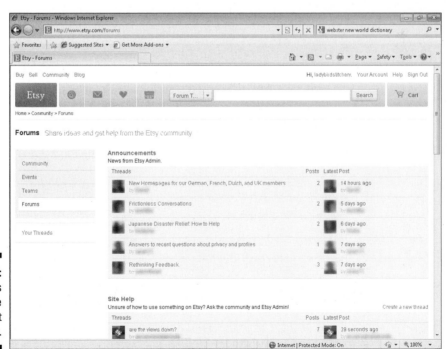

**Figure 19-2:**
Etsy's
forums are
a great
resource.

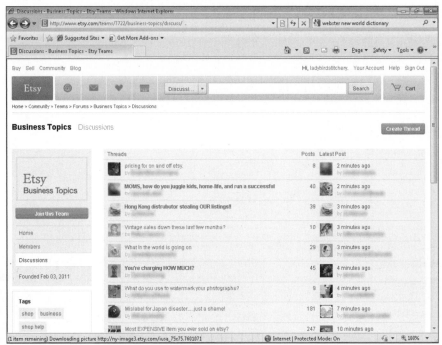

Figure 19-3:
An Etsy
forum.

1. **Click a thread that interests you.**

   A page opens, showing the post that started the thread, along with any responses to that post (see Figure 19-4).

2. **To respond to a post, either click the Post a Reply button at the top of the page or scroll down to the bottom of the page.**

   The Post a Reply box appears (see Figure 19-5).

3. **Type your reply and then click Post a Reply.**

   Your post appears at the end of the list of replies.

To view threads in which you've posted a reply, click the Your Threads link on the left side of any forum screen, click the Threads You've Posted In tab, and click the thread that you want to view (see Figure 19-6).

If you find a thread that's particularly interesting, you can mark it. That way, you can easily keep track of new posts in that thread. To mark a thread, open the thread and click the Mark button (refer to Figure 19-4). To view threads that you've marked, click the Your Threads link on the left side of any forum screen, click the Marked Threads tab, and click the thread that you want to view.

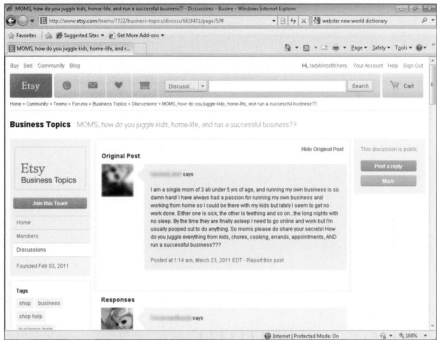

**Figure 19-4:**
An Etsy
thread.

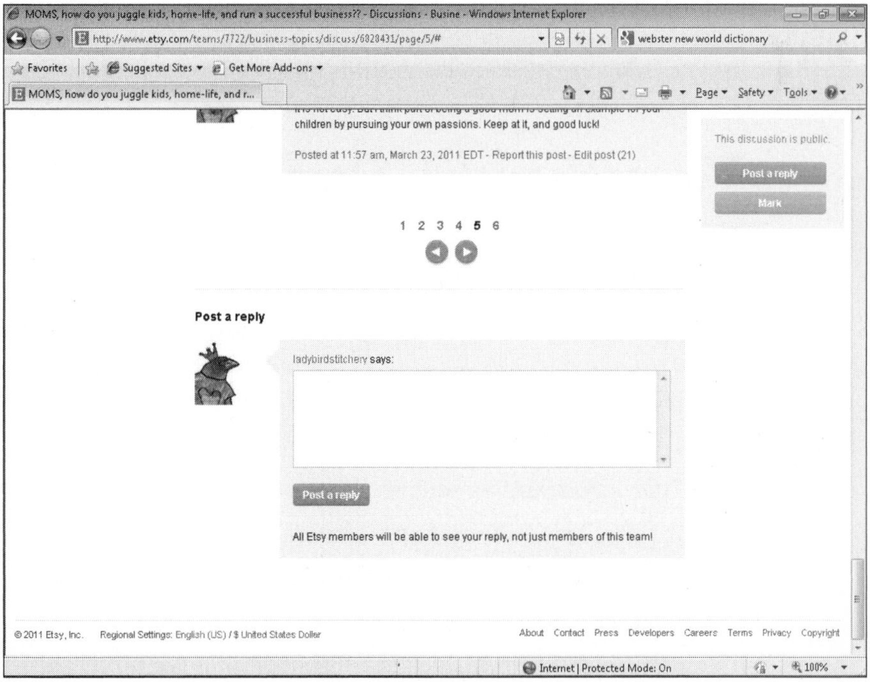

**Figure 19-5:**
Reply to a
post.

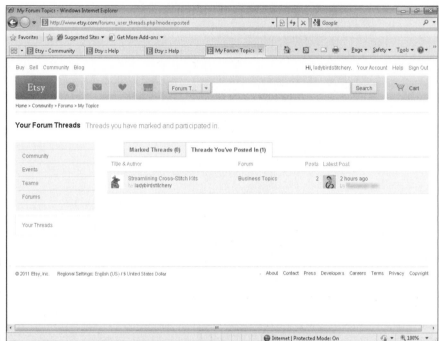

**Figure 19-6:**
View your
forum
threads.

Before you reply to a thread in an Etsy forum or start a new thread of your own (see the next section), be sure that your post doesn't violate Etsy etiquette (which we discuss later in this chapter).

## Thread Zeppelin: Starting a new thread

In addition to responding to posts in threads that others have started, you can start your own new thread. Here's the drill:

1. **Click the title of the forum in which you want to create a new thread.**

2. **Click the Create Thread button in the upper-right corner of the forum page.**

   The Create a New Thread page opens (see Figure 19-7).

3. **Type a descriptive, relevant title for your thread in the Title field.**

   For best results, type your whole question into the Title field (if it fits).

4. **Type your post in the Post field.**

5. **Click the Create Topic button.**

   Etsy creates a new thread, with your post at the top.

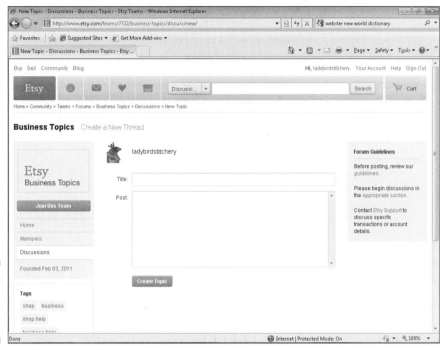

Figure 19-7:
Create a
new thread
in a forum.

When you start a new thread, be sure to start it in the correct forum. For example, don't start a thread asking for advice about your Etsy shop in, say, the Site Help forum. That discussion belongs in the Business Topics forum. Be aware that if you do start a thread in the wrong forum, Etsy may move it to the appropriate forum without notice.

Before you start a new thread, try searching for existing threads that cover your topic of interest. To do so, open the main Forums page, type a relevant keyword or phrase in the Search field in the header bar, and click the Search button. Etsy searches existing forum threads for the keyword or phrase that you entered. Etsy searches forum threads for the keyword that you entered and displays a list of matches.

# Go Team! Exploring Etsy Teams

As you find out earlier in this chapter, Etsy's forums are splendid — if your area of interest is announcements, site help, business topics, ideas, or bugs. But what if you're itching to explore some other topic? Say, product photography, quilting, Bauhaus style, or even a charitable cause? Or maybe you just want to connect with other Etsy members in your geographic area. In that case, Etsy's teams are for you.

Etsy teams act a lot like Etsy forums. People start discussion threads, and others add their two cents. The difference? With teams, you must join to participate. Although non–team members may be able to view posts in a team — when team members start new threads, they specify whether those threads are public (visible to anyone on Etsy) or private (visible to team members only) — they can't respond to those posts or start new threads of their own.

In addition, each Etsy team has its own captain (usually the person who started the team), who may appoint other members as "leaders." The team captain and team leaders are responsible for administering the team — that is, approving membership applications (some teams are open to any and all Etsy members; others require that you apply), moderating the team's discussion forum, and so on.

In the following sections, we show you how to search for a team, join a team, and start your own team.

Loads of great teams are out there, but one of our favorites is SASsy Critiques (www.etsy.com/teams/7702/sassy-critiques). Members can submit their Etsy shops to this team for critiques by Etsy's Sellers Assisting Sellers group, which mentors less experienced Etsy sellers. If you aim to spruce up your Etsy shop and boost sales, slide into your thick-skin suit and check out this team.

## Finders, keepers: Searching for an Etsy team

Literally thousands of Etsy teams exist, meaning that you can surely find one for you. To find a team, log in to your Etsy account and follow these steps:

1. **Click the Community link along the top of any Etsy page.**

   The Community page opens (refer to Figure 19-1).

2. **Click the Teams link on the left side of the page.**

   The Teams page opens (see Figure 19-8).

3. **Type a keyword in the Search box at the top of the page and click the Search button.**

   Etsy searches teams for the keyword that you entered and displays a list of matches (see Figure 19-9). You can sort your matches by Relevancy, Most Recent, and Least Recent by clicking the appropriate link at the top of the list.

4. **Click a team in the list of matches to learn more about it.**

   The team's page opens (see Figure 19-10). The team's page includes information about the team and who's eligible to join (see Figure 19-10a); a Discussions area, which lists recent threads (click the Discussions link to view more); and a sampling of team members (see Figure 19-10b).

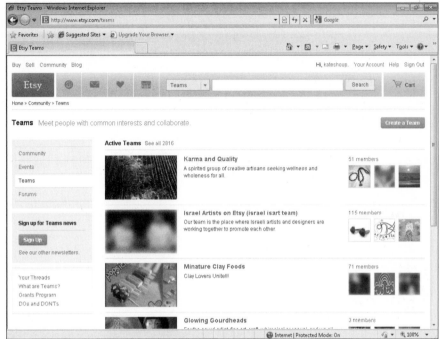

**Figure 19-8:**
The Etsy
Teams
page.

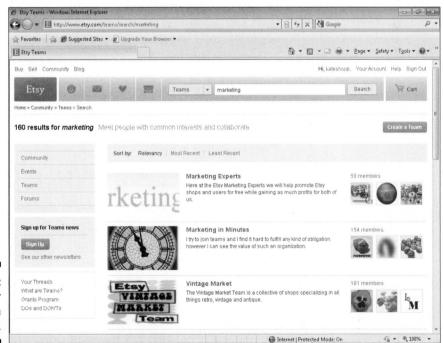

**Figure 19-9:**
View your
search
results.

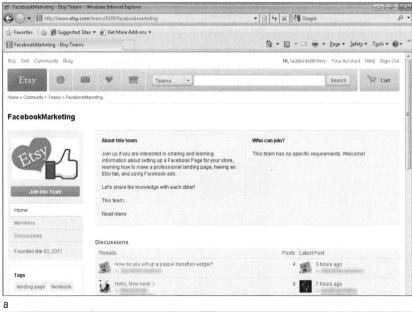

a

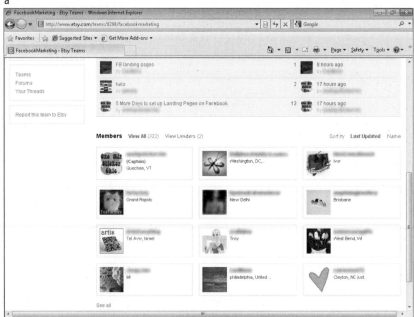

**Figure 19-10:**
An Etsy
team page.

b

## Sign me up! Joining an Etsy team

As we mention earlier in this chapter, some teams are open to any and all Etsy members. Others are moderated, meaning that they limit their membership based on certain criteria.

To join a team that's open to all, simply click the Join This Team button that appears in the top-left corner of the team's page (refer to Figure 19-10a). Then, when prompted, click Join This Team again. A welcome message appears at the top of the team page, and your avatar appears in the list of team members. The team that you joined also appears at the top of your main Teams page (see Figure 19-11).

**Figure 19-11:** When you join a team, it appears at the top of your Etsy Teams page.

Joining a team that restricts membership is a bit more involved. Instead of simply clicking a button, you must apply for membership, which sometimes means jumping through a few hoops. To join a moderated team, follow these steps:

1. **Click the Apply to Team button in the top-left corner of the team's page (see Figure 19-12).**

2. **An Apply to Team window appears (see Figure 19-13); read the information in the dialog box and answer any questions in the field at the bottom.**

**Figure 19-12:**
Click the
Apply
to Team
button.

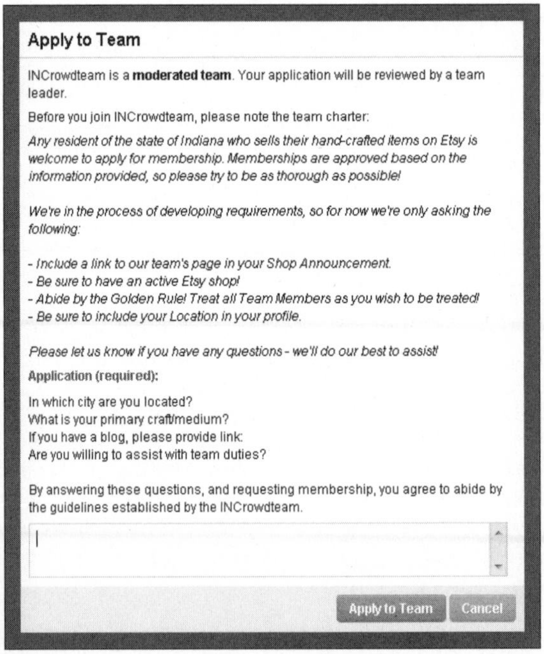

**Figure 19-13:**
The Apply
to Team
dialog box.

**3. Click the Apply to Team button to apply.**

Assuming that you meet the membership criteria, as determined by the team captain and laid out in the team charter, you'll likely be accepted — although the team leadership may deny membership at its discretion. Either way, after the team makes a decision, it'll notify you via e-mail.

When you become a member of a team, you can view and respond to posts in existing threads and create new threads, as described earlier in this chapter.

## Start me up: Starting your own Etsy team

If you don't find a team that meets your needs, you can start one of your own. For example, you may want to start a team for other Etsy members who share your passion for your medium, who live in your geographic area, who are devoted to a particular style of design, who share similar goals with their Etsy shops, or what have you. Note that when you create a team, you automatically become its captain, so administrative duties fall to you (unless you delegate them to other members).

To create a team, click the Create a Team button in the top-left corner of the main Etsy Teams page (refer to Figure 19-8). Etsy prompts you to enter the team details:

- ✔ The name and team type (see Figure 19-14a)
- ✔ A short description and (optionally) a long description
- ✔ Rules about team access and (optionally) who can join (see Figure 19-14b)
- ✔ Application questions (if needed)
- ✔ The team's logo (see Figure 19-14c)
- ✔ Tags to describe your shop (check out the sidebar "Tag, you're it! Tagging your Etsy team" for details on tags)
- ✔ Related links (for example, you may include a link to your own personal Web site or to some other relevant page online)

After you fill in the requested information, click Create Team.

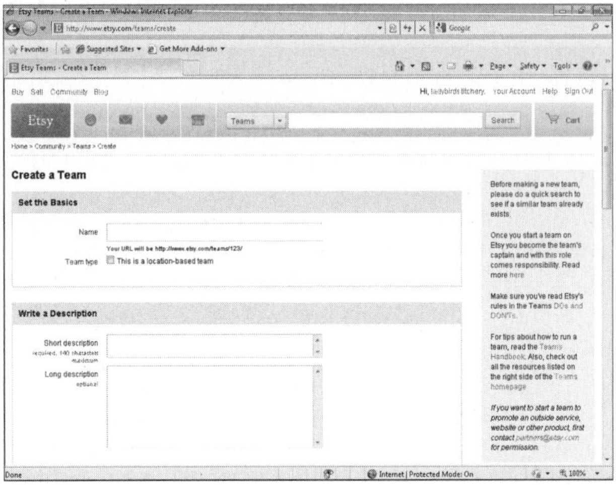


a

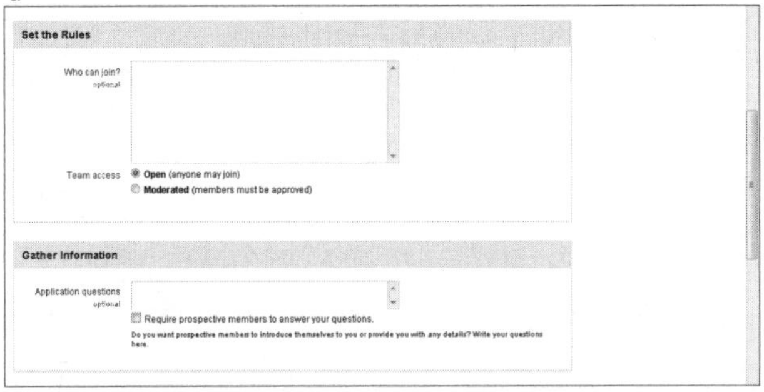


b

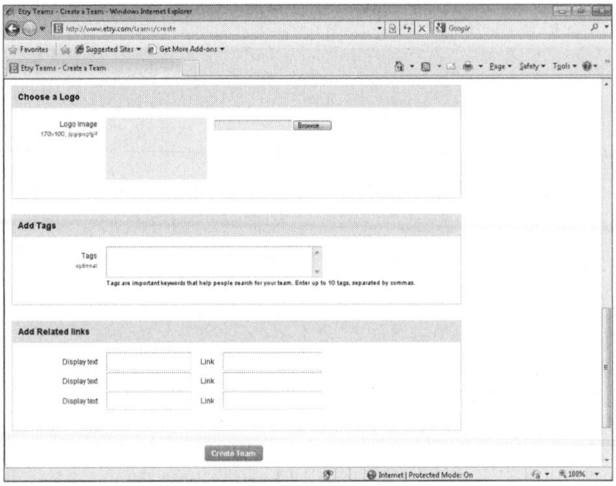


c

**Figure 19-14:** Create a new team.

---

### Tag, you're it! Tagging your Etsy team

When you create your team, you're prompted to enter tags that describe it — for example, where your team is based, the focus of your team, and so on. These tags act a lot like the tags that you add to your item listings (see Chapter 12); when someone searching for a team enters keywords that match your tags, your shop appears among the matches.

Note that the tags you enter to describe your Etsy team are different from what Etsy calls

"team tags." A team tag is a tag that team members use to tag their item listings, to identify themselves and their listing as being affiliated with a particular Etsy team. These tags must be unique terms — say, your team's name — and must contain the word *team* in them. When you create a team, you can establish a team tag for it, noting it in the team's description.

---

# Chatty Cathy: Using Etsy Chat Rooms

In addition to offering forums and teams to enable members to interact, Etsy hosts chat rooms — interactive spaces where you can *parlez* with other Etsy members. For example, you may join a chat organized by the captain of your favorite Etsy team, or one geared toward a specific Etsy-related topic.

In addition to joining existing chat rooms, you can create your own. For instance, if you're part of an Etsy collective (see Chapter 18), you may launch a chat with other members to discuss shop matters. Or if a buyer contacted you about creating a custom piece, you may want to launch a chat with that buyer to hammer out transaction-related details. And of course, you can also launch Etsy chats for the simple purpose of hangin' with your Etsy homies.

To access other Etsy chatters, open the main Etsy Community page (refer to Figure 19-1); then click the Chat link in the top-center area of the page. The Chat Rooms page opens, listing currently active chat rooms and giving you the option to create a new chat room of your own (see Figure 19-15). We discuss both of these choices and explain how to navigate any chat room in the following sections.

## Party crasher: Joining an existing chat room

To join an existing chat room, in the Chat Rooms page, click the Join button next to the entry for the chat room that you want to join (refer to Figure 19-15). If the chat is password protected, you'll see a field with a lock icon to the left of the Join button; you then need to enter the password before clicking the Join button to join the chat (see the next section for more about password protection). The chat room opens (see Figure 19-16).

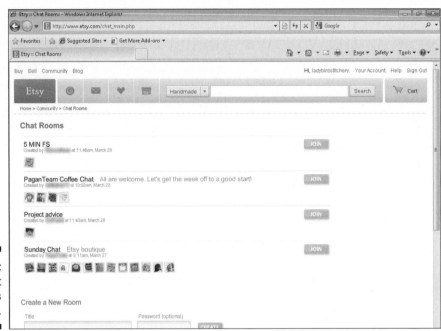

Figure 19-15:
The Chat
Rooms
page.

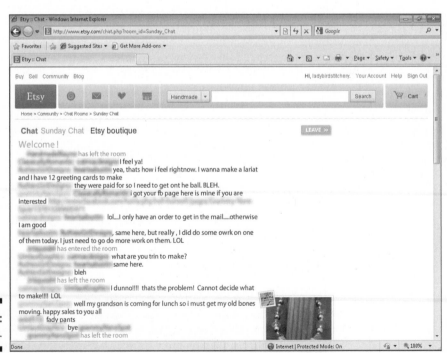

Figure 19-16:
Join a chat.

# Conversation starter: Creating a new chat room

Creating a new chat room is almost as easy as joining an existing one:

1. **Simply type a name for the chat room in the Title field, under Create a New Room in the Chat Rooms page (refer to Figure 19-15).**

2. **You have the option of password-protecting your chat room to keep it private; to password-protect the chat, type a password in the Password field.**

   If you password-protect the chat, you can send the password to other Etsy members via a convo.

3. **Finally, click Create to create the room.**

Other Etsy members can then join your chat room as they would any other.

*Note:* You can't close a chat room that you've opened, but it will disappear from the list of available chat rooms when it has been inactive for a prescribed period of time.

# Use your words: Navigating a chat

Every Etsy chat room, whether it's one that already exists or one that you created, has the same basic layout (see Figure 19-17):

- ✔ On the left side of the screen, you see lines of text scrolling upward, with each line preceded by the user name of the person who typed it. These lines of text comprise the conversation occurring in the chat room.

- ✔ To add your own two cents to the conversation, type in the Chat field below the scrolling lines of text; press Enter or Return or click Send to add them to the stream.

- ✔ On the right side of the screen, you may see a scrolling series of pictures. These are images from item listings shared by chat participants. You can click a photo to view more about the listing, including links to the listing itself. Each larger picture on the right side of the screen is accompanied by a smaller image. This smaller image is the avatar of the person who shared the item listing. If you click this smaller image, you're directed to that person's Etsy shop.

- ✔ To share your own listing photos, copy the listing's ID or URL and paste it in the field below the scrolling photos; press Enter or Return or click Send to add the photo to the stream. Note that you aren't limited to sharing your own listing photos; you can share any Etsy listing that you want in this manner.

**TIP**

Don't just barrage a chat room with images from your own listings; make it a point to share listings from other Etsy shops as well.

✔ Below the conversation stream and item listings, you'll notice several thumbnail-size images. These are the avatars of other Etsy members currently in the chat room. When you hover your mouse pointer over an avatar, Etsy displays three links: Shop, Profile, and /Msg. Click the Shop link to view the Etsy member's shop, click the Profile link to visit the user's profile, and click the /Msg link to send a private message.

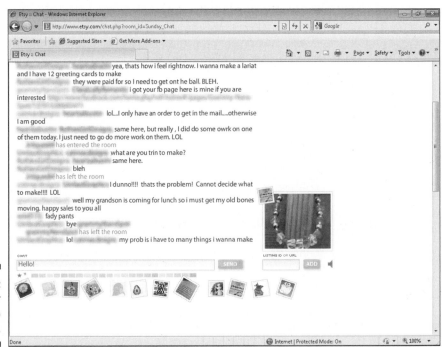

**Figure 19-17:** Adding your two cents to a chat.

To exit a chat room, simply navigate to a different Etsy page or click the Back button on your Web browser.

# Virtual Reality: Exploring Etsy's Virtual Labs

Etsy regularly hosts special events called Virtual Labs — special chat rooms in which Etsy staffers and members can run seminars, workshops, shop critiques, and other educational gatherings.

To view upcoming events and join Virtual Labs, open the main Etsy Community page (refer to Figure 19-1); then click the Virtual Labs link in the top-center area of the page. The Virtual Labs page opens. On this page, called the Virtual Labs lobby, you can view upcoming Virtual Labs and enter ones that are currently running (see Figure 19-18).

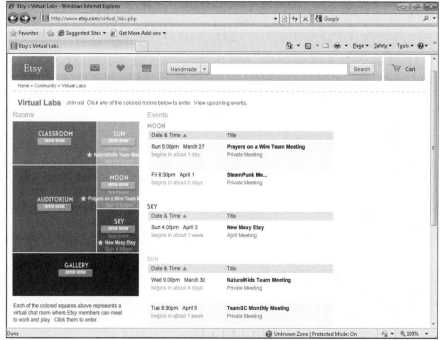

**Figure 19-18:**
The Virtual Labs lobby.

To enter a Virtual Lab, click its Enter Room button. When you do, you'll see your avatar in a screen that mimics a classroom of sorts, with a circle of "seats" (see Figure 19-19). To move an avatar to a seat, click the seat.

The Gallery room is a bit different from the others. In this room, you'll see loads of item listings, which you can peruse.

A Virtual Lab acts a lot like a chat room (which we describe earlier in this chapter). For example, as in a chat room, you can view the conversation occurring in the Virtual Lab along the left side of the screen, and you can contribute to the conversation by typing your comment in the Chat field and pressing Enter or Return or clicking Send. You can also share listing items with other Virtual Lab participants, as you can in a chat room; to do so, click the Items tab next to the Chat tab to display a special field where you can paste the listing's URL or its ID.

Virtual Labs offer you a few more tools than a chat room, though — namely, buttons below the Chat field that you can click to make your avatar spin, bounce, beat, or glow. In addition to these tools is a button that you can click to indicate that you're raising your hand (for example, to ask a question) or waving, as well as one that you can click to let other participants know that you'll be right back.

To exit a Virtual Lab, click the Back button that appears in the room's upper-right corner or simply navigate to another Etsy page.

# Event Horizon: Staying Apprised of Etsy Events

Etsy does more than host virtual gatherings; it also organizes real-world events, such as regular Craft Nights at its Brooklyn-based offices, as well as craft- and business-related summits at various locations worldwide. To stay apprised of Etsy events, click the Events link on the Community page; the Events page opens (see Figure 19-20). To see information about an event listed on the Events page, simply click it.

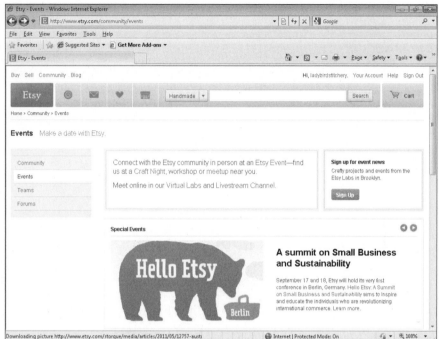

**Figure 19-20:**
View Etsy
events.

# Miss Manners: Respecting Community Etiquette

When it comes to interacting with the Etsy community, whether in the forums, within a team, in the Virtual Labs, or during a chat session, some important ground rules apply. Etsy's Dos and Don'ts spell out these rules in detail (see www.etsy.com/policy/dosdonts#thecommunity). If you violate any of these rules, Etsy may take action, ranging from removing your post or closing your thread to booting you from the site entirely.

Chief among these rules is this: For Pete's sake, *be nice.* It should go without saying that you need to treat all Etsy members with respect, but we're saying it anyway, just so there's no confusion. Also, never knowingly harass, insult, abuse, or otherwise dog another site user. Additionally, don't "call out" an Etsy member, shop, or item — that is, discuss her or it in a negative manner. (Duh.)

Beyond that, keep a few other points in mind as you mingle in the Etsy community (for a complete list, check out the aforementioned Dos and Don'ts page):

✔ **Don't post angry.** Yes, discussions in Etsy's community spaces sometimes get tetchy. After all, the Etsy community consists of millions of passionate, creative types. But if you find yourself getting your dander up, step away from the keyboard. In the history of the world, no good ever came from firing off a message in anger! Besides, if you do, you'll likely violate the aforementioned "Be nice" rule.

✔ **Stay on topic.** Sure, tangents happen. But if the tangent intensifies to such a degree that it threatens to smother the main discussion, others interested in the "real" topic can't find the info they need. If you find yourself part of a discussion that's gone off the rails, consider starting a new thread to handle that tangential issue.

✔ **Protect your privacy.** Don't share private information of any type, such as your (or someone else's) e-mail address, phone number, address, or what have you, on Etsy's public spaces. Also, put the kibosh on public discussions about specific transactions or feedback that you've received. For help on those issues, contact Etsy support (`support@etsy.com`).

✔ **Don't solicit.** Even if you're raising money for the best, most important charity on the planet, Etsy members are prohibited from trolling for donations or engaging in other types of fund-raising on the Etsy forums. Similarly, spamming Etsy forums — that is, posting unsolicited advertisements — is prohibited.

# Chapter 20

# OMG, Did You Hear? Keeping Up with Etsy News

*A*s big and active as Etsy is, staying abreast of all its goings-on can be as challenging as solving a Rubik's Cube during a blackout. Fortunately, Etsy maintains several news sources to help members stay on top of Etsy-related info, including a blog, multiple e-mail newsletters, and various social media pages. In this chapter, you discover all the ways you can keep up with Etsy news.

## All the News That's Fit to Print: Exploring the Etsy Blog

Maybe you're looking for tips to improve your Etsy shop. Or perhaps you want to explore a new craft medium. Or maybe you want a glimpse into the lives of other Etsy sellers. In any case, The Etsy Blog, formerly called The Storque, is for you. The Etsy Blog acts like a community newspaper of sorts, serving up loads of fresh content daily. To access The Etsy Blog, shown in Figure 20-1, simply click the Blog link that appears in the upper-left corner of any Etsy page. (You can also type www.etsy.com/storque.)

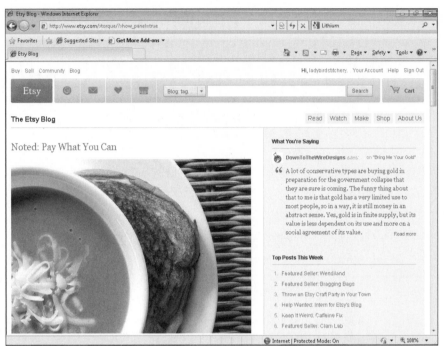

**Figure 20-1:**
The Etsy
Blog.

Etsy has organized The Etsy Blog into several handy sections to help you find the info you need. (Simply click a section's link along the top of the main Etsy Blog page to access that section.) These sections include the following:

- **The Etsy Blog:** This section is the main page for The Etsy Blog. Here you'll find articles from each section of the blog.

- **Read:** Click this link for quick access to written pieces on The Etsy Blog.

- **Watch:** The Etsy Blog doesn't just feature the written word. It also boasts video content, including visual how-tos, profiles of Etsy sellers, and more. To access this content, click the Watch link.

- **Make:** Looking to master a new crafty skill? Check out The Etsy Blog's Make section, with links to loads of how-to articles and videos.

- **Shop:** This section of The Etsy Blog is where you can track down Etsy's Featured Sellers, chosen by Etsy administrators (see Chapter 3). You can also read other regular segments, such as "Get the Look Decor" (in which Etsy spotlights a charming home and then flags listings of the same style), "Keep It Weird" (which highlights Etsy oddities), "Quit Your Day Job" (a Q&A-style segment featuring successful Etsy sellers), and more.

✔ **About Us:** Want to meet the magicians behind the curtain? Check out the About section of The Etsy Blog. In addition to spelling out The Etsy Blog's mission statement, the About section reveals the Etsy staffers behind the blog's content and includes an area where you can pitch your own story ideas.

To read an article or view a video in any section of The Etsy Blog, simply click the article title. Etsy opens the article in its own page, as shown in Figure 20-2.

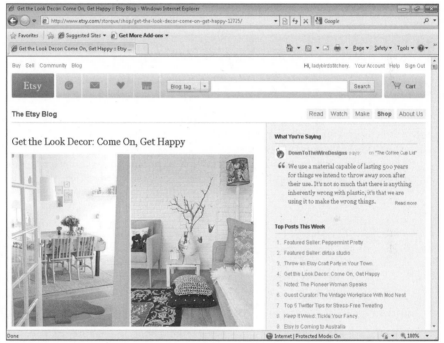

**Figure 20-2:**
Read an article on The Etsy Blog.

To search for an article in The Etsy Blog, follow these easy steps:

1. **Type your keyword in the Search box in the header bar.**

2. **Click the down arrow to the left of the Search box and choose Blog: Tags Only; Blog: Tags, Titles; Blog: Tags, Titles, Body; or Blog: Authors.**

3. **Click the Search button.**

   Etsy displays a list of blog articles containing the keyword you typed; click an article to view it.

In addition to reading the articles on The Etsy Blog, make it a point to peruse the comments left by Etsy members. These comments are often as enlightening as the article itself. If you've got something to add, don't hesitate to weigh in; just scroll to the bottom of the comments, type your two cents in the Add Your Comment box, and click the Add Your Comment button.

If you have an idea for an article for The Etsy Blog, why not pitch it? Although The Etsy Blog is written primarily by various Etsy staffers, members of the Etsy community sometimes contribute. To pitch your idea, click the About Us link on The Etsy Blog to open the About Us page. Type your e-mail address in the field provided; then type your story idea, optionally including an image to pique Etsy's interest. Finally, click the Submit button. If Etsy likes your idea, it'll let you know!

# Mail Bonding: Signing Up for Etsy E-mail Newsletters

If you've ever felt overwhelmed by the sheer number of fantastic items on Etsy, or you wished you could employ a personal shopper to sift through them for you, or you just feel adrift on the Etsy sea, you'll want to sign up for Etsy e-mail newsletters. When you do, you'll receive handy messages featuring all manner of kicky items, right in your e-mail inbox (see Figure 20-3). Click any entry in an Etsy e-mail to launch Etsy and view the associated item listing.

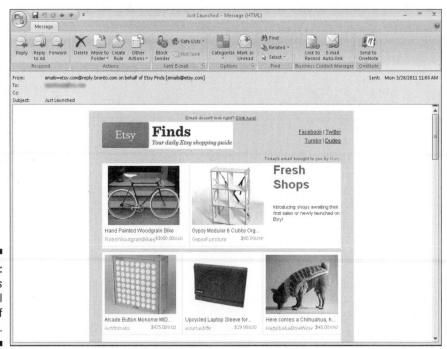

**Figure 20-3:**
Etsy e-mails feature all kinds of kicky items.

In the following sections, we describe the kinds of e-mail newsletters that are available and explain how to sign up to receive them.

## Red-letter day: Sifting through different types of e-mail newsletters

You can choose to subscribe to any or all of the following Etsy e-mail newsletters:

- ✔ **Etsy Dudes:** Yes, it's true, Etsy members are overwhelmingly female. But when you're talking about a community as large as Etsy, you'll still find thousands of guys around. If you have a Y chromosome (or buy presents for someone who does), you'll love this weekly e-mail newsletter geared toward dudes.

- ✔ **Etsy Fashion:** If fashion's your bag, you'll enjoy tracking fashion trends on Etsy with this biweekly e-mail newsletter.

- ✔ **Etsy Finds:** This daily e-mail is chock full of clever goodies from a variety of Etsy sellers.

- ✔ **Etsy Labs:** Do you live in or near Brooklyn, N.Y., where Etsy's offices are located? If so, you'll want to sign up for the weekly Etsy Labs e-mail newsletter, which includes a schedule of events at Etsy Labs.

  A community workspace of sorts, Etsy Labs play host to free weekly Craft Nights, as well as other handmade-centric events. To make sure that out-of-towners aren't left out, Etsy broadcasts these events in the Virtual Labs, which we discuss in Chapter 19.

- ✔ **Etsy News:** For a monthly rundown of administrative announcements, site news (such as updates), and upcoming events, sign up for the Etsy News e-mail.

- ✔ **Etsy Success:** For tips from top sellers, subscribe to the Etsy Success e-mail, sent biweekly.

- ✔ **Etsy Teams:** The Etsy Teams e-mail, sent once a week, broadcasts team-related news (see Chapter 19 for more about teams).

- ✔ **Etsy Weddings:** Sure, all weddings are special. But let's face it, weddings featuring handmade or vintage items are special-er. If you're in the midst of planning your own nuptials or you craft items that are made just for brides, grooms, or other members of the bridal party, this weekly e-mail newsletter is for you.

In addition to the e-mail newsletters listed here, Etsy sends newsletters in French, German, and Dutch, as well as ones for the U.K. crafting community.

# Subscription prescription: Subscribing to e-mail newsletters

To sign up for Etsy e-mail newsletters, log in to your Etsy account and follow these steps:

1. **On any Etsy Blog page, scroll down until you see the Etsy Finds field, and then click the See Our Other Newsletters link.**

   The Etsy E-mails page opens (see Figure 20-4).

2. **Click the check box next to each newsletter to which you want to subscribe.**

3. **Click the Save button.**

   Etsy signs you up to receive the newsletters you selected.

If you decide that you no longer want to receive a newsletter, simply click the blue Unsubscribe link that appears along the bottom of any Etsy newsletter.

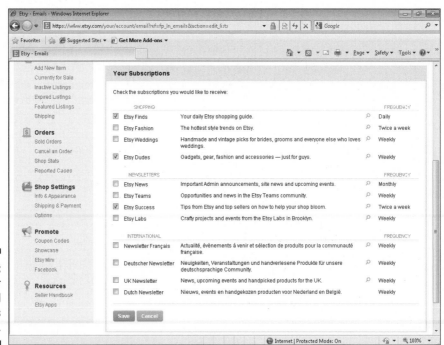

**Figure 20-4:**
Sign up for Etsy e-mail newsletters here.

# Social Skills: Staying in Touch Using Social Media

If you're like more than 500 million other people, you maintain a Facebook account. Not surprisingly, Etsy does, too! If you're on Facebook — or you use Twitter or enjoy YouTube — you can stay on top of Etsy's goings-on even when you're not on Etsy:

- ✔ **Facebook:** Etsy's Facebook page provides links to The Etsy Blog, inspirational quotes, kickin' music, thought-provoking videos, and more. To ensure that Etsy's Facebook posts find their way to your own Facebook news feed, simply click the Like button on Etsy's Facebook page (`www.facebook.com/Etsy`).

- ✔ **Twitter:** Citizens of the Twitterverse can follow Etsy, ensuring that timely Etsy-related tweets alight in their Twitter timeline. To follow Etsy, visit its Twitter page at `www.twitter.com/Etsy`; then click the Follow button.

- ✔ **YouTube:** In addition to sharing videos on its own Videos page, Etsy posts them on its own YouTube channel. To subscribe to this channel, thereby receiving e-mail notifications anytime Etsy posts a new video, simply click the Subscribe button on the Etsy YouTube channel page, found at `www.youtube.com/etsy`.

If you maintain a blog or other Web site, feel free to embed Etsy videos found on its YouTube channels in your own content. Just be sure to give credit where credit is due, and link back to the original source!

# Chapter 21

# A Love-Love Relationship: Showing Your Love for Other Etsy Sellers

. . . . . . . . . . . . . . . . . . . . . . . . . . . . . . . . . . . . . . . . . . . . .

### In This Chapter

▶ Flagging your favorite items and shops

▶ Building your Etsy Circle

▶ Creating a Treasury

. . . . . . . . . . . . . . . . . . . . . . . . . . . . . . . . . . . . . . . . . . . . .

*H*ow do we love Etsy? In lots of different ways, actually. One way you can love Etsy is to heart the items and stores you adore — that is, mark them as favorites. Another is to add an Etsy seller to your Circle so that you stay apprised of their goings-on. Yet another is to create a Treasury to showcase your favorite goodies. This chapter is devoted to all the ways you can love — and be loved on — Etsy.

## Heart and Sold: Hearting on Etsy

If you've spent any time at all on Etsy, you've no doubt run across a pajillion pieces and shops that you positively adore. Fortunately, Etsy enables you to keep track of all these gorgeous goodies by "hearting" them. When you heart an item or shop on Etsy, you essentially flag it as a favorite. You can view all these hearted must-haves from one easy-to-access page. In addition, others who visit your Etsy profile can see what items and shops you've hearted.

Why heart an item? Lots of reasons. For example:

✔ You may heart an item that you're dying to buy but that will have to wait until payday.

✔ Or you may heart your favorite supplier's shop so that the next time you need to stock up, you'll be able to find it more easily.

✔ Or you may heart an item or shop simply to let another Etsy seller know that you appreciate her work.

In the following sections, we explain how to heart items and shops and view them in a handy list. We also note how to keep your hearted items and shops private.

## A piece of my heart: Hearting items and shops

Hearting an item is simple. First, make sure you're signed in to your Etsy account (see Chapter 2 for details). Then click the Add Item to Favorites link on the item's listing page; it's on the right side (see Figure 21-1). Etsy adds the item to your list of favorites and adds a "Favorite" label to the right of the item's Add to Cart button. The hearted item also appears in your Etsy Activity Feed (more on that later in this chapter).

As an aside, you can also click the Like button in an item listing to post it on Facebook, or click the Tweet button to share it on Twitter.

Hearting an Etsy shop is just as easy: Simply click the Add to Favorites link along the left side of the shop's main page, or click Add Shop to Favorites on the right side of any of the shop's listing pages.

## Turn on your heart light: Viewing hearted items and shops

To view items and shops that you've hearted, click the Favorites button (the one with a heart on it, of course!) in the header bar that appears along the top of every Etsy page. The Your Favorites page opens, with hearted items displayed by default, as shown in Figure 21-2. (If hearted items don't show up, click the Items tab to reveal them.) To view shops you've hearted, click the Shops tab.

To remove a hearted item or shop from your list, place your mouse pointer over the item or shop on your Favorites page and click the X that appears.

Over time, you may collect so many favorites that finding them in your list is hard. To help you, Etsy includes a handy-dandy Search field in the Items tab (refer to Figure 21-2). Simply type a relevant keyword in the tab, click the Search button, and voilà! Etsy displays items you've hearted that match your criteria.

**Figure 21-1:**
Heart an
item on Etsy
to mark it as
a favorite.

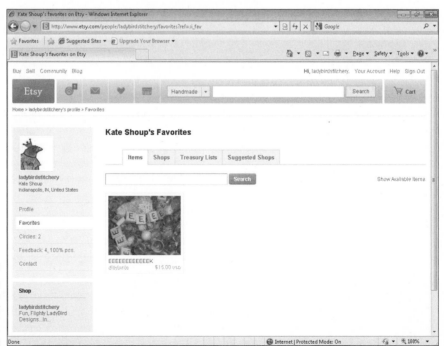

**Figure 21-2:**
Your
hearted
items.

As you heart items and shops, Etsy suggests other shops you may like, based on your selections. The more items and shops you heart, the better these suggestions are likely to be. To view these shops, which Etsy updates daily, click the Suggested Shops tab on the Favorites page (refer to Figure 21-2).

## *A private matter: Being a secret admirer*

Normally, when you heart an item or shop, it's visible to anyone who clicks the Favorites link in your Etsy profile. Similarly, if someone visits an Etsy shop or views an item listing, she can see which Etsy members have hearted that shop or item by clicking the See Who Favorites This Shop link or the See Who Favorites This Item link, respectively. (You can see these links in Figure 21-1.)

If you prefer to keep your favorites private — maybe you're a secret agent or a ninja, or perhaps you're just shy — you can easily do so. Here's how to become a secret admirer (after you log in to your Etsy account):

1. **Click the Your Account link that appears along the top of any Etsy page.**

   The Your Account page opens.

2. **Click the Settings link on the left side of the Your Account page.**

3. **Click the Privacy tab (see Figure 21-3).**

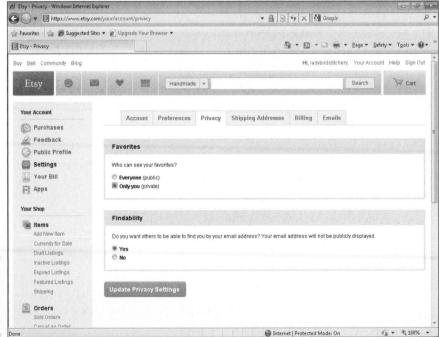

**Figure 21-3:** Keep your favorites to yourself.

4. **Click the Only You option button under Favorites.**

5. **Click the Update Privacy Settings button.**

   Etsy updates your settings.

# Circle du Soleil: Creating an Etsy Circle

Yes, Etsy's *raison d'être* is to serve as a marketplace for artisans. But as you find out in Chapters 19 and 20, Etsy also supports a vast and vibrant community of fascinating individuals. To help you build your own place in this larger Etsy community and generally share the love, Etsy has developed a feature called Circles. Circles enable you to keep track of other Etsy members — say, family members on the site, friends who run their own Etsy shops, or other Etsy members you admire. When you add someone to your Etsy Circle, you can stay on top of that person's activity on Etsy; for example, if a person in your Etsy Circle lists a new item or posts a Treasury, you'll know. (If you're curious, we discuss Treasuries later in this chapter.) You'll also know if someone in your Circle hearts an Etsy store or item or adds someone else to her own Circle. We explain everything you need to know about Circles in the following sections.

## Circle of life: Adding someone to your Etsy Circle

Adding someone to your Etsy Circle is a cinch. To do so, first make sure that you're signed in to your Etsy account. Then open the person's profile page by clicking the Profile link that appears in the Shop Owner section of her Etsy shop or by clicking her user name on any item listing page. Next, click the Add to Circle button on the left side of the person's profile page, as shown in Figure 21-4. When you add someone to your Circle, Etsy notifies that person via e-mail, by default.

A great way to grow your Etsy Circle is to use Etsy's Find Your Friends feature. With Find Your Friends, you can search your Gmail, Yahoo! Mail, or AOL Mail accounts to locate people in your address book who are also on Etsy. To use Find Your Friends, follow these steps:

1. **Click the Activity button in the header bar (the one next to the Etsy button) to view your Activity Feed (more on that later in this chapter).**

2. **Click the Find Your Friends button in the upper-right corner of the screen.**

3. **Click the appropriate tab (Gmail, Yahoo! Mail, or AOL Mail), click Find Friends on *X* (where *X* is Gmail, Yahoo! Mail, or AOL Mail), and follow the onscreen prompts.**

Of course, if you don't use any of these services, you can always use Etsy's Search feature to search for your friends by name.

**Figure 21-4:**
Add some-
one to your
Etsy Circle.

## Circle up: Viewing your Etsy Circle

To view your Etsy Circle, make sure that you're logged in to your account. Then follow these steps:

1. **Open your Etsy profile page by clicking your user name in the upper-right corner of any Etsy screen.**

2. **Click the Circle link on the left side of the screen to open your Circle page.**

3. **Click the Your Circle tab (see Figure 21-5).**

To remove someone from your Etsy Circle, click her entry in the Your Circle tab to open her profile page. Next, hover your mouse pointer over the In Your Circle notification and click the blue X that appears. Etsy prompts you to confirm the removal; click the Yes button.

Figure 21-5:
View your
Etsy Circle.

Interested in finding out who has added you to her Circle? You're in luck. By default, Etsy notifies you via e-mail anytime someone adds you to her Circle. (If you don't want to be notified, click the Your Account link that appears along the top of every Etsy page, click the Settings link on the left side of the page, click the E-mails tab, click the Edit link in the General Notifications area, uncheck the Someone Adds Me to Their Circle check box, and click the Save button.) In addition, you can view a list of people who have added you to their Circle by clicking the In *X* Circles tab on the Circle page (you can see this tab in Figure 21-5). Note that just because someone has added you to her Circle doesn't mean you'll see her info in your activity feed (discussed in the next section). You must add her to your Circle for that to happen.

If you've gone the secret admirer route with your favorites (as we describe earlier in this chapter), anyone who adds you to her Circle isn't able to see items and stores you've hearted. Otherwise, this info is visible for all to see.

# *Active ingredient: Checking your activity feed*

To keep abreast of goings-on in your Etsy Circle — for example, who in your Circle has increased her own Circle by adding new members — you can check your activity feed. In addition to broadcasting news from your Etsy Circle, the activity feed lists items and shops you've hearted, a smattering of new items in your favorite shops, Etsy teams you've joined, items you've sold, Etsy members who have hearted your shop or items you've listed in it, and Treasuries that feature your item. (More on Treasuries in the next section.) You can also see when members of your Circle add people to their Circle — a great way to find new Etsy shops and sellers.

One way to view your activity feed is to click the See Your Activity Link in the Your Circle tab (refer to Figure 21-5). An easier way is to click the Activity button (the one with a spiral shape on it) in the header bar that appears along the top of every Etsy page; your activity feed opens (see Figure 21-6).

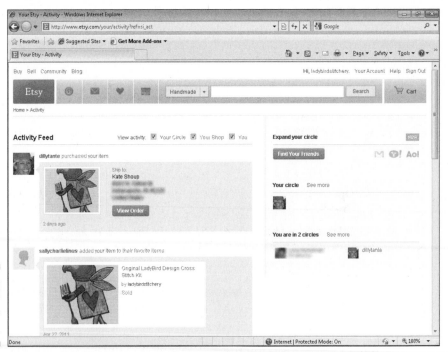

**Figure 21-6:** View your activity feed.

# Treasure Island: Creating a Treasury

A great way to spread the love on Etsy is to create a Treasury. A Treasury is a collection of as many as 16 Etsy listings. These listings may be your favorite things or maybe items that relate to a particular theme (say, bunnies or boats or the color blue). You can then share this list with the larger Etsy community on the Treasuries page. If your Treasury is super beautiful and interesting, it may land on the site's main page — a major karmic boost for you!

It's considered bad form to include your own items in a Treasury. The idea is to call attention to others. Also, limit your list to one item per shop.

Creating a Treasury is easy. After logging in and gathering the items you want to highlight, follow these steps:

1. **Click the Treasury link under Ways to Shop, on the main Etsy page.**

   The Treasury page opens.

2. **Click the Create a List link in the upper-right corner of the Treasury page.**

   The Create a List page opens, as shown in Figure 21-7.

3. **Type a catchy title for your list in the Title field (refer to Figure 21-7a).**

4. **Type a snappy description of your list in the List field.**

5. **Under Privacy, click the Everyone option button to share the Treasury with everyone.**

6. **To help people find your Treasury, type tags in the Tag field, clicking Add after each tag.**

   Flip to Chapter 12 for an introduction to tags.

7. **Open the listing page for the first item you want to add to your Treasury, select the page's URL, and copy it.**

8. **Click in the first Listing URL box in the Create a List page, paste the link you copied, and click OK.**

   A photo of the item appears in the box.

9. **Repeat Steps 7 and 8 to add the remaining items that you selected to your list.**

   You can include as many as 16.

10. **To change the order in which the items appear, click on an item you want to move, drag it to the desired order in the list, and release your mouse button to drop it there.**

To remove an item from the list, hover your mouse pointer over the item and click the Remove link that appears.

**11. Click the Save button to save your list (refer to Figure 21-7b).**

Etsy creates your list, as shown in Figure 21-8a, and cites you as its "curator" (see Figure 21-8b). Etsy also adds it to the Treasury page (see Figure 21-9).

**Figure 21-7:**
Use this page to create your Treasury.

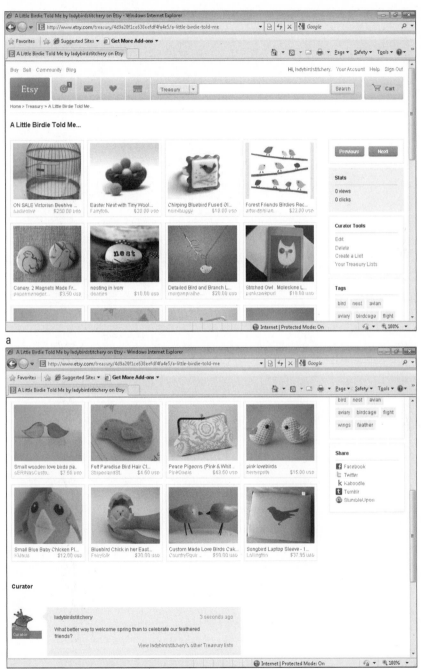

**Figure 21-8:**
Etsy creates your Treasury.

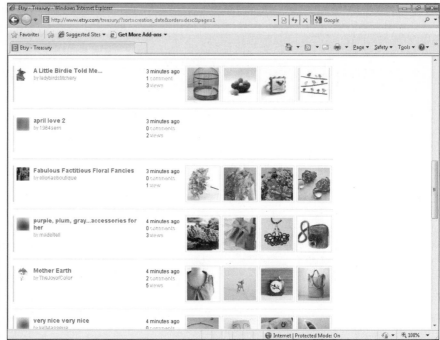

**Figure 21-9:**
Your list
appears on
the Treasury
page.

# Chapter 22

# Help! Getting It When You Need It

. . . . . . . . . . . . . . . . . . . . . . . . . . . . . . . . . . . . . . . . . . . . . . . .

. . . . . . . . . . . . . . . . . . . . . . . . . . . . . . . . . . . . . . . . . . . . . . . .

*Y*es, Etsy is super easy to use. But that doesn't mean you won't ever need a little help. Fortunately, Etsy maintains copious resources to help members find answers to all their burning questions. (Well, answers to their burning questions about using Etsy, anyway.) In this chapter, you discover all the ways you can get help on Etsy.

## Search and Rescue: Searching for Help on Etsy

Given the proclivity of Etsy users for DIY, it's no surprise that the site offers tools for finding help on your own. Perhaps the easiest of these is the Search Help tool, which enables you to search the site's help information for the answers you need by entering a keyword or phrase.

To use the Search Help tool, follow these steps:

1. **Click the Help link that appears along the top of any Etsy page.**

   The Help page opens (see Figure 22-1).

2. **Type a keyword or phrase in the Search Help field at the top of the page, as shown in Figure 22-2.**

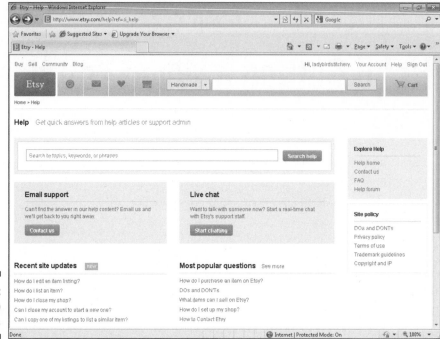

**Figure 22-1:**
The Help
page.

**Figure 22-2:**
Use the
Search Help
field to enter
a keyword
or phrase.

3. **Click the Search Help button.**

   Etsy displays a list of articles, or answers, that match your criteria (see Figure 22-3).

4. **Click an answer link.**

   Etsy displays the answer (see Figure 22-4).

   Etsy displays links to other answers related to the one you just read at the bottom of the help article. Simply click a link to view it.

If your search efforts fail to yield useful results — for example, Etsy returns too many matches — try the search techniques in Chapter 5.

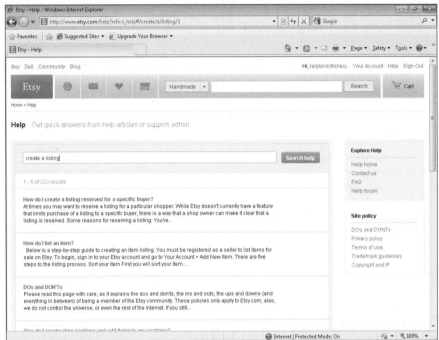

**Figure 22-3:**
View your
matches.

**Figure 22-4:**
Click a link
to view your
answer.

# That's a FAQ Jack: Accessing Etsy FAQs

With as many members as Etsy has, odds are, you're not the first person in the history of the site to have thought of the question you need answered. In fact, certain questions — How do I purchase an item on Etsy? How do I set up my shop? How do I list an item? — get asked a *lot.* For this reason, Etsy has compiled a FAQ (that is, a list of frequently asked questions, and their answers) for your perusal.

To access the Etsy FAQ, follow these steps:

1. **Click the Help link that appears along the top of any Etsy page.**

   The Help page opens (refer to Figure 22-1).

2. **Click the FAQs link under Explore Help on the right side of the Help page.**

   A list of frequently asked questions appears, as shown in Figure 22-5. Notice that the FAQs are organized by category.

3. **Scroll through the list to find a question that you want to answer.**

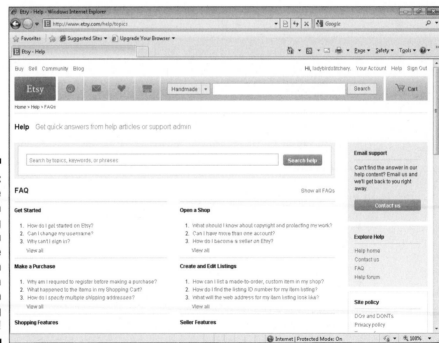

**Figure 22-5:**
Take comfort in knowing that you aren't the first person to have a question about using Etsy!

If the question you want answered doesn't appear in the first batch shown, click the View All link that appears at the bottom of the appropriate category to view all questions in that category. Alternatively, click the Show All FAQs link directly below the Search Help button at the top of the page to view a list of all FAQs (see Figure 22-6).

4. **Click a question in the list.**

Etsy displays the answer (refer to Figure 22-4).

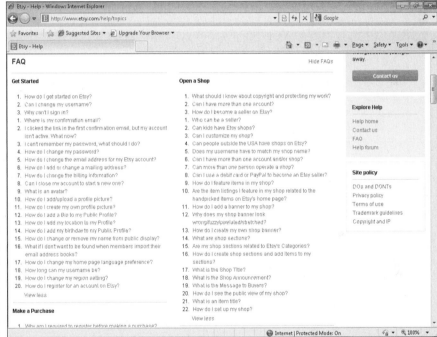

**Figure 22-6:** Click Show All FAQs to view all Etsy FAQs on one page.

# Getting Personalized Help from the People at Etsy

Sometimes you simply want to be able to ask a question and have it answered by an actual *person*. Fortunately, Etsy can accommodate you! With Etsy, you can Live Chat with actual people on Etsy's support team. You can also e-mail Etsy support to find the answers you need. Finally, you can use Etsy's Help forum to get help from other Etsy users.

# Can we talk? Chatting with an Etsy helper

If you have a fondness for humans, Etsy's Live Chat feature is for you. With Live Chat, you can connect with an Etsy staff member and pose your question; the Etsy staffer can then answer it. Easy, peasy!

Help via Live Chat is available Monday through Friday from 10 a.m. to 6 p.m. EST.

Be aware that the Live Chat help feature is for general support requests only — for example, if you need help uploading an image to a listing or you're not sure how to leave feedback. It's not for help in handling issues that require investigation. See the next section for information about handling those types of queries.

To get help via Live Chat, follow these steps:

1. **While logged in to your Etsy account, click the Help link that appears along the top of any Etsy page.**

   The Help page opens (refer to Figure 22-1).

2. **Click the Start Chatting button at the top of the page.**

   As soon as a representative is available, Etsy launches a chat window, with a message from the Etsy representative with whom you're connected (see Figure 22-7).

3. **Type your question in the bottom portion of the window, and click Send or press either Enter or Return to transmit it.**

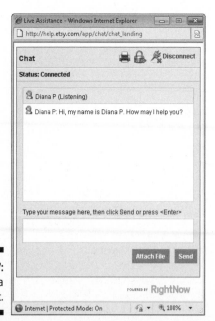

**Figure 22-7:**
Launch a chat.

The question that you typed appears in the top portion of the chat window. When your Etsy representative responds, her response appears below your question in the top part of the window, as shown in Figure 22-8.

4. **Repeat Step 3 to chat with the Etsy representative, typing in the bottom portion of the window and reading her response in the top portion.**

5. **When you're finished chatting, end the session by clicking the Disconnect button in the upper-right corner of the chat window.**

Etsy terminates your session.

To print a transcript of your session, click the Print button in the upper-right corner of the Chat window.

6. **Click the Close button in the upper-right corner to close the chat window (see Figure 22-9).**

Etsy e-mails you a transcript of your chat session, in case you forget the specifics of what went down during the session.

**Figure 22-8:**
Chat with an Etsy representative.

# *Life support: Contacting Etsy support*

Suppose that you have a problem with your account. Or maybe you need help with a transaction. In either case, you can send a message to Etsy support right from the Help page. You can also send a message to Etsy support to notify that group of a problem on the site. Here's how:

**Figure 22-9:**
Terminate
your chat
session.

1. **While logged in to your Etsy account, click the Help link that appears along the top of any Etsy page.**

   The Help page opens (refer to Figure 22-1).

2. **Click the Contact Us link on the left side of the page.**

   The E-mail Etsy Support page opens, as shown in Figure 22-10.

3. **Click the Please Select a Topic down arrow and select a category. Choices include the following:**

   • General site help

   • Report something you saw in a shop or a listing

   • Help with disputes, harassment, or a suspicious convo

   • Help with Etsy shop fees

   • Questions en Français

   • Fragen auf Deutsch

4. **Type a subject for your message in the Subject field.**

5. **In the Message field, type your message.**

6. **Optionally, you can attach a file; to do so, click the Choose a File button, and then locate and select the file that you want to attach.**

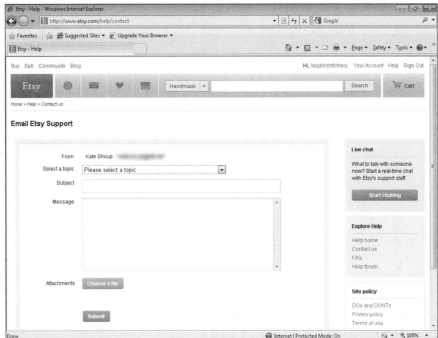

**Figure 22-10:**
The E-mail
Etsy Support
page.

For example, if you're experiencing a problem with your shop page, you may capture a screen shot of the page and attach that image file to your message.

7. **Click Submit.**

8. **Etsy notifies you that your question has been submitted (see Figure 22-11); it also sends you a confirmation e-mail to that effect.**

When it has your answer, Etsy sends it to you via e-mail. You can reply to the person who sent the e-mail if you have further questions.

## Forum letter: Using the Etsy Help forum

As you discover in Chapter 19, Etsy's forums serve as public message boards where members can discuss all manner of topics — including help. Specifically, Etsy's Site Help forum, shown in Figure 22-12, is a great resource if you have general questions about how to use Etsy, questions about site features, or queries related to site policy. Odds are, someone in the Etsy community or on the Etsy staff can — and will — answer your question!

You can access the Site Help forum directly from Etsy's Help page. Simply click the Help Forum link under Explore Help on the right side of the page. For info on using the forum, refer to Chapter 19.

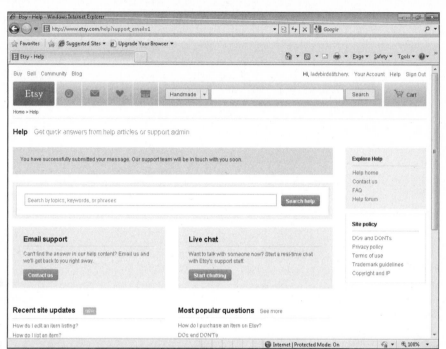

**Figure 22-11:**
Your message is sent.

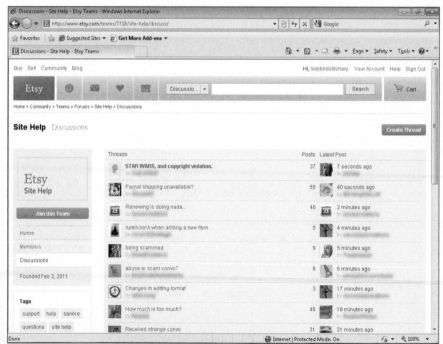

**Figure 22-12:**
The Site Help forum.

# Part VI
# The Part of Tens

"No, I'm not selling lawn gnomes. I'm selling knit hats like the one my husband's modeling in the picture."

## In this part . . .

Every *For Dummies* book features the Part of Tens, and we're not messing with a winning formula! In this part, we offer our (admittedly unsolicited) opinions on a variety of topics, including ten things we think sellers must know, ten strategies for marketing your shop, and ten tips for saving money and time as an Etsy shop owner.

# Chapter 23

# Ten Terrific Tips for Etsy Sellers

*In This Chapter*

▶ Getting (and staying) organized

▶ Serving customers and networking

▶ Loving what you do

**R**unning an Etsy shop — even if it's just a hobby — is no small undertaking. Organization is critical, as is offering top-notch customer service. Here's the place where we offer a neat, concise roll call of ten terrific tips for Etsy sellers. Drum roll, please!

## Have a Place for Everything

Nothing is as frustrating as trying to find just the right bead, button, ribbon, or supply when you have 11 orders breathing down your neck. Do yourself a favor: Get organized! Figure out the best way to store all your supplies, both for your craft and for your business. First, sort all your supplies by type or color. Then stash everything in a place where you can easily find it.

In our experience, clear boxes with labels are the only way to go.

## Save Time with Twosies

We've wasted too much time looking for the scissors, and then tracking down the tape, and then wondering where the heck that marker went. Save yourself a ton of time and aggravation by buying many, *many* multiples of oft-used supplies.

Our advice? Head to the dollar store and knock yourself out. Get a dozen pairs of scissors, a zillion rolls of tape, and lots of whatever else you need. Live a little!

# Organize Your Paperwork

Even if it's just a shoebox, have a place to stick all your business-related receipts, whether they're for crafting tools, packaging supplies, or what have you. Then have *another* place for your other paperwork — invoices, bank statements, and such. Tax time is tough enough without having to sort through all that stuff at the 11th hour! (Flip to Chapter 18 for more details on handling paperwork and other business-related issues.)

# Use What You Discover from Other Shops

Before you start selling on Etsy, buy a handful of items from a handful of sellers. Pay attention to the way each seller communicates with you, the packaging she uses, how long it takes for her to ship to you, and so on. What are the sellers doing right? Where can they improve? Then put what you learn to work in your own Etsy shop.

# Offer Service with a Smile

No, your online customers can't see you. But that doesn't mean you can cop an attitude with them. In fact, even though you're "out of sight," your lousy outlook will ooze into everything you do. Remember, on Etsy, it's all about the customer service! Offering service with a smile is a good way to ensure that you get a smile in return. (Check out Chapter 17 for more customer service tips.)

# Network, Network, Network

Networking is a wonderful way to grow your Etsy business. Whether you're interacting with others in the Etsy community (see Part V) or just going about your day in the real world, make it a point to connect with people. Ask questions. Coax those you meet to share their stories. Offer to help others. Engage in the kinds of behaviors that let people know who you are, what you're about, and, eventually, what you do. (Chapter 16 has plenty of guidelines to get you started.)

# Keep a Blog

If you're serious about your Etsy shop, consider starting a blog. A blog can serve as an excellent marketing tool to help you grow your customer base. Blogging is a great way to share tips and ideas, and you can even run contests and giveaways. Plus, a blog is easier to maintain than a newsletter, and you can add to it anytime.

Popular blog-hosting sites include Blogger.com (www.blogger.com), TypePad (www.typepad.com), and WordPress (www.wordpress.com).

# Learn to Say No

As an Etsy seller, you'll almost certainly be inundated with requests for freebies, donations, and discounts. You know what? It's perfectly okay to say no to some or even all of these requests. Pick and choose. Say yes to the requests that make you feel good and that are good for your business; to everything else, say no.

# Never Give In

Take a lesson from the great British Prime Minister Winston Churchill: "Never give in. Never give in. Never, never, never, never." Although Churchill uttered those words in an attempt to galvanize the British against their Axis foes, they apply equally to Etsy sellers — with a spin: If you have an original idea for a product that you love, never stop pushing yourself. Never stop developing and finessing and improving and learning and changing and working hard. Never, never, never, *never*.

# Have Fun!

You're not out to change the world here, one beaded necklace at a time. Selling your work on Etsy needs to be fun! Do your best to maintain perspective. Chortle on the inside when a customer requests a gum-wrapper purse made entirely of Teaberry wrappers, and enjoy yourself!

# Chapter 24

# Ten Strategies for Marketing Your Etsy Shop

## In This Chapter

▶ Bringing folks to your Etsy shop (and keeping them there)

▶ Using technology to your advantage

▶ Marketing your wares in the real world

Marketing is the key to any successful business, your Etsy shop included. Here we offer ten tips you need to know to successfully market your Etsy shop (flip to Chapter 16 for even more guidance).

## Offer Tiered Pricing

If all you had to offer were $25 gumball machines, you'd really be limiting your customer base. By offering a $5 item as well as a $100 item, you open your shop to buyers with different-sized pocketbooks. With so-called "tiered pricing," you can include big-ticket items to make your shop seem more exciting, while at the same time offering goodies for entry-level shoppers so they can test the waters of your shop, so to speak.

## Understand That Giving Begets Giving

Helping someone by giving her more than she asked for makes that person want to return the favor. Build trust and develop relationships with your customers by offering something for nothing, whether it's advice on your blog or a gift with purchase.

But don't go the cheap route; it may actually work against you by turning off customers. Make sure that you offer only good-quality stuff.

# Provide a Guarantee

No doubt about it, you can engender a lot of trust by offering to replace or refund an item if the customer isn't happy for any reason. Buying online can be a scary proposition; you can break down a barrier by letting shoppers know that you're willing to work with them. We guarantee it!

# Consider a Loyalty Program

Loyalty programs, or frequent-customer cards, can be a great way to bring back return customers. Your loyalty program may offer prizes, future discounts, and other incentives designed to keep customers doing repeat business with you.

As you develop your loyalty program, don't forget your branding. Design customer cards that reflect your shop's color, logo, design, and feel.

# Impose a Deadline

Research shows that procrastination is the leading factor in delaying doing things. Overcome the customer's natural tendency to put things off by offering a sale with a deadline. Add a sense of urgency to your marketing message, and customers will respond.

# Create a Great E-mail Signature

Most e-mail programs enable you to create an e-mail signature — a bit of text or an image that appears at the bottom of every e-mail message that you send. Take advantage of this feature! Creating an e-mail signature gives you a chance to share your contact info and reinforce your branding.

Your e-mail siggy is the last thing the person reading your message will see — you want it to reflect your personality!

# Connect with Social Media

It's really easy to get so caught up in sharing our own stories online that we forget to listen to others. Instead of using Facebook and Twitter as one big opportunity for you to advertise your wares, use them to reach out to others. Read and comment on others' posts. Congratulate a fellow seller on her successful sale or cheer up a Twitter buddy who's down in the dumps. It's karma, baby!

# Make Google Your Best Friend

With this newfangled interweb thingie, you can find the answer to literally any question you have (including marketing questions). Don't be afraid to turn to Google as you grow your Etsy shop! You'll find everything from tips on developing a logo to the best marketing strategy for your craft business.

# Use Your Items in the Real World

One of the simplest ways to promote your work is to use or wear your pieces in everyday life, and to always have a business card handy. That way, when Aunt Sarah compliments you on your beautiful feathered and bedazzled bracelet, you can hand her your business card and tell her where to get one of her very own (and one for Uncle Frank, too).

# Help Your Community

Get your craft business some publicity by doing something to benefit your community. For example, create a special breast cancer awareness necklace to honor a neighbor, or hold a special sale to help someone in the area. Make sure you let the local paper know what you're up to!

# Chapter 25

# Ten Pointers for Saving Money and Time as an Etsy Shop Owner

Time is money. It's a cliché because it's true — especially when you run your own business. Here you find ten great tips for saving money *and* time as you run your own Etsy shop.

## Plan Before You Shop

You can save a lot of money by doing some planning before you purchase. Don't wait until you're totally out of supplies before you go shopping; making a special trip to the store because you ran out of shipping envelopes is going to cost you! Buy when stuff is on sale, and be sure to use coupons.

## Buy in Bulk

I know, the local office-supply store is close and convenient, but trust us when we say that they're gouging into your profits. Buy in bulk online, and you can save a boatload. If you've got the storage space, get more than you think you'll need; you'll use it eventually.

Respected providers of bulk supplies include ULINE (www.uline.com), PaperMart (www.papermart.com), and Nashville Wraps (www.nashville wraps.com).

## Know That Bartering Can Be Better

Bartering is all about trading goods and services directly with other businesses, for the benefit of all. If you need a beautiful banner for your Etsy shop, and you make gorgeous hand-knitted sweaters, why not browse Etsy to find a graphic designer who lives somewhere cold and propose a trade? Talk about a win-win situation!

## Create Master Forms

With your Etsy business, you're probably going to repeat yourself in e-mails a lot, either answering questions or thanking customers for sales. Designing a master e-mail template for frequent responses not only eliminates spelling errors, but helps you appear more professional.

## Create a Shipping Station

Don't waste time turning the house upside down to find tape and scissors every time you have a sale. Instead, set up a shipping station, even in a little corner of the house, where all your supplies are waiting for you when you need them.

## Ship from Home

Every once in a while, there's a *really* long line at the post office. Save time and money by shipping from home. Just stick your outgoing mail in your mailbox, and your postal carrier will pick it up when she drops off your mail.

If you're shipping at least one Priority Mail or Express Mail package, you can even schedule a pickup online at www.usps.com.

# Recycle Your Shipping Supplies

Purchasing premade shipping boxes and bubble wrap can be expensive. You can save cash *and* the environment by reusing shipping boxes and supplies — provided, of course, that they aren't tattered and filthy. (The idea is to be green, not gross!) If you opt to go the recycling route, be sure to mention this point in your shop's policies.

Make friends with local businesses that may have unwanted supplies. That candle store downtown may be the source of enough Styrofoam peanuts to keep you in business for a long time.

# Deduct from Your Tax Bill

As you discover in Chapter 18, if you work at home, you may be able to take advantage of significant tax deductions. For example, if you use a room in your house specifically for your business, if you use your car to purchase supplies (and who doesn't?), or if you have a separate business phone line, you may be able to save money with tax deductions.

Contact a trustworthy tax advisor or accountant for details, and be sure to keep great records.

# Set a Daily Objective

Short-term goals can help you accomplish a little something every day toward making your business work for you. You're way more likely to get something done if you set even a small everyday goal. Consider setting goals like spending a certain amount of time on marketing, or creating your craft, or prettying up your Etsy shop to help your business grow.

# Get Off the Computer!

There's only one problem with Etsy: It's addicting! You may find yourself spending way more time browsing than crafting. That's fine and dandy — unless your time is valuable! Set a timer if you have to, but limit your computer time to make sure that you focus on your business, too.

# Index

### • F •

## • *M* •

### • Z •

## Apple & Macs

iPad For Dummies
978-0-470-58027-1

iPhone For Dummies,
4th Edition
978-0-470-87870-5

MacBook For Dummies, 3rd
Edition
978-0-470-76918-8

Mac OS X Snow Leopard For
Dummies
978-0-470-43543-4

## Business

Bookkeeping For Dummies
978-0-7645-9848-7

Job Interviews
For Dummies,
3rd Edition
978-0-470-17748-8

Resumes For Dummies,
5th Edition
978-0-470-08037-5

Starting an
Online Business
For Dummies,
6th Edition
978-0-470-60210-2

Stock Investing
For Dummies,
3rd Edition
978-0-470-40114-9

Successful
Time Management
For Dummies
978-0-470-29034-7

## Computer Hardware

BlackBerry
For Dummies,
4th Edition
978-0-470-60700-8

Computers For Seniors
For Dummies,
2nd Edition
978-0-470-53483-0

PCs For Dummies,
Windows
7 Edition
978-0-470-46542-4

Laptops For Dummies,
4th Edition
978-0-470-57829-2

## Cooking & Entertaining

Cooking Basics
For Dummies,
3rd Edition
978-0-7645-7206-7

Wine For Dummies,
4th Edition
978-0-470-04579-4

## Diet & Nutrition

Dieting For Dummies,
2nd Edition
978-0-7645-4149-0

Nutrition For Dummies,
4th Edition
978-0-471-79868-2

Weight Training
For Dummies,
3rd Edition
978-0-471-76845-6

## Digital Photography

Digital SLR Cameras &
Photography For Dummies,
3rd Edition
978-0-470-46606-3

Photoshop Elements 8
For Dummies
978-0-470-52967-6

## Gardening

Gardening Basics
For Dummies
978-0-470-03749-2

Organic Gardening
For Dummies,
2nd Edition
978-0-470-43067-5

## Green/Sustainable

Raising Chickens
For Dummies
978-0-470-46544-8

Green Cleaning
For Dummies
978-0-470-39106-8

## Health

Diabetes For Dummies,
3rd Edition
978-0-470-27086-8

Food Allergies
For Dummies
978-0-470-09584-3

Living Gluten-Free
For Dummies,
2nd Edition
978-0-470-58589-4

## Hobbies/General

Chess For Dummies,
2nd Edition
978-0-7645-8404-6

Drawing
Cartoons & Comics
For Dummies
978-0-470-42683-8

Knitting For Dummies,
2nd Edition
978-0-470-28747-7

Organizing
For Dummies
978-0-7645-5300-4

Su Doku For Dummies
978-0-470-01892-7

## Home Improvement

Home Maintenance
For Dummies,
2nd Edition
978-0-470-43063-7

Home Theater
For Dummies,
3rd Edition
978-0-470-41189-6

Living the
Country Lifestyle
All-in-One
For Dummies
978-0-470-43061-3

Solar Power Your Home
For Dummies,
2nd Edition
978-0-470-59678-4

## Internet

Blogging For Dummies,
3rd Edition
978-0-470-61996-4

eBay For Dummies,
6th Edition
978-0-470-49741-8

Facebook For Dummies,
3rd Edition
978-0-470-87804-0

Web Marketing
For Dummies,
2nd Edition
978-0-470-37181-7

WordPress
For Dummies,
3rd Edition
978-0-470-59274-8

## Language & Foreign Language

French For Dummies
978-0-7645-5193-2

Italian Phrases
For Dummies
978-0-7645-7203-6

Spanish For Dummies,
2nd Edition
978-0-470-87855-2

Spanish
For Dummies,
Audio Set
978-0-470-09585-0

## Math & Science

Algebra I
For Dummies,
2nd Edition
978-0-470-55964-2

Biology For Dummies,
2nd Edition
978-0-470-59875-7

Calculus For Dummies
978-0-7645-2498-1

Chemistry For Dummies
978-0-7645-5430-8

## Microsoft Office

Excel 2010 For Dummies
978-0-470-48953-6

Office 2010 All-in-One
For Dummies
978-0-470-49748-7

Office 2010 For Dummies,
Book + DVD Bundle
978-0-470-62698-6

Word 2010 For Dummies
978-0-470-48772-3

## Music

Guitar For Dummies,
2nd Edition
978-0-7645-9904-0

iPod & iTunes For
Dummies, 8th Edition
978-0-470-87871-2

Piano Exercises
For Dummies
978-0-470-38765-8

## Parenting & Education

Parenting For Dummies,
2nd Edition
978-0-7645-5418-6

Type 1 Diabetes
For Dummies
978-0-470-17811-9

## Pets

Cats For Dummies,
2nd Edition
978-0-7645-5275-5

Dog Training For Dummies,
3rd Edition
978-0-470-60029-0

Puppies For Dummies,
2nd Edition
978-0-470-03717-1

## Religion & Inspiration

The Bible For Dummies
978-0-7645-5296-0

Catholicism For Dummies
978-0-7645-5391-2

Women in the Bible
For Dummies
978-0-7645-8475-6

## Self-Help & Relationship

Anger Management
For Dummies
978-0-470-03715-7

Overcoming Anxiety
For Dummies,
2nd Edition
978-0-470-57441-6

## Sports

Baseball
For Dummies,
3rd Edition
978-0-7645-7537-2

Basketball
For Dummies,
2nd Edition
978-0-7645-5248-9

Golf For Dummies,
3rd Edition
978-0-471-76871-5

## Web Development

Web Design
All-in-One
For Dummies
978-0-470-41796-6

Web Sites
Do-It-Yourself
For Dummies,
2nd Edition
978-0-470-56520-9

## Windows 7

Windows 7
For Dummies
978-0-470-49743-2

Windows 7
For Dummies,
Book + DVD Bundle
978-0-470-52398-8

Windows 7 All-in-One
For Dummies
978-0-470-48763-1

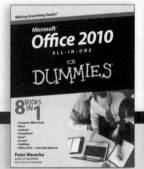

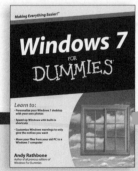

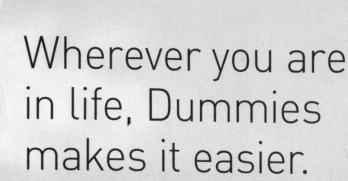

Wherever you are in life, Dummies makes it easier.

From fashion to Facebook®, wine to Windows®, and everything in betwee Dummies makes it easier.

Visit us at Dummies.com

# Dummies products make life easier!

DIY • Consumer Electronics • Crafts • Software • Cookware • Hobbies • Videos • Music • Games • and More!

For more information, go to **Dummies.com®** and search the store by category.